The Center of the Web

The Center of the Web

Women and Solitude

edited by

Delese Wear

State University of New York Press

Published by
State University of New York Press, Albany

© 1993   State University of New York

Printed in the United States of America

For information, address State University of New York
Press, State University Plaza, Albany, NY 12246

Production by Christine M. Lynch
Marketing by Fran Keneston

Library of Congress Cataloging-in-Publication Data

The Center of the web : women and solitude / edited by Delese Wear.
     p. cm.
    Includes bibliographical references and index.
    ISBN 0–7914–1545–7 (cloth). — ISBN 0–7914–1546–5 (pbk.)
     1. Women—Psychology. 2. Solitude. 3. Women—Religious life.
    4. Loneliness. I. Wear, Delese.
    HQ1206.C39   1993
    155.6'33—dc20   92–31366
                                           CIP

10 9 8 7 6 5 4 3 2 1

To Wear women—my mother Frances,
my sisters Tracye and Rachel, my daughter Meredith

CONTENTS

ACKNOWLEDGMENTS

My personal life and my work life—as if the two could be neatly separated!—are full of people who quietly or loudly encourage, advise, care for, and admonish me. I am blessed, and I offer my gratitude to those who helped me with this book.

Martin Kohn, Mark Savickas, Michelle Wimer, Jeannette Stoffer, Marge Wilkinson, and Nancy McDonald make coming to my office a pleasure. I value their opinions, insights, and presence enormously. Carolyn Simon and Jamie Evans were efficient and patient with the seemingly endless word-processing that goes into a project like this. And I thank my sister Rachel for the cover design.

When reading similar acknowledgments in other books, I had always been a bit mystified about the kudos some authors gave to their editors. Now I know why. From my first tentative inquiry through the months of writing and editing, Priscilla Ross's perceptiveness, honesty, wit, and unwavering encouragement gave me much-needed confidence and made the entire experience gratifying.

And of course, always, my partner Steve Broderick, and my children Ben and Meredith, lovingly but mostly unknowingly center my life. My projects have more joy, vitality, and meaning because of them.

INTRODUCTION

"I know you are reading this poem as you pace beside the stove
warming milk, a crying child on your shoulder, a book in your
hand because life is short and you too are thirsty." (Rich 1991, 25)

Just about the time I received the last essay for this book, I had a phone conversation with Susan Laird, one of the contributors. After we talked awhile about what and how some of the other authors had written about solitude, she asked me what I was going to write in the introduction. I thought for a moment and then answered, "I can't even think about an introduction. After reading and thinking about what everyone has written, I just want to go back and rewrite my own essay."

The way I think about solitude and the personal meanings it holds for me keeps changing since I first wrote my essay over a year ago, the essay from which the idea for this collection emerged. These changes in meaning did not result from a change in life circumstances—I'm still a daughter, partner, mother, teacher of the same courses at the same college. Rather, I am changed because of the year I've spent talking with and reading the essays of nineteen women who, like me, have been puzzling over the meaning of solitude in their varied lives.

The idea of women and webs is, of course, not new. My own image of the metaphor appeared when I first read Gilligan's description of women in webs of relationships and connection. When reading that account, I visioned the delicate intricacies of webs, gently binding me to others, situating me in my network of family and friends, and in the circumstances and particularities of my unique but connective life. I, the spinner of my web, was at the center, but it was a center that existed within the architecture of the rest of the web. The threads leading outward and around were essential, reassuring, and secure.

Since that time, I've come to realize that webs are also structures where we can get caught. The recollections of many of the authors found here portray the painful experiences of being tangled in the webs of heterosexist, racist, patriarchial cultures. When caught in a web, spinning is wearisome, often impossible; connections are difficult and knotted.

Both of these images of webs—places of creation and security, or fixed places of confinement—may be helpful as we read these essays and think about the place of solitude in the lives of women not represented here. If we think of our women's lives as webs, we may consider how and where we are situated; our abilities to influence the method and direction of our spinning; and the issues confronting many women living in webs in which they are caught, or living in webs they try to create.

"Writing in the feminine. And on a colored sky. How do you inscribe difference without bursting into a series of euphoric narcissistic accounts of yourself and your own kind?...How do you forget without annihilating?" (Minh-ha 1989, 28)

It all began several years ago when the idea of solitude and my pursuit of it became an important focus in my life. As I am apt to do, I thought I was an irregularity in the category Woman (as if some unitary category even existed); I wondered if and how other women thought about solitude. I don't mean that exhausted plea for a momentary, essential respite from duties and work that most of us yearn for in our overstuffed, overextended lives. Rather, I was referring to a more ethereal (although often literal) kind of shelter in order to think and reflect and often create, *away* from others we care for and about—children, friends, parents, students, partners. How did other women seek solitude? Did they seize it or thoughtfully construct it, or was it just there? Or was I way off base, all this merely my educated, middle-class privilege allowing me to ask questions about, seek, and live solitary moments? I wanted to know, and finally summoned up enough courage to ask.

It's wonderfully odd, now that I think about it, that I felt *familiarity* and *connection* to the women who contributed to this collection when we talked about writing essays on *solitude*! I was again reminded that once we name our thoughts and experiences, only then are they brought into a kind of visibility where now we can see and recognize not cloned images of a universal experience, but what Fraser and Nicholson (1988, 35) call a "patchwork of overlapping alliances." In her essay in this collection, Magda Lewis similarly writes of the importance of the feminist focus on experience, not as "the vacuous and gratuitous telling of our private stories as a cathartic moment but indeed to emphasize that subordinate groups live subordination and marginality through our subjectivity. We live it precisely in the context of the details of our individual experiences which to the extent that they can be made to seem to be private cannot then offer the ground for a collective political practice." Thus, these essays, even read individually, are not merely the subjectivities of self-representation. Rather, they are forms of what Quinby (1992, 127) calls "ideographic selfhood: an ethical self-stylization that refuses the particular forms of selfhood, knowledge, and artistry that modern systems of power have made dominant." In their collective form, they produce *externalized* subjectivities that are dialogical, multiple, and discontinuous (Quinby, 128).

Moreover, these essays are well-crafted examples of what Nancy K. Miller calls personal criticism, "an explicitly autobiographical performance...a self-narrative woven into critical argument" (1991, 1–2). Such writing dismantles the personal-public dichotomy, one of many dimensions of women's oppression, one which has sent most of us tenure-hungry academic women into the conformity underlying critical plausibility. Yet much feminist theorizing has built on the personal for nearly twenty years when the authority of experience became a stream of feminist theorizing; many such attempts were and are efforts to form resistance to the reigning critical positionings. In fact, Miller writes, "the efflorescence of personal criticism in the United States in the eighties—like the study of autobiography—has in part to do with the gradual and perhaps inevitable waning for a mode of theory, whose authority—however variously—depended finally on the theoretical evacuation of the very social subjects producing it" (24).

These essays, because they ignore the personal-public dichotomy, speak to readers in a fluid, back-and-forth between frank autobiography and the subject matter under discussion. These women have not inserted a catheter into their souls or memories, those places where experiences are stored. When we write from those places we can, as Miller describes it, "let it show." And when we write from those places we validate, finally, to ourselves and others, that our experiences count in the discourse of knowledge. Bound together by myriad difficulties induced by cultures that pull, twist, and push our various selves into conflicting roles and responsibilities, we can forge a collective alliance grounded, in part, by these politicized, circulating stories.

"Poetry is the way we help give name to the nameless so it can be thought. The farthest horizons of our hopes and fears are cobbled by our poems, carved from the rock, experiences of our daily lives." (Lorde 1984, 37)

As I read and reread these essays, I tried to resist the temptation to impose order and categorize; I thought that to do so even without intent might corral thought and possibility for readers. But it was evident that most authors began with a conception of solitude, then wove stories around several themes that seemed to recur no matter how I shuffled the essays. Of course these themes are not discrete: how can one talk of solitude and work without addressing issues of identity and culture? Thus, the borders here are open between all the themes, and I offer them tentatively, recognizing that each reader will bring to her reading particularities of her life that will evoke in ways I never considered.

Solitude and Identity

I found that many of the writers think of solitude as a respite for reflection on identities. Within these inquiries, solitude is often a condition/place to refurbish our spirits, to distill our thoughts, to confront the way we live, and often to work—separate from the other lives we live within the many kinds of families we've created. My essay, which begins this section, is via fiction a personal inquiry into solitude as a condition for intense reflection on my life, on my emotional and spiritual self, and my self as a site of creation. Lynne McFall, a philosopher, writes that "to become an individual requires solitude and suffering. To survive and develop as an individual requires the capacity to `stand alone': to think and feel and speak for oneself." Mara Sapon-Shevin writes of her changing experiences of solitude from childhood to present: as unchoseness, as alienation, as disempowerment, as hiding, as vulnerability, and finally coming to reclaim solitude as a potentially affirming experience. Through the writings of several African-American women, Jacqueline Jones Royster finds that she is better able to "breathe into myself hope, courage, and grit...[to] see myself beginning to fashion what I need: new pathways to solitude, new ways of looking at time and at time alone, new ways of conceiving a notion of place, and other ways, if not new ones, to create places apart." Similarly, Jo Anne Pagano writes of the relationship she has found between solitude and connection: "I can be alone because I know that I am connected. The world does not fade when I am in solitude because it is only in the world and in my connection to others in it that I am myself."

Some writers think about solitude and its place in the academy as they confront the deeply coded rules about productivity and "fitting in," and the devaluation of collaboration. Other writers think about solitude as giving them a place to acknowledge, confront, and nurture their lives as separate from the academy, or as different from the academy's template for its inhabitants. Elizabeth Ellsworth writes in her essay: "This additional, different self forged in solitude...gives me someplace else to stand in relation to the academy and refuse to present myself there as 'The One.'...That academic self becomes one among my many selves." Beth Rushing examines solitude from a sociological perspective as she posits that "we are...more aware of solitude if our surroundings constantly serve as a reminder of our solitude, thus heightening the sensation"—such as being alone amidst a crowd. Finally, Tuija Pulkkinen examines the dialectics of solitude and connection, and the dialectics of solitude and loneliness as she thinks about and compares the solitude associated with philosophy and her experience of connectedness with women.

Solitude and Culture

A number of writers view solitude through the lenses of difference and isolation imposed by racist, heterosexist, patriarchal cultures. Writing about the difficulties of trying to unravel the ironic dualities of isolation and solitude, Kal Alston reflects on the aesthetic qualities of a solitude where she consciously tries to reside "in moments of heightened awareness in which one's relation to the world is somehow made crystalline." Glorianne Leck writes of her solitude as a healing place in a world governed by heterosexual norms, a respite from loneliness and detachment, a safe landing in her "movement toward locations of plentitude." Darshan Perusek recounts growing up in India within a secure, happy, and connected family in contrast to many Indian women who grew up and continue to live in a patriarchal silence in which their "deepest needs and longings go unheard." Beverly Gordon describes the difference for her between solitude—"being alone in the quiet of one's spirituality"—and isolation—"being lonely for a critical mass of people, particularly African-Americans, to sustain, encourage, and collaborate within academic settings." The "insistent voices" of six young, white working-class women are found in Elyse Eidman-Aadahl's essay, voices that helped her "to rethink both solitude and connection, and how literacy work in schools operates to support and constrain both." Finally, Susan Laird examines the ambiguity of the concept solitude with the purpose of "illuminating its utility as a critical and constructive tool for a broad rethinking of curriculum," and poses questions for curriculum theorists and designers who "care about the quality of women's lives."

Solitude and Work

Other essays found here are more reflective of the author's examination of solitude in relation to her work. Noting that "women in the academy have not had our stories told very much one way or the other," Magda Lewis asks herself: "How much of my daily life is rationalized; how much is political strategy; how much is material, ideological, psychological and emotional constraint; how much is a particular discourse and a way of relating to the world that grows out of my appropriation of socially acceptable forms of femininity and my culturally contained reality as 'woman'?" Ellen Michaelson writes of the difficulties of finding solitude to do creative work amidst the pressures of being a physician, of "putting her muses above the pursuit of material objects and career advancement" in a medical environment that does not encourage or reward such activity. Elaine Atkins, a teacher and curriculum theorist, reflects on how she had previously "placed knowledge within the context of social or communal institutions [and] had never thought seriously about how solitude allowed an individual to interact with her own thoughts rather than with other people, other texts"; she now looks for ways to achieve a balance between the public and private. Janet Miller writes of the spaces within her that fill with the needs and desires and requests of others as she waits for a return of her own self in those spaces: "What I want and am still learning how to do is to construct moments of both solitude and connectedness for myself—those doubled spaces—in which I am fully present, neither sifted into others' spaces nor drained from my own." Ann Berlak reflects on writing autobiographically in solitude about teaching; she does so to "take the time both to see the coherence of my teaching in the face of the flowing, and to see it critically, to analyze the parts"—a time to question what she takes for granted more deeply than she "ordinarily, in the flux of daily life, can do." Last, Linda K. Christian-Smith reflects as teacher-educator: "Solitude was a key ingredient in my rethinking of schooling long ago and guides my struggles to attain a more democratic practice....Time away from the struggle gives me the courage to continue."

"Private speech in public discourse, intimate intervention, making another text, a space that enables me to recover all that I am in language, I find so many gaps, absences in this written text. To cite them at least is to let the reader know something has been missed." (hooks 1990, 147)

As the editor of this volume, it was I who invited the nineteen women whose essays appear here to write about solitude. I realize, uneasily, that for each unique and expressive voice we hear, many remain to be heard. My thinking and my work have suffered from class, racial, and other biases; my feminist awakening as a young woman was nurtured albeit narrowly by white, heterosexual, middle-class feminist traditions of North America and Western Europe; I strive now to confront and unlearn these biases. Thus, I hope that this volume, because it is a privileged discourse of educated women, is viewed by readers only as part of a compendium reflecting the diversity of women's needs and experiences. To that end, perhaps these essays fit what Fraser and Nicholson (1990, 35) would call an "appropriate and useful expression in a postmodern-feminist form of critical inquiry…[part] of a broader, richer, more complex, and multi-layered feminist solidarity, the sort of solidarity that is essential for overcoming the oppression of women in its 'endless variety and monotonous similarity.'"

While the thoughts of Margaret Atwood's cabin in the Canadian wilderness, or Alice Koller's beachhouse on Nantucket still sound delicious (and are opportunities I'd grab in a second), these days I find I don't need an exotic, or even separate place to live self-consciously in a deeply reflective, solitary way—one of *my* selves among many. Like several of the authors found here, I find myself writing best in restaurants, or to the rattle of the dishwasher at home, or with my office door open as the world traffics in and out. I *am* in a web; but it's good and important (for me) to weave back and forth instead of around and around, returning to the center where I began, where things look different each time, where as May Sarton writes, "all things are made new."

Author's Note

I owe a great debt here to Patti Lather, whose remarks as critic at the 1992 AERA symposium, "The Center of the Web," helped me to focus on issues surrounding autobiography that I had not considered previously.

References

Fraser, N., and L. Nicholson (1988). Social criticism without philosophy: An encounter between feminism and post-modernism. In *Universal abandon: The politics of postmodernism*, edited by A. Ross, 83–103. Minneapolis: University of Minnesota Press.

hooks, b. (1990). Choosing the margin as a space of radical openness. In *Yearning: Race, gender, and cultural politics*, 145–53. Boston: South End Press.

Lorde, A. (1984). Poetry is not a luxury. In *Sister outsider: Essays & speeches*, 36–39. Freedom, Calif.: The Crossing Press.

Miller, N. K. (1991). *Getting personal: Feminist occasions and other autobiographical acts*. New York: Routledge.

Quinby, L. (1991). *Freedom, Foucault, and the subject of America*. Boston: Northeastern University Press.

Rich, A. (1991). XIII (Dedications). In *An atlas of the difficult world*, 25–26. New York: W. W. Norton.

Sarton, M. (1980). Of the muse. From *Halfway to silence*, 61. New York: W. W. Norton.

PART I

Solitude and Identity

Chapter 1

A Reconnection to Self: Women and Solitude

Delese Wear

> *You quit your house and country, quit your ship, and quit your companions in the tent, saying, "I am just going outside and may be some time."*
>
> —Annie Dillard, *Teaching a Stone to Talk*

> *Now she can say without shame or deceit,*
> *O blessed Solitude.*
>
> —Denise Levertov, "A Woman Alone"

Introduction

Everywhere I turn, I'm connected, or supposed to be: at home with my partner, children, parents, and siblings; at work with my colleagues; at leisure with my friends. My way of thinking, feeling, and behaving is bound up in webs and intricate interrelationships. My self is known to me in my experience of connection and interaction with others. It seems, according to the work of Carol Gilligan, that even my conception of morality is grounded in values of care, connection, and interdependence.

Not enough professional kudos can ever be given to Gilligan and her colleagues whose work continues to inform our understanding of differences in the lived lives of men and women that may be attributable to gender. Reading *In a Different Voice* (1982) convinced me that the way I thought about the world wasn't blunted or restricted; that my intelligence wasn't wandering aimlessly in some soft, ethereal cloud with daily changes in form and composition; that I wasn't alone.

I'm affirmed by my connective life; I nurture and savor my attachments to others; I nourish my connectedness to mother, sisters, daughter, friends. I search for histories of connections to my unknown women ancestors. I eagerly read stories of my interdependence with other women, theirs with me. I hunger for women mentors; I mentor younger women.

Yet, I'm increasingly drawn to the idea of solitude. Days go by when I'm wearied by my interdependence, when responsiveness is mechanical and tedious. I want not just a room of my own; I want figurative space in my life. I'm slowly finding that my view of myself is not solely in relation to others, but is one that emerges in moments of impenetrable, profound silence, moments in which I am alone, moments in which I am no longer mother, daughter, teacher, wife. Anthony Storr captured who I am and who I strive to be, unconnected in these moments when one is "constantly seeking to discover [her]self, to remodel [her] own identity, and to find meaning in the universe through what [she] creates. [She] finds this a valuable integrating process which, like meditation or prayer, has little to do with other people, but which has its own separate validity. [Her] most significant moments are those in which [she] attains some new insight, or makes some new discovery; and these moments are chiefly, if not invariably, those in which [she] is alone" (1988, xiv).

Storr's right, I think: while there is inherent joy for many in living a life of care and response to others, there can be a toll for the sum of minutes and hours and years of moving "to the rhythms of others" (Olsen 1989, 68). In her book *Silences*, Tillie Olsen portrays the slow burn of one's need for solitude amidst the "joys and responsibilities and trials of family life" (1983, 38). But it didn't happen, as it doesn't—can't—for many women who, through duty or choice, weave their lives around others, their selves known only within the context of human connection. Olsen's need for aloneness, for separation from others in order to create, could not be first. It could have "at best, only part self, part time....It is distraction, not meditation, that becomes habitual; interruption, not continuity; spasmodic, not constant toil.... Work interrupted, deferred, relinquished, makes blockage—at best, lesser accomplishment. Unused capacities atrophy, cease to be" (1983, 37). This is not to suggest that women's connectiveness is necessarily distracting or disabling, sapping energy rather than charging it up. But our energy is often beamed to and from people, not toward the singularity of creation, introspection, reflection. And I fear that, with the intense focus on and celebration of women's connectiveness, we turn away from purposefully nurturing and validating not just the wish for or need to be alone, as Olsen portrayed, but the capacity to be alone (Storr, 18).

Storr argues that this capacity to be alone "becomes linked with self-discovery and self-realization; with becoming aware of one's deepest needs, feelings, and impulses" (p. 21). During these times, one is likely to discover and engage in the interests and creative work that play an important part in "defining individual identity and in giving meaning to a person's life" (p. 73). Here is the juncture at which Storr may offer women's developmental theories another perspective for which we need not apologize, fearing solipsism or selfishness or male-dominated patterns of relationships. Storr argues,

> If it is accepted that no relationship is ever ideal, it makes it easier to understand why men and women need other sources of fulfillment. As we have seen, many creative activities are predominantly solitary. They are concerned with self-realization and self-development in isolation, or with finding some coherent pattern in life. The degree to which these creative activities take priority in the life of an individual varies with [her] personality and talents. Everyone needs some human relationships; but everyone also needs some kind of fulfillment which is relevant to [her]self alone. (p. 84)

In the following pages I examine solitude as an essential condition for intense reflection on one's life, as a primary state for examination of one's emotional and spiritual self, and as a site of creation. My focus is necessarily personal; my own attempt at meaning-making has been grounded in a lifelong passion for literature during times I have been alone. Thus the examples I use are those from imaginative literature in the voices of women who have experienced solitude by choice or chance, solitude that has strengthened, nurtured, startled, or awakened their lives. While the sites and conditions of solitude are as varied as those who experience it, all the women in the following stories find a different kind of connectedness from that which we have grown accustomed to expect. That is, the solitude they experience is a reconnection of their outer, interpersonal, role-saturated selves back to their hidden, inarticulate selves—the part of us often parched or atrophied when our energy is only spent outward, on others.

Images of Solitude in Literature

Alice Koller's flight to an isolated beach house, documented in her book *An Unknown Woman* (1981), came after realizing at the age of thirty-seven that she "didn't have a life" and was merely "using up a number of days somehow" (p. 1). She decides to leave the familiarity of place and security of friends and acquaintances and lovers to go somewhere "quiet, without traffic or factories. Somewhere where I can be really alone, so that I don't have to be pleasant to people all day long, so that I don't even have to see other faces when I walk outside my door. Somewhere I don't have to do anything but think all day long" (p. 2). But why the *solitude* to think? She describes bits of intro-spective monologues she had in the presence of her psychiatrist that were helpful during her one-hour therapy sessions, but couldn't begin to unravel the difficult questions of days made up of twenty-four hours. Alone on Nantucket, she finds she doesn't have to separate that hour of introspection from the rest of her living, because there on the island "the hour has expanded to encompass the day....When I start thinking my way through some remembered torment, the only thing that stops my thinking is my endurance...no one can tell me more about myself than I already know. No one can care how it all turns out more than I do. And that's why no one is here with me now" (p. 61).

Still, Koller finds solitude to be an acquired capacity as she avoids the thinking she came to do, or loses the patience to sit down and write as she thinks, the thoughts coming too fast or too randomly. But slowly she becomes more adept at pursuing "one single thread all the way to its end" (p. 60). She begins to realize that she had never understood the meaning of what she needed or wanted, so dependent she had been on what other people said and believed: "I have turned other people into mirrors for me. I look at other people in order to see myself" (p. 69). She realizes how she had trusted what others saw, but not her own sight; thus she realizes her need for outside sources of validation—of her physical beauty, her intelligence. Yet once the sources dried up, she was set on a course of doubting herself. Without the mirrors supplied by others, she finds herself unable to know how to respond to things. No, that's not it, she writes. It's that "I don't know how *I* respond to things. I don't know how to find out what's going on inside of me" (pp. 111–12). Koller is not alone; Gilligan (1982, 16) describes women's ten-dencies to "question the normality of their feelings and to alter their judgments in deference to the opinion of others." Yet Gilligan presents the case that women's deference, rooted in social subordination, can also be regarded as the "substance of their moral concern. Sensitivity to the needs of others and the assumption of responsibility for taking care lead women to attend to voices other than their own and to include in their judgment other points of view" (ibid.).

But Koller finds in herself possible dishonesty in attending to oth-ers before she understands what she thinks and feels and wants, because being a person has to do with generosity and kindness only secondarily to being honest with myself. Suppose my generosity is the means I use to get someone to give me something. Suppose my kindness is my way of ignoring my anger. Suppose my thoughtfulness is my way of manipulating other people's lives....I feel naked and very small. But new. Nothing ever again has to be the way it was. If I can only hold back the world until I can catch up with my own unclad response to it. (p. 229)

There on Nantucket, alone without humans and mirrors, was where she set the process of self-understanding in motion. It was a process never to be completed, she believed; in fact, she didn't "even know how to begin learning how" to recognize what she felt (p. 123). But she was onto something, finally, an awareness and a yet-to-be-learned process that could deepen and magnify her experience, those lived in both separation *and* connection.

May Sarton writes of the similar challenge of her solitary confrontation with self in *Journal of a Solitude*. Living alone in her home in Maine, she describes the swings of emotion, the thinking, the tears of realization of truths, big and small, which compose the evolving story of her life. Living alone without any dependencies, she's aware of her position of privilege enabling her to ask the very questions themselves, to engage in a search for meaning, to mull and puzzle and think uninterrupted. She writes: "It is harder for women...to clear space.... Their lives are fragmented...[they] cry not so much for 'a room of one's own' as time of one's own. Conflict becomes acute, whatever it may be about, when there is no margin left on any day in which to try at least to resolve it" (1973, 56).

In Sarton's cleared space, she is able to dig deep enough to find a "bedrock of truth, however hard" (p. 150). She finds in herself not merely the capacity for solitude; she finds it imperative for finding meaning in the rest of her lived life. Yet this necessity is not without the risk of near-drowning in depths where there is nothing to "cushion against attacks from within" (p. 16). Here, alone, she is able to take up her "real" life again: "That is what is strange—that friends, even passionate love, are not my real life unless there is time alone in which to explore and to discover what is happening or has happened. Without the interruptions, nourishing and maddening, this life would become arid. Yet I taste it fully only when I am alone here and 'the house and I resume the old conversations'" (p. 11).

These essential, nourishing and maddening connections, if left unexplored, lead to what Sarton calls "clutter" when there is "no time to analyze experience. That is the silt…that literally chokes the mind" (p. 160). Without time to analyze experience, women *have* no center, so fragmented they become with the tugs and pulls and demands of others that their conception of self is a scatter plot, a labyrinth with someone always around the corner, a diagram of competing vectors. Without solitude, Sarton describes this as feeling "dispersed, scattered, in pieces" (p. 195). She finds that she must have time "to mull over any encounter…to extract its juices, to understand what has really happened to me as a consequence of it" (p. 196).

But what does one do when self and spirit are divided, and when human connections have disintegrated? Margaret Atwood's unnamed protagonist in *Surfacing* (1972) becomes primal, as far away from human contact as possible. For her, humans—the Americans—are the enemy in her search to discover her essential self, the self without "husks." Both the site and means to her search is the Canadian wilderness—"the truth is here"—where there is only the singularity and sacredness of nature. For her, solitude must be an inside-out, all-over, sensory experience, not merely in isolation in a room, a house, just anywhere. Her solitude is one in which her self becomes known only in connection with nature. Her search must be undistorted by humans, much like Thoreau's well-known flight to the woods where he went "to live deliberately…to reduce [life] to its lowest terms" (p. 67).

Atwood's protagonist lives deeply and deliberately, too, as she melds with nature: "I lean against a tree, I am a tree leaning.…I am not an animal or a tree, I am the thing in which the trees and animals move and grow, I am a place" (p. 210). Through her solitary experience in the wilderness, the awareness that comes to her helps her to hone and whet her humanness: she sleeps in lairs; she discards clothing and mirrors and other civilized accoutrements that restrict and blunt the authenticity of one's living; she dissects past relationships and revisits parents with sharper, more intuitive lenses; she identifies the enemy as anyone who "will not let you have peace…(or) anything they don't have themselves" (p. 215). She waits and watches and remembers. Finally she is able to reenter her own time with a newfound strength, awareness of self, and resolution: "This above all, to refuse to be a victim. Unless I can do that I can do nothing. I have to recant, give up the old belief that I am powerless" (p. 222).

A different perspective on solitude and the ravages of its absence in a woman's life is found in the voice of Eva in Tillie Olsen's *Tell Me a Riddle*. Unlike the other women I've described who are all in the midst of living in middle age, Eva is older, and dying. Her life has been one of continuous care for her husband and seven children, bound by a sense of unquestioned selfless duty, and confounded by the "humiliations and terrors" of poverty, leaving little time for herself. Even in those precious stolen moments when the house was quiet, nursing one baby with another on her lap, she would "try to stay awake for the only time there was to read," often to the coaxes of her husband to "put the book away, don't read, don't read" (1989, 67).

Now, in her garden and in the tranquility of an empty house "no longer an enemy, for it stayed clean," she had peace. And she was dying. But what to do with the manner of her dying? Her family thought they knew, based on the manner of her living: surround her with her children and her grandchildren, with the flurry of doing. Hiding the finality of her illness, and without asking what she wanted, her husband whisks her around the country to her children's homes. While she thought she might be able, finally, "to live within, and not move to the rhythms of others" (p. 68), she is faced with more noise, more chatter, more insistence from others to comfort, to mend, to tell stories and riddles. So what she did, instead, was pretend to nap,

> and hunch in the girls' closet on the low shelf where the shoes stood, and the girls' dresses covered....For that while she would painfully sheathe against the listening house, the tendrils and noises that knocked, and Vivi's spilling memories....Blows, screams, a call: "Grandma!" For her? Oh please not for her. Hide, hunch behind the dresses deeper....But a trembling little body hurls itself beside her—surprised, smothered laughter, arms surround her neck, tears rub dry on her cheek, and words too soft to understand whisper into her ear (Is this where you hide too Grammy? It's my secret place, we have a secret now)....And the sweat beads, and the long shudder seizes. (pp. 89–90)

Even in dying she is denied solitude, so seeped was her family in the belief that her connectedness to others was what, in the end, would give her the most comfort.

Summary

Through literary descriptions of solitude, I've attempted to reveal its absence and importance in women's lives. Solitude, the voices of these women posit, is essential if they are to examine themselves critically, deeply, and honestly, without looking at and listening to others first or exclusively for validation. While it may be that women depict "ongoing attachment as the path that leads to maturity" (Gilligan, 170), somewhere along that path should be forays into the woods, alone without companion or guide, where the "mirror of the soul" (Merton, 106) can be emptied of other images.

Yet, I'm uneasy. The women I've described are women of privilege, and none has the dailiness of dependents. With the exception of Eva, they are writers or academics, not bound by timecard or rigidity of being here or there for this person at that time. They are white, apparently well-educated, middle class. I worry that it is my position, like theirs, that allows me even to raise the issue of solitude. As I read Annie Dillard's account of writing *Pilgrim at Tinker Creek* in Roanoke, I thought how strange and mysterious her schedule must sound to women whose lives are framed by lunches to pack, mountains of laundry, bills that may not be paid, and tedious or routinized jobs: "I slept until noon, as did my husband, who was also writing. I wrote once in the afternoon, and once again after our early dinner and a walk. During those months, I subsisted on that dinner, coffee, Coke, chocolate milk, and Vantage cigarettes. I worked till midnight, one, or two. When I came home in the middle of the night I was tired; I longed for a tolerant giant, a person as big as a house, to hold me and rock me" (1989, 27).

I and many others rejoice in Dillard's solitude that allowed her to give us the gift of her craft. But to suppose that a literal escape, a place, is *necessary* for women to live reflective, creative lives is romantic, perhaps quixotic, a brass ring just out of reach, given the multiple lives many women live. Perhaps Tillie Olsen offers hope for many women wanting connection and separation, family and solitude, a life of giving and serving and a life lived within:

> Bliss of movement. A full extended family life; the world of my job...and the writing, which I was somehow able to carry around within me through work, through home. Time on the bus, even when I had to stand, was enough; the stolen moments at work, enough; the deep night hours for as long as I could stay awake, after the kids were in bed, after the household tasks were done, sometimes during. It is no accident that the first work I considered publishing began: "I stand here ironing, and what you asked me moves tormented back and forth with the iron." (1983, 38)

Through chance, oppression, or choice many women are not able to seize blocks of time in solitary places to think, reflect, or create like Sarton or Koller or Dillard, though we celebrate their lives that enable them to do so. Perhaps what some of us can do, however, is follow the example of lives like Olsen's that acknowledge, then stalk those moments of solitude often wedged in dailiness. We're far more than what we see of ourselves reflected in others; learning how and where to look for ourselves, to "dive deep" and still surface, seems to be what we can learn to do as we, too, stand here ironing.

References

Atwood, M. (1972). *Surfacing*. New York: Simon and Schuster.

Dillard, A. (1982). *Teaching a stone to talk*. New York: Harper Colphon Books.

———. (1989). *The writing life*. New York: Harper and Row.

Gilligan, C. (1982). *In a different voice*. Cambridge: Harvard University Press.

Koller, A. (1981). *An unknown woman: Journey to self-discovery*. New York: Holt, Rinehart and Winston.

Levertov, D. (1975). A woman alone. In *Life in the forest*, 16–17. New York: New Directions.

Olsen, T. (1983). *Silences*. New York: Dell. (First published 1965).

———. (1989). *Tell me a riddle*. New York: Dell. (First published 1956).

Sarton, M. (1973). *Journal of a solitude*. New York: Norton.

Storr, A. (1988). *Solitude: A return to the self*. New York: Ballantine Books.

Thoreau, H. (1962). *The Variorum Walden*. New York: Washington Square Press. (First published 1854).

Chapter 2

Solitude, Suffering, and Personal Authority

Lynne McFall

One of my clearest memories of childhood is of lying alone in a field of mustard flower, staring up at the sun, wondering whether it was true, as my mother said, that staring at the sun could cause blindness. I prayed to go blind or to suffer some other tragic loss, so that I could be brave and enigmatic and full of woe and would thereby earn my mother's bereaved smile. There is an aristocracy of great suffering done with grace and I wanted to belong to it.

To suffer is to begin to think. The infant cries; the mother or father comes but not soon enough; and in that space is born the idea of "I" and "not-I." So the psychologists tell us. If we got everything we wanted, exactly when we wanted it, there would be no impetus to change, no "growth," and we would never learn where the world stops and the individual starts. Suffering is the beginning not only of personal identity but of metaphysics. Pleasure is never problematic; it is pain that prompts the question "Why?" or, less philosophically, "Why me?" (Smolkin 1989, 1). Another requirement for membership in my imaginary aristocracy was solitude, which was necessary, I thought, for genuine suffering. If your mother was around, for instance, or someone to baby you when you were hurt, then you might be crying a little louder than necessary. You might be screaming your lungs out so she would hold you a while longer, or give you some ice cream to take your mind off the pain, and that would corrupt your suffering. To suffer one must suffer alone, out of reach of comfort and salvation. "Great is my sorrow, without limits. None knows of it, except God in Heaven," and He does not exist (Kierkegaard, quoted in Becker 1973, 67). This was the litany of my youth.

My aim in this essay is to suggest that while solitude and suffering are not guarantees of moral wisdom, they are rightly associated with it. The child lying in the field of mustard flower was not completely wrong.

As I grew up, my society of solitary sufferers became—slightly broader in conception—a society of the morally serious: those who told the truth whatever the cost. Suffering alone was not grand enough. One had to suffer for a noble cause, and only the Truth was noble enough. To prove one's seriousness, I thought, one had to die for it. Suicide was the ultimate proof.

Of those I granted membership in this imaginary society, one was Simone Weil, who lived a solitary life, a life of great suffering, and who was a self-appointed truth-teller. "They alone will see God who prefer to recognize the truth and die, instead of living a long and happy existence in a state of illusion" (Panichas 1977, xxii). She died of willful starvation at the age of thirty-four, in part to share her limited rations with her compatriots in France under the German occupation. A small plaque attached to her tombstone by an anonymous donor read: *La mia solitudine l'atrui dolore germivo fino all morte*: "My solitude held in its grasp the grief of others till my death" (p. xvii).

She suffered, it was said, from "vertigo of the absolute," a condition with which I could identify. I discovered Simone Weil the year I discovered moral philosophy, at the age of twenty-seven, and from then on believed I knew my destiny: to write down the absolute moral truths and give them to the world. This would take hard work, I thought, but not more than three years.

That same year—my first year at Reed College—a philosophy professor loaned me Norman Malcolm's memoir of Wittgenstein, and I immediately dropped death as a requirement in my imaginary society and gave Wittgenstein an honored place. The other conditions he clearly met. Most of his life he lived alone in a room furnished with a cot, a chair, and a writing table. George Henrik von Wright wrote: "It is probably true that he lived on the border of mental illness. A fear of being driven across it followed him throughout his life" (Malcolm 1975, 3). Wittgenstein's reply to his sister Hermine supports this. Upon hearing Wittgenstein's decision to become a country schoolteacher, Hermine said that imagining him with his philosophically trained mind as an elementary schoolteacher was like using a precision instrument to open crates. Wittgenstein replied: "You remind me of someone who is looking through a closed window and cannot explain to himself the strange movements of a passer-by. He doesn't know what kind of a storm is raging outside and that this person is perhaps only with great effort keeping himself on his feet" (Wittgenstein 1981, 5).

It's been said that Wittgenstein started two important schools of philosophical thought, both of which he renounced (Malcolm 1975, 1).

One of his mottoes, which I copied into a spiral-bound notebook: Go the bloody hard way. There was, in that brief quotation, all the breast-beating of which I was capable.

"Almost anything that consoles us is a fake," Iris Murdoch has written (1971, 59). This is true, I suppose, even of our moral heroes, if we imagine them too pure to be human. Simone Weil was an anti-Semite after all. Wittgenstein was hell on his friends, often harsh and self-righteous.

It is no less true of suffering, of which we may be tempted to be proud. I remember a party my husband and I gave when we were first married in 1967. We had no money then, were barely making it from paycheck to paycheck, but a good time was more important than solvency, so I pawned my wedding ring to pay for the necessities of entertainment. A few years later, at another gathering, the conversation turned to the topic of living in poverty. My story began, "We were so poor that we hocked my wedding ring for fifteen dollars to buy the makings of tacos and Margaritas." Every story after that sought to top this. "You call that poor? At least you had a wedding ring. We were so poor that we had to sell blood to buy our baby milk." "We couldn't afford a baby. We were living in my Chevy Impala, and our bedroom was the back seat." Then the next exploiter of grief would begin.

Last year in Syracuse, at a dinner party for a visiting poet, a similar discussion began among the writers at the table, this time of mental illness: who was manic-depressive and who merely depressed; who had been hospitalized, how many times, for how long; who suffered still.

Even among manic-depressives there is competition. "I thought I was John the Baptist and I was standing on my head naked in the bathtub doing the fourteen stations of the cross when my wife called the ambulance." "I thought I was Jesus Christ and I lay down on Interstate 90 like a crucifix and refused to get up." "I thought I was God." When I heard this conversation I decided that if there is an aristocracy of great suffering done with grace, it does not include those who brag about it.

I now believe that suffering—even where it isn't consolation or barter for attention—is highly overrated as a path to wisdom. The sadomasochist and the ascetic have too much in common. To Simone Weil one might fairly say, You love your affliction as much as your God. There is in her suffering too much self-obsession: not "Thy will be done," but that *I* do it. And even among ordinary mortals with no aspirations to sainthood, suffering may lead not to wisdom but to brutality. The prisons and mental hospitals are full of the abused children of alcoholics and drug addicts and others who were given early lessons in suffering.

Still, there is some truth in the thought that suffering is necessary for wisdom: we require that the insight be earned, not gotten second-hand—perhaps from a book or, worse, simply parroted from a parent or friend. When the adolescent says, "What's madness but nobility of soul at odds with circumstance?" we don't believe it. When Theodore Roethke says it, we do. The difference is personal authority proved through experience.

> In a dark time, the eye begins to see,
> I meet my shadow in the deepening shade;
> I hear my echo in the echoing wood—
> A lord of nature weeping to a tree.
>
> What's madness but nobility of soul
> At odds with circumstance? The day's on fire!
> I know the purity of pure despair,
> My shadow pinned against a sweating wall.
> That place among the rocks—is it a cave,
> Or winding path? The edge is what I have.
>
> A steady storm of correspondences!
> A night flowing with birds, a ragged moon,
> And in broad day the midnight come again!
> A man goes far to find out what he is—
> Death of the self in a long, tearless night,
> All natural shapes blazing unnatural light.
>
> Dark, dark my light, and darker my desire.
> My soul, like some heat-maddened summer fly,
> Keeps buzzing at the sill. Which I is I? (Roethke 1975, 231)

To suffer is to begin to think for oneself.

For this, solitude may be required, but not in the beginning, if D. W. Winnicott is right. The "I" is born in solitude but needs another person to develop. In an essay titled "The Capacity to Be Alone," Winnicott says: "It is only when alone (that is to say, in the presence of someone) that the infant can discover his personal life....In this setting the sensation or impulse will feel real and be truly a personal experience" (quoted in Storr 1988, 20).

This happens, according to Winnicott, when the baby is in a relaxed state, alone in the presence of the mother, and the baby's basic needs have been met: for food, warmth, affection, and so on. "The capacity to be alone thus becomes linked with self-discovery and self-realization; with becoming aware of one's deepest needs, feelings, and impulses" (Storr 1988, 21). This is contrasted with a "false self" based on compliance with the desires of others.

In *The Drama of the Gifted Child: The Search for the True Self*, Alice Miller (1981) provides support for this. An adult can only be fully aware of her feelings, Miller claims, if the adult has "internalized" an affectionate mother, one who "mirrors" the feelings of her child, who does not use the child to satisfy her own narcissistic needs. Those who have not are "never overtaken by unexpected emotions, and will only admit those feelings that are accepted and approved by their inner censor, which is their parents' heir" (p. 21). She quotes a patient: "I lived in a glass house into which my mother could look at any time. In a glass house, however, you cannot conceal anything without giving yourself away, except by hiding it under the ground. And then you cannot see it either" (p. 21). Forced to choose between one's true self and parental approval and love, the child chooses against himself.

Personal authority, then, begins with someone listening and encouraging us—not to say what she wants to hear, but to be ourselves. Without the "mirror" of an affectionate mother or father, there would be no self to be true to, much less the strength to achieve such moral independence.

Winnicott claims that being alone in the presence of someone is also the origin of the capacity for solitude in adult life."I am trying to justify the paradox that the capacity to be alone is based on the experience of being alone in the presence of someone, and that without a sufficiency of this experience the capacity to be alone cannot develop" (quoted in Storr, 20). We learn to be alone without anxiety step by step—first by being alone with someone who is there if needed but not directly concerned with us; then, when a sense of security has developed, being alone by ourselves for longer and longer periods of time.

So a gift for solitude and personal authority may be, paradoxically, proof that one was well-loved. I don't know whether this is true, or how it might be proved, but it has some plausible marks of truth: it balances two extremes (abject slavery to others and the myth of complete self-creation), and it provides no occasion for breast-beating, no easy consolation.

It also makes of the capacity for solitude a virtue instead of a reason to seek psychiatric help. If the necessity for constant approval in the form of everpresent others shows a lack of emotional maturity (and an unfortunate choice of parents), then the capacity for solitude may be evidence of emotional maturity.

In *Solitude: A Return to the Self*, Anthony Storr (1988) argues for just this view: that the capacity to be alone should be—along with the capacity for close emotional attachments—one of the criteria of emotional maturity. As one more solitary than social, I find this conclusion welcome.

Storr claims, further, that both suffering and solitude may have other benefits that have gone unnoticed. He quotes Freud—"we may lay it down that a happy person never phantasies, only an unsatisfied one" (p. 64)—in defense of the view that discontent may be the beginning of artistic creativity. And solitude, he says, may be necessary to the growth of the imagination necessary to become an artist. In Trollope's case, it produced a writer:

> As a boy, even as a child, I was thrown much upon myself. I have explained, when speaking of my schooldays, how it came to pass that other boys would not play with me. I was therefore alone, and had to form my plays within myself....Thus it came to pass that I was always going about with some castle in the air firmly built within my mind....There can, I imagine, hardly be a more dangerous mental practice; but I have often doubted whether, had it not been my practice, I should ever have written a novel. I learned in this way to maintain an interest in a fictitious story, to dwell on a work created by my own imagination, and to live in a world altogether outside the world of my own material life. (quoted in Storr, 107–8)

In *Art and Artist*, Otto Rank (1932) adds his weight (as Freud's chosen heir, who defied the overbearing "father" and went his own way) to this view. How does one become an artist? The first step, according to Rank, is the appointment of the artist by himself as artist. "The ability to appoint oneself is an act which reflects one's individuation, one's emergence from the matrix of childhood dependency. It is the precondition in the average individual for the creation of a mature, separate personality and for the creative artistic personality it is the first productive work" (quoted in Menaker 1982, 35). Thus Rank suggests that what individuation requires of every adult is found exaggerated in the artist: the ability to stand alone, to create her own meanings, the justification for her life. Personal heroism through individuation "is a very daring venture precisely because it separates the person out of comfortable 'beyonds'" (Becker 1973, 171). For most of us, the meaning of our lives is given by the culture: we're good citizens, dutiful daughters, faithful lovers, reliable mothers, good at our jobs, great beauties or great brains, followers of an accepted religion. The difference between the average person and the artist, other than talent, is that the artist is separated out of the common pool of shared meanings. There is something in his life experience that makes him take in the world as a *problem*; as a result he has to make personal sense out of it....Existence becomes a problem that needs an ideal answer; but when you no longer accept the collective solution to the problem of existence, then you must fashion your own. The work of art is, then, the ideal answer of the creative type to the problem of existence as he takes it in—not only the existence of the external world, but especially his own: who he is as a painfully separate person with nothing shared to lean on. (Becker 1973, 170)

My argument, then, is this: to become an individual requires solitude and suffering. To survive and develop as an individual requires the capacity to "stand alone": to think and feel and speak for oneself, even when terrified, traits found exaggerated in the artist. Solitude, like suffering, is a symbol, if not always proof, of personal authority, which is the beginning at least of wisdom.

Now that I am grown I no longer believe in absolutes or the beatitude of suffering. Solitude is not always my first choice, though I still think that without the developed ability to be alone one is not fully grown. My moral heroes now are more likely to be those capable of irony and self-mockery rather than breast-beating and suicide. Alice Munro. Raymond Carver. I still believe in something like truth, only now with a lower case "t": personal truths, the only defense of which is one's whole lived life. Truths one hopes not to die for, but might be willing to share. I'm too old for mottoes but there is a saying I like: "The only thing that we can hope for is that we lapse now and then into reality" (Munro 1974, 222).

The paragraph with which this essay began is from my second novel, *Dancer With Bruised Knees*, which dramatizes this transition: from a belief in absolute moral value to an acceptance of disorder, imperfection, and uncertainty; from a position of dependence on authority to an ability to stand on one's own; from self-dramatization to irreverent humility.

The narrator, Sarah Blight—a photographer whose right eye has been put out—is a thirty-nine-year-old woman who has come to doubt everything she has thus far believed. This is the way it begins:

It happened in my fortieth year that I fell into a depression so deep that even the thought of sex could not raise me from it. I began, during this year of which I am going to speak, to doubt everything I had believed and had built my life on. What was the genesis of this doubt? The losses were many. First Jake, then the accident. Then the split between my father and my brother. Then frosting on the poison cake: a devout and life-long pessimist, I was diagnosed a manic-depressive, pre-scribed lithium and antidepressants—in short, cured of my melancholia. And therein lay my grief. I had wanted all my life to get to the black heart of things. I discovered there was no black heart of things, only chaos. (Evil too is a kind of order.)

The novel is, in part, a continuing meditation on the meaning of a picture with which Sarah identifies, though she is not sure why. The picture is of her great grandmother, Victoria Blight: a tiny figure in a long dress dancing on a rock in Yosemite National Park. The rock sticks out like a tongue from a rock mountain, with a drop of thou-sands of feet on three sides.

One thing the picture is meant to depict is our belief in individual-ism and self-invention. But in Sarah Blight's moral "coming of age" this belief is modified: Victoria Blight also represents Sarah's heritage, which suggests that our creation of ourselves is not from scratch but is limited by what has been passed down to us, both genetically and morally.

I come from a long line of suicides, lunatics, and lushes. Some had more flair than others. My great grandmother on my father's side, Victoria Blight, jumped to her death from a rock in Yosemite National Park around 1900. Either that or she fell. There's a picture of her that I keep on top of my desk. She is dancing at the edge of the abyss, one leg flung up so high it threatens her ear, her arms raised in jubilation, her skirts fly-ing. The expression on her face is unclear, though I imagine it to be one of ecstasy or defiance or abject terror, depending on my mood at the time. Did she know in the picture that she would die that afternoon? Was the decision her own, or some-thing ineluctably come to, like Uncle Ad's fist wrapped around a scrap of wet paper covered with words even Aunt Martha couldn't decipher? I search the place where her eyes must be, hidden by what looks like a man's hat with a Dick Tracy brim. I can't tell.

Sarah's heritage includes a set of conflicting beliefs drawn from her forebears: a Christian Scientist with Alzheimer's, a skeptical Catholic who is alleged to have killed a man, a utilitarian addicted to gambling, an atheistic mother who reads Anne Sexton and Sylvia Plath to her children at bedtime instead of fairy tales. Among others. Faced with the breakdown of her beliefs, and given a moral heritage full of contradictions (much like the moral heritage of all of us in the late twentieth century), Sarah Blight must recreate herself, must formulate "rules for living in a state of siege."

Take a broken woman, invent a few more calamities, and then see how she manages to live, what she can love. That was my "literary method," learned more from life than from philosophy or fiction. What Sarah Blight, one-eyed photographer, will come up with as a solution, or a way to go on, I have not yet fully invented and/or discovered. (Her wisdom is, unfortunately, limited by my own.) But it will include a modified belief in the value of both suffering and solitude. In deference to reality one must admit the existence not only of grief but of happiness. Even the artist cannot stand completely alone and survive.

In my own life, women have been the major caretakers.

My mother encouraged my gifts and my "true self." When I showed a talent for music she bought me a piano and paid for the lessons. When I decided to become a dancer, she bought me tap shoes and ballet slippers. When I totaled the second family car, she encouraged me to buy my own and become a stock car racer. I didn't know until I went to kindergarten that I wasn't quite right: too aggressive for a girl, too smart-mouthed, stubborn, nowhere near selfless. Always there if needed, she left me to my wanderings in the field. And she taught me to tell the truth in the loudest voice I knew.

At the age of twenty-seven, when I left my husband to study philosophy at Reed—a decision of which many in my family disapproved—my grandmother said, "To thine own self be true." Later on, when I wanted to become a novelist, she said, "I always thought your name would look good on a book." A learned and self-taught person, she lived alone the last twenty years of her life, had more than her share of grief, a great sense of irony, and the personal authority of a religion she chose for herself at the age of nineteen and never wavered from in spite of social pressure. She was devout but not dogmatic, if that is possible. We spent many hours arguing over whether God is dead or just not listening. President of the Christian Science church, she allowed her granddaughter to be a skeptic. In the months before she died, when she had forgotten my name, she could still laugh at her predicament and say, "T'ain't funny, McGee."

I have had at all times of my life at least one close friend, in spirit if not in distance: someone I could tell everything to, someone who believed in my improbable dreams. In the novel, Sarah Blight says: "My sister was a hard act to follow in high school—head majorette, Homecoming Queen, beautiful, smart, universally admired—but she loved me unconditionally and so I tried to forgive her for being perfect. She often expressed the wish that she could be like me (hell on wheels and who cares), which went a long way toward making me feel at home in the world." This part is true.

Romantic love has come and gone several times but these relationships have lasted.

The image of the dancer on the rock exalts solitude and personal authority; in response to terror, grace. But it is also meant to convey thanksgiving, for the long line of women—from my grandmothers Lucille Carter and Amelia Salmon, my mother Louise McFall, my sister Sharon Benn, my friends Inger Van Wagner and Rebecca Holsen, to my daughter Hope McFall—whose love has made this solitary and sometimes risky life possible; who have, unseen, held me up.

Author's Note

I am indebted to Storr's essay, both for his discussion of Winnicott and for the quotation from Trollope.

I would like to thank Rebecca Holsen for valuable criticisms of this essay.

References

Becker, E. (1973). *The denial of death*. New York: The Free Press.

McFall, L. *Dancer with bruised knees*. In manuscript.

Malcolm, N. (1975). *Ludwig Wittgenstein: A memoir*, with a biographical sketch by Georg Henrik von Wright. London: Oxford University Press.

Menaker, E. (1982). *Otto Rank: A rediscovered legacy*. New York: Columbia University Press.

Miller, A. (1981). *The drama of the gifted child: The search for the true self*. New York: Basic Books.

Munro, A. (1974). Memorial. In *Something I've been meaning to tell you*, 207–26. New York: New American Library.

Murdoch, I. (1971). *The sovereignty of good*. New York: Schocken Books.

Panichas, G. A. (ed.) (1977). *The Simone Weil reader*, xvii–xxxiii. Mt. Kisco, N.Y.: Moyer Bell.

Rank, O. (1932). *Art and artist*. New York: Knopf.

Roethke, T. (1975). In a dark time. In *The collected poems of Theodore Roethke*, 231. Garden City, N.Y.: Anchor Books.

Smolkin, M. T. (1989). *Understanding pain: Interpretation and philosophy*. Malabar, Fla.: Krieger.

Storr, A. (1988). *Solitude: A return to the self*. New York: Ballantine Books.

Winnicott, D. W. (1965). The capacity to be alone. In *The maturational processes and the facilitating environment*. New York: International Universities Press.

Wittgenstein, H. (1981). My brother Ludwig. In *Ludwig Wittgenstein: Personal recollections*, edited by R. Rhees, 1–13. Totowa, N.J.: Rowman and Littlefield.

Chapter 3

Reclaiming the Safety of Solitude:
Being With, Not Hiding From

Mara Sapon-Shevin

I am six years old. My family is spending a year in Spain, and the first summer in the little town of Palamos on the Costa Brava. We have just moved into a house on the edge of town, near the sea. Several blocks from our house is a very steep hill, and at the bottom of that hill is the Mediterranean. I descend the hill, almost running because it is steep and my legs are short. I am at the rocks. Later I will learn that there is an official name for this place, but for now, they are my rocks. These are not small rocks, but huge boulders, a vast expanse of oddly shaped stones that end at the sea. I find a rock to sit on. I choose carefully, being cautious not to step on the sea urchins that are attached to the rocks' sides, avoiding the jellyfish that have washed up onto the rocky shore. I am alone. Truly, stunningly alone. There are no people any-where in sight. The whole world is mine: the crashing blue-green breakers, the rush and hiss of the water approaching and then reced-ing, always safely away from me, the blue sky, the silent, salty air. And I am safe.

It is years before I will learn that I am not safe alone, that girls are never safe, that there is much to fear. It is long before I will have to learn to choose my solitude carefully, to listen cautiously to approach-ing footsteps, to be constantly aware of what is outside, unable to con-centrate fully on what is inside.

I am seventeen years old, a freshman in college, away from home for the first time, relishing my freedom. And I have found another quiet spot. The women's dormitory where I live is connected by underground tunnels to many other buildings on campus, and I know the tunnels well. It is late at night. I am awake studying for an exam. Deciding to get something from the food machines in the basement of the psychology department, I travel the tunnels alone. There is no one else awake, it seems. It is completely still. I am an explorer, an adventurer. I reach the machines, buy my snack and then curl up on what I have come to think of as "my ledge" by the machines, my back to the wall. It is totally still. I feel powerful and safe. I relish and delight in being somewhere no one else is. Perhaps they have been here at other times, but now there is just me. Alone. Quiet. Safe.

It is over thirty years since I was a little girl sitting on the rocks, over twenty years since I was a freshman sitting by the candy machine in the tunnel. But there have been very few times when I have been happy to be alone, have chosen to be alone. My life, like that of many other women, has been spent trying to make connections with others, trying to construct myself in a social context. And now, at a very different time in my life, I am only beginning to understand why being alone has rarely felt good to me, am trying to reclaim the safety of being alone, trying to find ways to be alone without being lonely, apart from others but not isolated, on my own, but not bereft.

This essay traces my thinking about solitude and safety. My attempt is to understand and explore the many meanings that being alone has had for me, to construct the contexts in which those meanings were formed. I try to explore the original contexts in which I first learned how to "read" being alone and then explore ways in which my current life as a university professor feeds some of those old meanings and makes redefinition difficult. Finally, this essay represents my attempts as a woman to reclaim spaces for myself, spaces of safety and solitude, to transform the concept of solitude in my own life as I regain power, trust and choices.

Aloneness as Unchoseness

I am at my first sixth-grade dance. My parents have refused to let me wear stockings and flats like the other girls, so I wear black and white oxfords and ridiculous little white ankle socks. They will not let me shave my legs, so my dark, hairy limbs stand in sharp contrast to my white socks. No one asks me to dance. All evening I wait on the side of the gymnasium, but no one asks. None of the other girls talk to me, either, although occasionally, one snickers at me. I hear muffled calls, "Can I hide in your legs?" I am devastated, alone, rejected.

Already I have learned, if you are different, you will be alone. You are alone because no one wants to be with you. To be alone is to be unchosen, unwanted, unworthy. People who are popular are constantly surrounded by others; it is good to be popular, it is bad to be alone.

Sixth grade was, for me, a marker. I was new to town, having just moved to New York from California, and I was different in many ways. I had a different name, different clothes, but worse yet, for a girl, I was smart. I did well in school. Daily, I saw my choices hover before me as painful alternatives: do well in school and have the teachers like you; do poorly and have friends. "Curve buster," "teacher's pet," "smarty pants," "goody two shoes." You can't have both. If you do well you will be alone. Teachers held up my work as an example: "This is what I expect from an essay. Mara will you read yours to the class." The rejection was instantaneous. No one to sit with at lunch, sixth-grade parties to which I wasn't invited. Always, the punishment for excellence took the same form, the same ultimate public humiliation: being left alone. Time spent alone did not feel like a gift, a treasure of freedom for contemplation and reflection. Time to spend alone was an indicator that no one wanted to be with you.

As an adult, I find myself still wrestling with what feel like similar choices: can I be as good as I can be and still be liked, still have friends? If I am too smart or too powerful or too successful, will I be rejected by my friends and colleagues? A colleague approaches me in the hall and asks bitingly: "Why do you write so much?" I feel a rush of guilt and alienation: how dare I do well and make others look or feel bad? Is it worth it? Some of my colleagues form a "non-writers' support group." Weekly they meet for breakfast to share their work and their struggles to write; they are warm and friendly to one another. I am not invited to join, not even permitted to attend, because, as one member explains when I ask: "You write a lot. It's not hard for you." My mother's old warning, "Never beat a boy or he won't ask you out," comes back to haunt me in new and painful ways. I am not looking for dates, only acceptance, but doing well makes that goal seem elusive. Many years later, I feel some of the same struggle, face some of the same difficult choices: fit in, conform, be like others, or you will end up alone. Aloneness as unchosenness.

Aloneness as Alienation

If you are bad, if you are disagreeable, if you yell or cry, we will send you to your room. If you are sick, if you are in pain, we will send you to your room. There you will be alone. You will not receive support, or nurturance or solace. You will be there by yourself. How many times as a child was I told, "You go to your room now and think about your behavior. And don't come out until you're prepared to apologize/recant/redo."

To be alone was to be isolated from the rest of the world. Alone was where you were sent if you had feelings, and if you expressed them. People with feelings were not permissible, and they were sent away. People who cry must be sent away. People who yell must be banished. In solitude, you must learn to conform; you are "fit" to be around other people only when you act like they tell you to.

In schools, we banish "misbehaving" children to the "time-out" room; sent away from the action as punishment, as time to reflect, as a place to cool off. But always sent away. At home we send children to their rooms. Away. Small wonder, then, that being alone can come to connote punishment, isolation from real emotions and real feelings.

Years later, as a woman academic, I face the isolation that results from having feelings and expressing them. I learn that to express passion or emotion in the academy is to be suspect, less than professional, inappropriate. At a faculty meeting when we are discussing a faculty candidate who I have judged to be racist, I speak out strongly about my concerns. I voice my commitment to supporting the diversity in our own student body, make my fervent plea to hire faculty who are open to differences. I speak with passion, and at the end of my speech I begin to cry. In tears I leave the meeting and return to my office, and there I remain. Alone. No one comes to comfort me. No one comes to see if I am okay. Later, I am told that I acted "unprofessionally," and that my "personal and professional agendas are too closely related."

It is appropriate to cry alone in your office (or at least acceptable), but not in public. You can only be in the public arena, the professional world, if you remain calm and neutral, unemotional and dispassionate. Different setting, same message: if you display emotion, if you have feelings, you will end up alone. People are not comfortable around people who are feeling things, particularly women who get angry or cry. Aloneness as alienation.

Aloneness as Disempowerment

My parents are summoned to school to discuss a problem I am having. I am told to wait at home, alone. This is something for adults to discuss. Yes, it concerns my life, yes, decisions will be made which may change my immediate future, but I am not invited. Grownups have important conversations, and children must go away and leave them alone. Alone to their power, to their decision-making, power and decisions from which I am excluded, disenfranchised. Important things happen away from you, and you are informed of them later. The same is true for many positive events: adults have parties, share jokes, and children are sent away. I remember a chronic feeling that I was "missing something," and that it wasn't safe to be away from the action because I would get left behind, excluded. I remember the sense of panic, the tight feeling in the chest that if I went off by myself, spent time alone, then I would miss being in the center of the action, would miss "something good," or, worse yet, would miss knowing what was happening, things I needed to know to stay powerful, in charge, safe.

Now as an adult academic, there is often the same feeling; somewhere, important people are making decisions that will affect my life, and I am excluded. I have watched senior members of the faculty closet themselves in an office before a faculty meeting and decide on both the agenda and the outcome of the meeting. And then, I have been a spectator at such meetings, meetings in which people went through the motions of deciding when, in fact, the important deliberations all went on outside, away from me, went on while I was alone in my office. During the time of my tenure committee's deliberations, I was left awkwardly alone. Friends and colleagues who had previously talked to me and included me in conversations now seemed strangely distant. Disempowerment became coupled with fear; important things were happening, things which would affect me, and I would be the last to know. The feeling was clear: if you spend time alone, you will be away from the action, away from the power. Power does not rest within you, but with other people. If you are off by yourself, you won't know about what is happening: the latest office gossip, the latest departmental mandate. And not to know is to be unsafe. Aloneness as disempowerment.

Aloneness as Hiding

Like many Jewish children, I was raised by adults for whom the Holocaust was a powerful, life-altering event. And, like many Jewish children, there were both the tales told (of concentration camps, of relatives murdered, of homes destroyed) and the tales untold but still powerful, the sub-texts: there are dangers out there for you as a Jew. You are never really truly safe. The Jews thought they were safe in Germany, but their neighbors sold them out. You may think you fit in, but you must always be careful, always be wary, always have an escape route.

And, of course, there was the *Diary of Anne Frank*. Anne, a young Jewish girl, in danger from the Nazis, must go into hiding with her family in a small annex above a warehouse. Only by hiding does the family have any chance of staying safe, of surviving the destruction of the Jews. And, ultimately, they are not successful. Shortly before the end of the war, they are discovered, taken to concentration camps, and killed. Anne, the young Jewish girl, a Jewish girl like me, was unable to stay safe, even by hiding.

I read this book in religious school and also in public school, saw the movie, saw the play, and always, there was the unspoken terror: you can hide, but you can never really be safe. You cannot stay safe by being around other people, and you cannot even stay safe by hiding. Then where was safety? Being alone is what you do to avoid others who would hurt you. To be alone is to affirm that you are in danger. Perhaps if you hide, you will avoid harm, but perhaps, even by hiding, you will not be safe.

Years later, I have organized a Holocaust Conference on my campus, and I return one evening to my office and find a note on my chair: "Shut up and get out of here or your reproductive capacity will be sharply diminished." On the back it says "Holocaust—destruction of the Jews." Suddenly, old fears are rekindled—am I safe as a Jew? Will my colleagues come to my aid, or will they allow horrible things to happen to me? Several colleagues are shocked and supportive, but another tells me "not to take it personally," and another tells me she "doesn't feel comfortable" coming to a meeting called to discuss better security for me in the building. My private space—my office—has been invaded. Where does one hide on a university campus?

The meanings of being alone again become transformed. One is alone, hides, to stay away from fearful things "out there," but what happens when those cannot be easily discerned, when the parameters of the danger become nebulous and uncertain? How can one hide to be safe when it is not clear what or whom one is hiding from? And, perhaps worse yet, one can be alone even surrounded by other people, can feel separate, apart, unsupported. Aloneness as hiding.

Aloneness as Vulnerability

And last, sadly, I have learned as a woman, that there can be great danger in being alone. Talking to women who have been raped, abused, and harassed because they were "alone," I have come to doubt that women are ever really safe. Women who have been assaulted are often chastised: "What were you doing there alone? Didn't you know that was dangerous?" And so, we must choose our aloneness carefully. Going out running early in the morning may not be a safe way to be alone. Going hiking alone in the mountains may be foolhardy. It is hard to relish being alone when it is tinged with fear and dread. Will my boundaries be invaded? Will I be safe here alone? Why should being alone be dangerous?

In response to the dangers of being alone, women are taught early on that the best way to be safe is to have a male close by: "let your brother walk you to the party," "don't go into that neighborhood without a male date/bodyguard." But what happens when women find out that the very men that are supposed to offer them protection can in fact assault them, that brothers, fathers, and colleagues may not be safe either. Last year, at a conference at the O'Hare Hilton, I realized that I had dropped my wallet in the restaurant in the airport. Frantic, I set out to retrace my steps through the underground walkways in search of what I had lost. A sympathetic man in the elevator said, "You don't want to walk over there alone at night, let me go with you." I accepted gratefully, glad for the company and, yes, for the protection. Half way there, however, he began to make advances to me; did I want to come up to his room for a drink, was I staying alone, was I married? I never did recover my wallet, but I did reclaim some of my anger: we are not safe alone, but the danger is not from being alone, it is from suddenly being "not alone" and we are not necessarily safe when we are being protected either.

In childhood movies, the frightened child runs home and closes the door behind her, safe at last. But what happens when home is not a safe haven? What about the hundreds of thousands of children who experience sexual abuse at home, abuse at the hands of fathers, brothers, uncles? What happens when those we are taught to trust most are not to be trusted at all? The outside world might not be safe, but neither may it safe to be at home alone. The danger lies not in being alone, but in the disruption of that aloneness, in the transformation of safe spaces into dangerous ones. Where are there safe spaces for women? Aloneness as vulnerability.

Reclaiming the Safety of Solitude

Most of my life has been spent avoiding being alone, seeking, sometimes desperately, to fill my life with people and activity. But there have been moments of solitude that have felt wonderful: sitting in the highest row of a huge auditorium after a rehearsal, after everyone had gone home, relishing the quiet and the peacefulness; time writing in my new office in the attic, savoring my own rhythms and my own presence. And so, I have begun to ask myself: what are the conditions that make being alone a positive experience, and how can these be reclaimed? My answers at this point are inevitably partial, only somewhat digested, difficult to articulate. But I share my own thinking as a way of furthering my own understanding. I sit here writing, in solitude, in order to understand my own solitude.

At this point, I have been able to discern three conditions or components of solitude which can make it, for me, a positive, valuable condition. These are choice, power and trust.

First, I must be alone because I have chosen to spend time alone, not because I have no choices, not because there is no one who wants to be with me. Spending time by myself must be a decision, not simply the default option of my life. Thus, I may choose to have lunch by myself, or to spend an afternoon reading alone and have it feel good. But if I have tried to find someone to have lunch with and have come up short, or would have preferred to spend my afternoon leisure time with others, then solitude becomes, again, punishment, alienation, loneliness. I can enjoy time alone when I know that it is not a permanent or defining condition in my life, will not represent the totality of my experience.

Secondly, I must trust that if I choose to spend time alone, the rest of the world, my world, will still be there for me when I am ready to return. I must trust that my friends will not abandon me if I choose to spend time by myself; I must trust that I will not lose control or power by being alone, apart for a while. My professional community will not forget about me if I spend time away from the action, away from conferences and meetings—"Mara who? Didn't she used to be in education?" I must trust that my office will not be cleaned out and redecorated for a new person, that my teaching load will not be altered while I am not there, that I will not get appointed head of a committee in my absence. I must have trust in those who make up my world, trust that I will still be real to them, still important to them, still of value, even if I am not immediately present.

And, lastly, in order to relish being alone, I must feel my own power, my own worth. I must know that I am not in jeopardy if I am alone, that I can take care of myself, that I don't need other people around to keep me safe.

Of these three conditions, the first is relatively easy, the second more difficult, and the third, the most challenging. How have I addressed these in my own life? What is my trajectory towards completely reclaiming my own life and dazzling set of possibilities? First, I have tried to sort out the underlying motivations and feelings associated with the choices I have made and continue to make about the role of solitude and "other-devoted" time in my life. More and more, I am trying to think about what I really want and really need, and less about what others will say or think, trying to make rational choices from a position of safety and not desperate choices from a position of fear. If I choose to spend time connected with others, I want it to be because I enjoy their company and want to be with them, not because I don't want to be perceived as antisocial or a loner. I want to connect with people in whose presence I feel good; I don't want to connect with people because I need them to keep me safe, people as bodyguards or buffers against the world. This rethinking and redeciding is constant; I must continually be vigilant in monitoring my own thinking and decisions.

Learning to trust has been more difficult. Academia breeds alienation and isolation—people in their own fields, in their own offices, teaching their own courses. Much of the work that academics do is done in isolation: reading papers, writing articles, planning for teaching. My approach here has been to try to change some of the conditions under which I work, breaking down barriers of separateness and individual achievement, reaching out to others in my writing, my teaching and my research. And I must continuously remind myself that I am connected to others, that being alone does not negate or call into question my relationships. On my desk sits a large picture frame with photos of me with many of my friends and dear ones. As I sit working, in isolation, it serves to remind me that all those people are still there for me, a phone call, a letter, a Bitnet message away. I can relax in my aloneness because I know that it does not tell the whole story. Yes, I am working in my office alone. No, I am not alone in the world.

Reclaiming full power and worth continues to be the most challenging and exciting process. I recently completed a women's self-defense class called FIGHTBACK in which women learn to defend themselves against a fully-padded male mugger, learn to kick and hit and yell "no," learn to reclaim their bodies as their own and their space as inviolable. Watching us as a group of sixteen women become more powerful, feeling myself gain in confidence and strength, has confirmed many of my beliefs about power and safety. Feeling powerful involves, at least partially, feeling safe, safe against violation and confident in my own strength. As women we are typically taught to define ourselves in relation to other people: how do others feel about us, like us, treat us. When I am alone, those traditional markers are absent, or at least temporarily obscured. When I am alone, in order to feel good about myself, I have to like myself. And for me and for many of the women in our class, feeling good about being alone is directly related to feeling safe being alone.

As I realize the ways in which my own reality has been constructed, I observe others as well, wondering how they construct meaning in their own lives. I watch my older daughter, at twelve, curl up on the couch with a book. She spends considerable amounts of time by herself, and relishes it. Although she has friends, she also enjoys her own company. I am delighted and awed to see the ways in which she renews herself by spending time alone. My younger daughter spends time alone drawing or playing with her dolls. She talks to herself, sings to herself, hums and whistles. She is affectionate and social with others, but she is happy to be by herself as well. I asked her who she played with at recess yesterday, and she responded: "No one, I played by myself." And then, because I have not fully hidden my own hurts in this area, she added, "But don't worry, Mama, it wasn't that I didn't have anyone to play with. I like spending time by myself."

I think of my daughters as models, as positive images for my own life: women who are pleased by who they are, confident that they will continue to connect well with the outside world, and able to enjoy time alone. I wonder whether this stage of comfortable solitude will last, worry about the forces and experiences which will disrupt their sense of safety in solitude. And I think about a mantra for myself:

> I can choose to be alone
> I can be alone and still be fully connected
> I can be alone and completely powerful
> I can be alone with myself, not hiding from others
> I can be alone and safe, alone and strong.

I repeat this mantra to myself, to myself when I am alone. I grieve what I have lost in my life—perfect trust, perfect safety, untarnished confidence and power—and I struggle to reclaim myself.

Chapter 4

Time Alone, Place Apart: The Role of Spiracy in Using the Power of Solitude

Jacqueline Jones Royster

Growing up as an only child, I found myself alone frequently, and in the early years, I struggled mightily to distinguish between being alone and being lonely, being apart and being isolated, living differently and being different. Ultimately, I came to understand distinctions among solitude, loneliness, isolation, and alienation, and across the matrix of these experiences, I learned to appreciate the power of solitude. I consider myself fortunate that I had parents who helped me to like and to value myself without external affirmation. I grew to enjoy my own company. With their guidance, times alone became opportunities to enter the worlds of books, to reflect, to explore possibilities, to process observations and experiences, to act out in my own head untold possibilities, to imagine. My parents listened to my ravings and my cravings, and they encouraged me to study, to grow, and to develop.

Further, during the times alone, I learned to focus my energy toward action and productivity. I was able to crystallize my imaginings in words, in pictures, in colors. Perhaps my greatest asset, beyond loving and supportive parents, was that there was no shortage of books, paper, pencils, crayons, or other tools that might facilitate such explorations. I harbored theories and concepts, neither of which I would have labeled such high-sounding words. I identified solutions to little problems in my own life and big problems out in the world. In other words, in the safe space of my own solitude, having time alone and place apart, I let myself loose in the world.

As a young child, then, I had the luxury of time. I had the security of places that were my own. I had spiritual and physical nourishment from my parents, and I had a peace of mind that comes with respecting one's own talents and abilities. I was able to feel the joy and power of solitude, and I experienced its blessings as evidenced particularly by the validation of academic success. I was able to see first hand what the solitary activities of thinking and writing alone with one's self can do. I learned early to rejoice in the potential of being alone.

Life, however, has a way of continuing and changing. As an adult who has adult responsibilities, I have been plagued by this image of solitude, by the challenge of finding time alone and place apart. These are luxuries that get harder and harder to come by. When we have jobs that are time-consuming; when we value relationships with others (partners, children, parents, friends, other significant others) that require maintenance and demand time, thoughtfulness, and energy, how do we maintain a balance that allows time and space for self in solitude? What happens if this luxurious image of solitude cannot hold? If we do not have ready access to this potential, how, then, do we remain productive? How do we reach and sustain a state of being that allows us to make good use of our talents and abilities as thinkers and writers?

I am an active teacher, writer, scholar; a mother of two; a wife of an active professional; a daughter of a woman from whom I still draw strength and who deserves to know my love and appreciation; a friend to a relatively small group of people who are invaluable in my life; a person within a closely knit family who lives in a city filled with family; a member of a socially conscious community organization that dedicates itself to public service and political action. I have multiple loyalties beyond myself, and there is never enough time to do all that ideally either I would want to do or should do. Or, on the occasions when I do have time alone, there are still multiple obligations across which to divide my thinking and my energy, and few spaces, large or small, that I can claim as exclusively my own. When I feel most distracted by the fullness of my life, I allow myself the luxury of imagining a future state when my felt needs are ideally met. In the meantime, however, I resist the desire to let myself drown in a sea of obligations that are at the same time also my pleasures and my passions. Instead, I look for inspiration and for alternatives.

Again and again, I have turned to the world of African-American women writers. They have articulated my thoughts and desires, helped me to name my struggle, and demonstrated with their lives that productivity is possible even when conditions are not at their best. Across the generations, these women have been, for me, beacons of light in what can often feel like pervasive darkness. From their lives and words, I breathe into myself hope, courage, and grit, and I can see myself beginning to fashion what I need: new pathways to solitude, new ways of looking at time and at time alone, new ways of conceiving a notion of place, and other ways, if not new ones, to create places apart.

I feel kinship, for example, with Gertrude E. H. Bustill Mossell, who in 1908 wrote *The Work of the Afro-American Woman* under the name Mrs. N(athan) F(rancis) Mossell. Mossell was a journalist who wrote for the periodical press, both white and African-American. In one of the essays in this collection, "A Lofty Study," Mossell describes a visit to the home of a member of the Society of Friends during which she has a moment of insight. The woman took Mossell to a room in the attic, the woman's study. Mossell describes its suitability for work (i.e., for writing): "It was so quiet, so peaceful, the air was so fresh and pure, it seemed like living in a new atmosphere" (p. 127). The sight of this room, so pleasingly decorated, so specifically appropriate for study showed her what was missing from her own environment. She was amazed that she had not thought of such a thing, a place of her own, if not a room in the attic, then "at least a corner" (p. 128). She says: "What a satisfaction to put everything in order, turn the key, and feel that all is safe—no busy hands, no stray breeze can carry away or disarrange some choice idea kept for the future delectation of the public! Besides this, one who writes much generally finds that she can write best at some certain spot. Ideas come more rapidly, sentences take more lucid forms. Very often the least change from that position will break up the train of thought" (p. 129).

A reader of this short essay can easily receive the impression that between these lines Mossell alludes to the encumbrances on her own work, or in the very least, to her understanding of adjustments that women often must make in anticipation of the hands of children or the needs and preferences of professional husbands who are "educated to work alone" (p. 128). The reader can also infer that Mossell recognizes that the woman's own work, her own intellectual enterprises rather than her household/family duties, may not have central priority in the home. We can infer that she understands that women may not be "educated to work alone" or "educated" to feel entitled to the privilege of time and place alone. We may also infer that at some level Mossell seems to understand that the first barrier to a place of one's own is, perhaps, in the woman's own mind. She writes: "I just sat down and wondered why I had never thought of this very room for a study" (p. 127).

With the sight of this room, Mossell awakens to a need for solitude, for a place apart. Twenty-one years later, Virginia Woolf makes this same case quite powerfully in *A Room of One's Own* (1929). Eight decades later in our own day, often women like myself who think and write still must awaken or be awakened to the necessity of recognizing, naming, and claiming a need for solitude. We must also awaken to the necessity of feeling entitled to a place apart.

I feel similar kinship with Anna Julia Cooper whose thoughts extend the sense of need beyond solitude as a place apart. Cooper was a former slave who went on to become a teacher, a writer, a scholar, a social activist, a woman who was among the first African-American women to earn a Ph.D., and the first from this group to be named president of a college. Sixteen years earlier than Mossell, in 1892, Cooper wrote in *A Voice from the South*:

> One mind in a family or in a town may show a penchant for art, for literature, for the learned professions, or more bookish lore. You will know it when it is there. No need to probe for it. It is a light that cannot be hid under a bushel—and I would try to enable that mind to go the full length of its desires. Let it follow its bent and develop its talent as far as possible: and the whole community might well be glad to contribute its labor and money for the sustenance and cultivation of this brain. Just as earth gives its raw material, its carbons, hydrogen, and oxygen, for the tree which is to elaborate them into foliage, flower and fruit, so the base elements, bread and money furnished the true brain worker come back to us with compound interest in the rich thought, the invention, the poem, the painting, the statue. (pp. 262–63)

In this passage, Cooper brings to life images that are elemental, basic, foundational. She conjures visions of growth and development from the realm of the ordinary, and through the implied contrasts with the ways in which we do and do not support the development of human beings, she places American society before a tribunal of reason and justice as she appeals for a place in which academic pursuits and learned enterprises are valued and specifically nourished, given the context of the book, even for women. Cooper appeals for "bread" to sustain both body and soul and entreats her audience to understand that "base" elements (bread, money) are the foundation from which excellence grows and through which the society reaps reward. In her own case, with a mind so ingenious and vibrant, she received precious little of either, such that she says, "I constantly felt (as I suppose many an ambitious girl has felt) a thumping from within unanswered by any beckoning from without" (p. 76). We hear an undernourished spirit. We know her pain and her frustration. But if we look at her life and contributions, we also see her resiliency and her determination to be productive and to make a difference.

Like Cooper, I sometimes long for easier access to conditions—the time, space, resources, circumstances, the peace of mind—that would allow me to devote sustained energy to thinking, reading, writing as I feel inclined to engage in them and not at the will and/or demand of others; to exchanging ideas with others in the interest of spiritual and intellectual stimulation and not just toward the completion of assigned tasks; to searching for truth/sense/understanding and not just for ways to get things done in the face of encumbrances and constraints amid balances of power, policy, or privilege that are not tilted in my direction. I would like the time and space that money can buy but also spiritual nourishment so that I can sustain and insulate myself as well as conserve and maximize my energy as I work. Like Cooper, sometimes, I feel "a thumping from within." Unlike her, occasionally I hear resonant chords in the distance, but still I long for them to be closer, clearer, more full-bodied, and more consistently available. I look at Cooper, however, and all that she was able to do with less than I, and I am renewed.

A third African-American woman writer from whom I gather strength and inspiration is Maria W. Stewart, a free-born woman who wrote in the 1830s and who is generally acknowledged by scholars as the first African-American woman political writer. She was a pioneer in a day when precious few women, and certainly not African-American women, either spoke or wrote in public arenas. In her very first publication, a tract addressed to the people of color in Boston, Massachusetts, Stewart reflects on her actions in a way that helps me to implant, not just the need for solitude, but more the need to make use of the power of solitude within a more meaningful framework. She wrote that

> what I have done, has been done with an eye single to the glory of God, and to promote the good of souls. I have neither kindred nor friends. *I stand alone in your midst* [emphasis mine], exposed to the fiery darts of the devil, and to the assaults of wicked men. But though all the powers of earth and hell were to combine against me, though all nature should sink into decay, still I would trust in the Lord, and joy in the God of my salvation. For I am full persuaded that he will bring me off conqueror, yea, more than conqueror, through him who hath loved me and given himself for me. (p. 41)

As an academic, I have found that time alone and place apart are vitalized by what I have come to call, for lack perhaps of a better term, a sense of spiracy. I have come to understand this term as a recognition of the ways in which I am situated or situate myself within the worlds in which I live and breathe. It is not just a sense of self. It is more a sense of self in particular space as such territory may be defined in variable but meaning-filled ways. I find that with a sense of spiracy, there is the capacity to be propelled toward solitude as a state of consciousness.

Maria Stewart wrote, "I stand alone in your midst," and like her, at some point along my way, I sensed in myself the need to find a breathing space, even in the midst of others, from which I could do more than just breathe and experience the world, but also from which I could envision it. The process of trying to meet this need has felt like a cleansing, clarifying process, one that I have had to manage in the midst of "the fiery darts of the devil, and the assaults of wicked men." Moreover, as I have gained a better notion of good breathing and greater visibility, I have discovered that often these spaces are very personal, solitary ones, places that are hand-fashioned to meet individual needs, but in being so, they tend to be, as I have come to recognize and understand them, well-fortified, richly generative, and wondrously self-sustaining, even in the face of ongoing darts, devils, and wickedness.

In my life as an academic, this sense of spiracy seems to emerge from points of convergence in literacy studies, women's studies, and African diaspora studies. This is the space from which I envision the world. In each discipline, separately, I can feel connection, but I feel most energized, most capable of productivity at a point of convergence. In Black women's studies, a point at which women's studies meets African diaspora studies, I have found many moments of intellectual and spiritual synergy, which, in my experience, seems essential to our abilities to maximize our uses of the power of solitude. I feel most synergetic, however, when all three disciplines converge at points that allow for a multidimensionality of connection and vision. Through this multidimensional experience, I live and breathe, sense my own potential, and feel capable of productivity. I feel in focus, attuned to my thoughts.

As I have reflected on this process, I have become aware that the synergy, the sense of connectedness, the sense of spiracy comes, in part at least, from a coalescing of values, beliefs, priorities, interests, experiences, and training. However, I recognize the three disciplines—

sites of training, research, and learning—as lenses through which I can make sense of this spectrum, see the world, think, write, and search for truths. On a spiritual level, therefore, I feel well-seated and generously endowed with possibility.

As in Stewart's case, this process seems to have brought me to a sense of mission, and in keeping with the tradition of Black feminist thought (see Royster 1990), intellect, ethics, and action seem to have become one. Stewart considered herself to be chosen as an instrument of God and dedicated herself to "the Glory of God" as she sought to "promote the good of souls." One might say that she was a politically conscious evangelist, seeing evils in the world that could be addressed through the good will, hard work, and good sense of men and women.

In similar manner, I consider myself to be an academic activist, a person who has chosen (even if I have not been chosen) to be a politically conscious watchdog, a sentry for the need for positive change in the world of education. My mission is two fold: (1) to document to the extent that I can the lives, conditions, and achievements of women of African descent, both historically and currently; and (2) to use the understanding that I acquire of life, literacy, and learning in the interest of academic excellence, intellectual growth, and the individual development of my students. At this point in my understanding, then, I am beginning to see solitude less as a physical state of being, which I cannot always maintain, than as a state of consciousness, which I can maintain more easily. I find that, even though I still look toward some future state of solitude within which I am ideally nurtured, I am more at peace than I might have been about finding ways to use the power of time alone and place apart, despite the limitations in access that are imposed by my circumstances.

First of all, I find that I am much better at creating illusions than I used to be. As Mossell has urged, I create the illusion of space at the corner of a table, at a chair in an otherwise crowded room, in piles of file folders with descriptive labels, or boxes of diskettes, all of which help to provide for me a sense of order and organization to a sometimes chaotic existence. I maintain a sense of continuity, order, and privacy, and I name these small organizers of my life and my work the exclusive room of my own. I find my own place within the covers of multicolored folders and within the tiny spaces of little boxes.

In addition, I take time where I find it. With a heightened consciousness of good, meaningful work, I find solitude even amid a crowd—on an airplane, among children at play, during any of an endless number of meetings, lectures, or other public events; or I find it in atypical places, like my favorite place this year—the shower. I listen, not to the chaos around me, but to myself. My thoughts claim authority regardless of my physical surroundings, and I listen. I find it wise, therefore, never to be far from my journal, the encoded key by which I can go about the business of my days and still have a mechanism that can record my movements toward focus and unlock both potential and productivity.

This conglomeration of things is the way that I have found to make use of the power of solitude when I do not have the luxury of sustained times alone or exclusive places apart. Through such mechanisms, I try to maintain balance, sometimes with more success than others. I make time for family, for job, for friends, occasionally for community service, and I feel that all is relatively well. However, when illusions become too inadequate, I stop pretending and also make time for myself in more traditional ways. I claim at that point, as I feel that I am entitled to claim, more substantial chunks of time and a literal room of my own, temporary though they will have to be. I understand clearly that my solutions are not magic ones, but they are workable ones. For me, they have become the truth until some other truth arrives.

At the base of it all, I distinguish the vital role that my parents played in the formation of fundamental notions of potential and productivity, and I feel privileged. At base, also, is a sense of spiracy that has brought me focus, and with sincere gratitude, I honor the lives and legacies of African-American women writers for being so instructive and so inspirational. With their help, I feel even greater privilege. I count this two fold heritage as my intellectual ancestry (see David 1987), and from this place, I find solace and solitude, and feel empowered to make whatever use I can of whatever potential is available in my efforts to preserve, to carry forth, and to add to the legacies of Black women's writing.

References

Cooper, A. J. (1988). *A voice from the south*. New York: Oxford University Press (Schomburg Library of Nineteenth-Century Black Women Writers).

David, D. (1987). *Intellectual women and victorian patriarchy: Harriet Martineau, Elizabeth Barrett Browning, George Eliot*. New York: Cornell University Press.

Mossell, Mrs. N. F. (1988). *The work of the Afro-American woman*. New York: Oxford University Press (Schomburg Library of Nineteenth-Century Black Women Writers).

Richardson, M. (ed.). (1987). *Maria W. Stewart, America's first black woman political writer*. Bloomington, Ind.: Indiana University Press.

Royster, J. J. (1990). Perspectives on the intellectual tradition of black women writers. In *The right to literacy*, edited by A. Lunsford, H. Moglen and J. Slevin, 103–12. New York: Modern Language Association.

Woolf, V. (1989). *A room of one's own*. San Diego, Calif.: Harcourt Brace Jovanovich.

Chapter 5

Who Am I When I'm Alone with Myself?

Jo Anne Pagano

I recall (or do I remember? I think I do both—I recall and I remember) first hearing what it meant for Adam to know Eve or for all of those other people in the Bible to know one another, whether licitly or illicitly. After Adam and Eve, after Moses I suppose, it all gets tied up with judgment and the law. Adam and Eve were innocent of judicial processes, and that's probably how Eve came to get Adam into all that trouble. I heard about Adam and Eve's acquaintance at the sixth-grade lunch table at about the same time the boys would grab our hands, scratch our palms with their forefingers and laugh uproariously. We girls blushed, even though we didn't know exactly why we were blushing. We knew there was something that we did not know, to our shame.

Actually my Bible does not say that Adam knew Eve or that Eve knew Adam, whatever the boys in my sixth grade class thought *they* knew. It does say that Joseph did not know Mary until after the birth of Jesus (Matthew 1:25). Adam and Eve did know that they were naked, and that seems to be the first thing that they knew (Genesis 3:7). Ham knew Noah's nakedness, and for that he was punished (Genesis 4:22–23), and Moses who gave us the commandments was the first to know the invisible and indivisible (and perhaps fully clothed) God's name (Exodus 6:3); therefore, could he command— therefore his legitimacy.

We must be struck in paging through the Bible by the coiled figures of knowledge, morality, sight, desire, and the body. In the prelapsarian state, ignorance is bliss. Knowledge leads to painful exile, knowledge conceived of Eve's desire. What did Eve desire? The serpent promised that when she would eat of the tree, she would have her eyes opened, being as the gods, knowing good and evil. Adam's and Eve's eyes were opened, and they knew that they were naked. The story of knowledge

seems to be interestingly complicated by difference and sexuality identified with the sight/site of the genitals. When Adam and Eve knew that
they were naked, they made aprons to cover their genitals. In covering
their nakedness they confessed to their crime, the crime of wanting to
be *like* gods. Their crime teaches them that they are different, sexually
different from each other. The knowledge of good and evil turns out to
be the knowledge of sexual difference.

God's punishment is not simply exile from his presence. Adam
and Eve who had been pronounced one flesh are given a life sentence
to a state of sexual enmity, their bodies to be the prison houses of their
souls. And the woman, for having succumbed to the desire for knowledge is sentenced to a lifetime of sexual desire for her husband, a
desire that legitimates his rule over her (Genesis 3:15–16). At the
moment of Eve's creation, God said, "Therefore shall a man leave his
father and his mother, and shall cleave unto his wife: and they shall be
one flesh" (Genesis 2:24).

In the governing narratives of psychoanalysis, the first knowledge
is said to be the knowledge of separation, a knowledge coincident with
the knowledge of sexual difference. This is obviously a male story, and
in many important respects, resembles the story of the exile from the
garden. The infant experiences itself as continuous with its mother, its
body an extension of hers, one flesh. It is blissfully unaware of its
dependence, its feebleness, the precariousness of its existence, or of
good and evil. Its relationship with the mother is symbiotic. When the
knowledge of its dependence on the maternal body, which is in fact
separate and distinct, and for the boy sexually different, intrudes, the
infant experiences rage and sorrow. It *knows*; it knows the evil of separation. And it desires; it desires that which it can never have—union
with the maternal body. It desires the unity expressed in the fantasy
that Adam and Eve are one flesh.

Eve's betrayal of Adam results in the knowledge that they are
naked. Her desire is his undoing, condemning him to an eternity of
desire for prelapsarian ignorance. This is rightly called the fall of *man*.
At the moment of the Oedipus Complex, the little boy sees that boys
and girls are different, and he is horrified. He begins to build a moral
structure based on his sense of horror. He acquires his capacity for
abstraction, a talent which will produce symbolic substitutes for the
maternal body. That girls lack two things and not just the one most
often fixed on is important. Girls lack not only the mark of sexual difference, the phallus, they lack also sexual difference from the mother,
and this is the sign of their moral defect. Because women are like their

mothers they are more closely confined in the prison house of the body. Similarity results in partial separation only, and vitiates the generation of symbolic substitutes.

Like Adam and Eve, deprived of the presence of God, deprived of the knowledge of the gods, bound together and eternally separate, the infant is deprived of the power of the mother and of the immediate, unmediated presence of the maternal body, and of the knowledge of connection to the mother. The punishment for desire in both the religious and the psychoanalytic narratives is enduring desire. In both narratives, the superstructure of civilization emerges as part of a compensatory process, a process designed to defend against an originary loss, the unendurable knowledge of our own lack of knowledge and of our vulnerability. Knowledge is instinct with tragedy.

So much is familiar to readers of Freud and Lacan. These tales of human origins are predicated on an invisible god in the one case, and on an inaccessible maternal body in the other. Both god and the primal mother possess a knowledge forbidden human beings. They see without being seen; they know without being themselves known. Loss, frustration, and fear then are the conditions of human knowledge. Human consciousness is born in an anguished moment; its history and fate in this tale of origins lead us directly to a kind of wisdom—Stanley Cavell calls it the wisdom of skepticism. Cavell argues that skepticism originates in the very condition of being human. The legacy of philosophy, he argues, is a repression or denial of our knowledge of this condition. Cavell distinguishes two species of skepticism: material-world and other-minds skepticism. For Cavell other-minds skepticism is the real problem, and one not dispatched by the solutions which mitigate our anxieties about the material world. Common sense and methodological rules of testing and evidence leave us with good enough knowledge regarding the existence and identity of material objects. At the same time, our optimistic faith in common sense and methodology serve only to repress what Descartes "knew"—we can never *know* the existence of other minds. Descartes was able to intuit his own existence through consciousness of his own act of thinking. But Descartes' intuition will never give us access to, knowledge of, *self*-consciousness of the Other's thinking. As Cavell notes, something is always in the way; something separates us, and that something is the body. The body stands in the way of the penetration of knowledge. In brilliant readings of Shakespeare, Cavell (1979) demonstrates that the repression of the failure of knowledge, the sense of lack, is at the heart of human tragedy.[1]

Cavell shows us that the question of other minds, of the Other, is not an epistemological or a methodological problem. I read him as claiming that it is a moral, a psychological, and a political problem. It has everything to do with what it means to be a human being dependent on integration into a world of human desire and human care. The legacy of skepticism is the problem of trust. The skeptical, the biblical, and the psychoanalytic tales are all expressions of the same grief and anger and fear—the tragedy of being human. These tales are also uniquely male, expressions exemplary of the male original relation to the lost female object, an object once the source of perfect pleasure. They all report different aspects of male rage and fear.

The hero of all these tales is the autonomous, individuated, unitary self. The individuated unitary self is the one, who at the moment of awareness of separation and individuation, is aware of himself as sexually different from the Other from whom he did not previously distinguish himself. In all of these tales, the moment of separation, the experience of lack and exile, is read as the beginning of knowledge. This epistemology is a result of a denial of epistemological status in our intellectual traditions to an alternative tale of origin which posits a knowledge prior to the knowledge of separation—knowledge of connection. Selfhood, and the knowledge of selfhood along with the knowledge of others, is as plausibly traced to our original attachment as to our original separation.

Raymond Williams (1961) notes that the medieval understanding of "individual" was rather different from our own, therefore also our understanding of selfhood. The word "individual" was employed principally in theological arguments to refer to the trinity—three beings constituting an indivisible and inseparable whole. Only as members of the whole do the entities have being. By extension, it was understood that persons exist as part of an inseparable whole, identity taking its meaning from membership in a group. Somewhere around the seventeenth century, individual identity came to be conceived as absolute, having reference only to itself, wholly separable and wholly distinct, *and different* from other individuals.

This is the individual we find in solitude, a word which, according to the *OED*, like "individual," did not come into common use in England until the seventeenth century. Descartes was alone in his dressing gown when he faced the horror, the tragedy of human existence, that is, the possibility that life is but a dream. I have argued (1990) elsewhere that this is a paranoid fantasy spun by an imperial self, dependent on a world he would know absolutely, absolutely unknowable to him. His thoughts become substitutes for that world, and even for his own existence. He is because he thinks. The only certainty regarding *this* world is the certainty of his own solitary existence, a certainty from which others will follow.

He is the inheritor of God's curse on Adam and Eve, the curse of exile and separation, forbidden the knowledge of the gods, bequeathed only the knowledge that he cannot know, like the original exile who is sentenced to live in enmity with his companion. He who would see fears instead that he is seen by an invisible other—an invisible god, a forbidden female body. This is the individual of the myth of psychoanalysis whose foundation is the knowledge of separation. He is alone, and his solitude has made him crazy.

Adam and Even were once as one in God's garden. In the infantile Eden, mother and child are one. The price of knowledge, or more precisely, the price of the desire for knowledge is separation and uncertainty. In a curious way, the condition of knowledge, that is the foundation of knowledge, is unknowableness, for knowledge is said to come of absence—the absence of god, the absence of the mother. In the psychoanalytic tale, the radical maternal absence demanded as the condition of knowledge is possible only for males who are sexually different, and therefore, totally distinct from their mothers.

Matters are different for females, who are not sexually different from their mothers and who, therefore, never experience themselves as totally distinct. This circumstance has been advanced to explain women's seeming superior capacity for attachment and nurture, or alternatively, women's seeming incapacity for abstraction and principled judgment, tied as we are to the claims of this world because incompletely distinguished from our mothers. The talent for attachment is said to come "naturally" to women; it is the expression of the persistent precognitive and prerational element in women's psychic economy. Freud (1933) advanced this state of affairs to account for his claim that women are doomed to moral imperfection and intellectual inferiority. The essentialist strain in such thinking is to be resisted, especially by women who may be tempted to make a virtue of necessity in acknowledging that women have small talent for solitary labor and little inclination for abstraction while asserting the superiority of communal work and its supposed cognitive corollary—relational or concrete thought. But all such arguments, both Freud's patriarchal argument and those feminist oppositions that accept the initial characterization, rest on a prejudice, or more charitably, on a paradigmatic proposition that can be displaced easily.

Women's stories are different from men's. In women's fiction, isolation is often the condition which the female must overcome in order to achieve identity. She must find others with whom she identifies. Jane Eyre's journey to selfhood and her achievement of mature identity is the lonely pilgrim's progress of a young woman without family or friends. Jane's solitude, her isolation, begins when she is placed, a young orphan, with a false family—a family who acknowledges no connection to Jane. Her journey takes this lonely and insubstantial being, insubstantial in property, in strength, in size, and in beauty from one unwelcoming prisonhouse to another, from one set of false relationships to another until she finds her true family in St. John, Diana, and Mary Rivers. Jane must find her true home and her true family before she finds herself. Only then are she and Rochester able to join as equals in true marriage.

In *Villette*, Lucy Snowe's solitude is the root of Lucy's descent into madness. An orphan, too, Lucy is without friends or attachments. Left alone during the summer days in the school at which she teaches, Lucy falls into delirium and is found by her only acquaintance wandering the streets. Pale and slight, she haunts the streets as she haunts her own life. Lucy suffers from detachment. Detachment leads to dislocation. Lucy's recovery depends not on any medicine dispensed by her acquaintance and distant kinsman, Dr. John, but on her acceptance into the household he shares with his mother.

In *Villette* things are never what they seem. A nun's ghost turns out to be a flighty and worthless young man seducing a girl of slight intelligence and dubious character. Characters are always trying to read each other and always failing. On Lucy's first appearance to *Villette*, the proprietress Madame Beck asks her kinsman and a teacher to read Lucy's physiognomy. The teacher, M. Paul, turns out be a gentle and generous man, capable of deep love and deeper sacrifice, rather than the self-indulgent petty tyrant he seems at first to be. Madame Beck runs her school by the method of surveillance—that is, she snoops among the belongings of her staff and pupils; she runs a sophisticated domestic espionage ring.

College students often have difficulty making sense of *Villette*. Nothing really happens in the novel. All of it is interior, an exploration of the geography of the imagination of the solitary intelligence. Its central problem is the problem of other-minds skepticism. Lucy's episodes of madness are expressed in hallucination and lead to a distrust of her own perceptions because she cannot trust the appearances of others. Nor can they trust her appearances. Over and over again other characters ask, "Who are you Miss Snowe?" The truth is that that is just what Lucy must learn, and she learns who she is only by learning others and by learning to trust and to accept.

Charlotte Bronte was ambivalent. The ending of the tale shocks readers, striking some as vengeful and angry. Like Jane Eyre, Lucy comes at last to know her true family in Dr. John and his mother, and in the young woman who will marry Dr. John. Still, Lucy remains eccentric to this family, not quite inside, but not altogether out. But felicity is promised through Lucy's intended marriage to M. Paul, who is lost at sea on the eve of their marriage. Charlotte Bronte refuses at the moment to acknowledge what the novel until then asserts—that identity is a matter of attachment.

It is as if Bronte associated human attachment with women's subordinate place in our culture. The marriage of apparent equals that marks the end of *Jane Eyre* is, in fact, one in which Rochester is dependent on his wife, maimed and blind as he is. This is Bronte's dark side and repeats Jane Eyre's angry outburst: women want what their brothers want. In Charlotte Bronte's case they want to be accepted as artists. And the artist's intelligence is, in our culture, solitary.

Our culture is loaded with stories about women trying to escape attachment, to get away and be by themselves. She who is named but does not name, she who occupies the place of the absent and voiceless Other, she who is trapped in the claims of attachment seeks the desperate drug of extreme detachment. But there are other ways of thinking about attachment and separation, and about difference. There are more than two things in the world.

Why should we believe that the process of identity formation begins, that self-consciousness and the objects known by the conscious self, depend *only* on a moment of violent detachment? It is merely prejudicial to accord foundational status to the knowledge of separation. Surely there is an experience preceding that of separation—the experience of attachment, unconscious though that experience is. Why can the child not be said to *know* that it is connected to the mother, even if this knowledge must wait on that second experience of separating from the mother? The moment of separation is a moment which disrupts the primal connection, the sense of oneness. But only an act of repression obliterates all trace of the primal connection. This primal connection acknowledged, taken together with the fact of separation and awareness of difference, makes possible a transformation of the original attachment such that the child is capable of multiple attachments and connections which nurture and sustain its singularity. We may say that we know one thing only when we know at least two. Knowing ourselves detached depends on the possibility of knowing ourselves attached, however unconscious the experience that permits us to acknowledge its possibility. Perhaps knowledge and experience have a double foundation. Assigning privilege to one pole of experience, to one mode of knowing, of necessity situates the other precariously, and sets the stage for Descartes' psychotic break and for a politics of gender domination.

I am, therefore I think; I think therefore I am. But who am I? Where and how do I find myself? Just as our religious and philosophical traditions depend on an economy of difference and distance, of separation and loss, so do our aesthetic traditions which raise these questions most immediately. The nineteenth-century myth of the romantic genius tells the story of the fate of the singular one, born in exile, alienated and self-alienated—Adam or Descartes. The artist-hero found in so much of nineteenth- and twentieth-century literature achieves himself through his own creative power and his struggles against a social, feminized world that threatens to swallow him, or a female nature which threatens his very life. His power must be exercised in solitude, often in poverty and ignominy as well. We find him in the wilderness, overcoming danger; we find him in solitary attics, alone and misunderstood, often betrayed. Often he is betrayed by a woman. But he gets his revenge. The object of his art is not infrequently, a woman—figured as Woman. She is trapped in the canvas or trapped on the page. She compensates his loss; he knows her absolutely, and in his creation of her he finds himself. Even his own existence falls victim to his ideas of his existing. He becomes as Virginia Woolf said, "the *I* that casts its shadow across the page."

In *A Room of One's Own* (1929), Virginia Woolf's exploration of "women and fiction," led her to the conclusion that if women are to write, they must have five hundred pounds and rooms of their own. Hers is at least in part a materialist account of women's prominent absence in our literary tradition. But it is also a psychological account in which writers of both sexes are criticized for different flaws: the male writer for the excessiveness of his presence, the female for her excessive awareness of the presence of others. Woolf fantasized an alternative to the two-sex model. Our two-sex model simply favors prejudicially the procreative function in human sexuality, and in human existence in general. Supposing that there are several sexes in body and mind alike, Woolf says, makes possible a figure of the writer whose psychic economy involves cooperation among all elements—

between the masculine and the feminine. Such a writer, a writer like Jane Austen or William Shakespeare, has an incandescent mind, according to Woolf.

Virginia Woolf had a room of her own where she struggled with her "Angel in the House" for her right to think of herself and her work, to write with integrity rather than to think always of others, rather than to privilege always the claims of attachment. We, too, contributors to this book have rooms of our own and offices which receive us as we cross the threshold of the private house daily.

In my private room, I see clearly Jane Austen in the drawing room writing her novels of courtship and friendship, family and human fallibility. I see her raise her head as she listens for the give-away creak of the door and hastily shoves her manuscript under the blotter. I can hear the gossip and the movement in the rooms below as I watch Jo March scribbling away in her attic, munching apples and tossing the cores to her pet rat, hoping that her writing will ease her family's poverty. I have just returned to my own desk having left to begin dinner preparations, empty the clothes dryer, and feed the animals with whom we share our lives. I thought about this essay as I went about my business. I hear the printer in the room across the landing where my husband has a room of his own. The sound must mean his work is going well, and I am pleased.

Women and solitude. It sounds in some ways too grand a topic or else too slight. Who am I when I'm alone with myself? Am I a teacher? A curriculum theorist? A wife? A friend? A daughter? Sister? Or am I ever really alone with myself? And if I answer, "No," as I am inclined to do, is that because I am a woman? Am I a self who just happens to teach, to write, to be married, have friends and relatives; and who is that self and what is her relationship to all of these? I find that I am myself *because* I teach and write, have married the person I have and claim the friends I claim. And I find that I make the choices I make and do the things I do because I am myself. And I find myself in those with whom I am in conversation, even when I am alone. I can be alone because I know that I am connected. The world does not fade when I am in solitude, because it is only in the world and in my connection to others in it that I am myself. In solitude we must be at home to others. In retreat or in enforced isolation, we lose the world in our ideas of it. We lose ourselves only to construct an illusion of selfhood, unitary and self-contained.

In Doris Lessing's novel, *The Golden Notebook* (1973), Anna Wulf is a writer who says that she wants to write a book that will change the world, that will provide a whole new way of looking at things. In fact, Anna is unable to write any book. She suffers from writer's block, and from an inability to trust her own perceptions, her sense of herself, or her understanding of her relationship with others. Hers is presented as a psychological, epistemological, and political dilemma. We meet Anna, often, in solitude, in a solitude in which she records in notebooks of various colors accounts of a life and events which she is unable to transform into the book her art and her desire demand of her. This set of four notebooks is an index of her psychic fragmentation.

The book opens with the following sentence: "The two women were alone in the London flat." That first sentence of *The Golden Notebook* was given, at the end of the book, to Anna Wulf. Written in Anna's gold-colored notebook by her one-time lover, Saul Green, it is his parting gift to her as he receives from her the first sentence of his next short story. This is the perfect exchange of gifts. This is a vision of the artist very different from the better-known solitary romantic genius. The final sentence of *The Golden Notebook* reads as follows: "The two women kissed and separated."

The Golden Notebook is informed by a psychoanalytic perspective and treats just those questions of separation and attachment we are concerned with here. It does so by probing the solitary intelligence, and concludes by asserting that art is a passage through which the world enters our solitude and through which the solitary intelligence makes its way into the world.

Like *The Golden Notebook*, Zora Neale Hurston's *Their Eyes Were Watching God* (1978) suggests a third way of understanding identity and attachment. Henry Louis Gates (1988), Barbara Johnson (1987), and Michele Wallace (1990) have all read this novel as making problematic the fastness of the distinction between inside and outside, even while asserting the necessity of this distinction.

The novel begins with Janie Chadwick's return to Eatonville, the all Black town in Florida where she had once lived with her second husband Joe Starks and where she owns a house still. Her arrival is commented on and chewed over by the townspeople who serve as a Greek chorus announcing the ignominy of her homecoming. Janie was raised by her grandmother, a former slave who bore all of the marks of slavery, including Janie's mother who was a child of rape. Up from slavery, Janie's grandmother worked hard and cherished hopes that her daughter would become a schoolteacher. She was instead raped by a schoolteacher. Janie and a ruined life were the results.

Janie's beginning awareness of sexual desire provokes fear in her grandmother, and the first tale in this multiply framed tale of tales is the grandmother's slave narrative. Fearing a life of sexual degradation for Janie, the grandmother seeks protection for her by marrying her to the much older Logan Killicks who offers the security of "sixty acres." Janie tells the story of this marriage, and her subsequent marriages to Joe Starks and Teacake Woods, to the only townsperson still friendly to her, Pheoby Watson.

The relationship with her first husband was a sorry affair; Killicks was a man of small imagination and little understanding or appreciation of his young wife. Joe Starks, fast-talking and determined to be a "big voice," had small work to entice Janie to accompany him to Eatonville where he quickly became a "big voice," the mayor who owned the general store and shut his beautiful young wife up in the grandest house in town. Following his death, the young widow does not lack for suitors. She will have none of them, preferring her new command over her own life. Her solitude suits her. Until Teacake Woods comes to town, owning only a guitar and having no connections anywhere. Teacake teaches Janie to play, and together they take off for the Everglades, abandoning house and store for a life working on the muck. This is Janie's ideal love.

But Janie knows, and so do Hurston's readers, that nothing good can come of such happiness. A hurricane brings floods to the muck, and Janie and Teacake, having been heedless of warnings to abandon their house in time, are swept up in the fury. Saving Janie from a rabid dog in the flood waters, Teacake is himself bitten. To end Teacake's eventual suffering from hydrophobia and to save her own life, Janie shoots him. She is charged with murder, but is finally acquitted by an all-white jury. The black men who pack the courtroom during her trail will not acquit her, however.

Barbara Johnson's analysis of this novel invokes the "double-voicedness" of African-American literature (1987). The problem of the authentic voice central to this novel is a problem of those who speak from a position of Otherness, from the place defined in discourse as Other, in a language which demands of them that they speak as Other to themselves. Theirs is a condition of self-difference. At the same time, the condition of identity, of the existence of a self different from itself, is the ability to fashion one's own story of difference. The author Zora Neale Hurston meets this problem by fashioning a novel which alternates between third-person and first-person narrative, between dialect and standard English, and between enactment and representation.

Janie's first-person story is framed by a third-person omniscient narration. Her own first-person story is framed by the situation of its telling; she is telling it to Pheoby Watson, who interjects questions at intervals, who leaves to prepare dinner and returns to continue the story. The telling of the story, then, is framed by a specific relationship. The story Janie tells includes the activity of storytelling as the men gather on the porch of the general store to "mule talk," a form of discourse known in African-American literary criticism as "signifying." When Janie attempts one day to join in the mule talking, Joe Starks sends her inside, as he stops every effort of hers to speak. He says that men see one thing and understand ten, whereas women ten things without understanding one. Janie learns to keep her lips shut tight. She learns the difference between her inside and her outside at this moment; she acquires boundaries and an inner self as well as a self defined by others. That is, she keeps her mouth shut until the day she loses her temper, and in public taunts Joe with his impotence, saying that with his pants down he looks like the change of life. Joe immediately falls ill and dies of Janie's speaking. Joe of the "big voice" knows that he is naked. This must be among the most literal representations of the castration complex.

The self is always divided from itself, divided between an inside and an outside, and between a self and an Other. The history of identity is the history of self-divisions. The first of these divisions according to Lacan and his followers occurs at the "mirror stage." The child sees its reflection at this moment, grasping the irreducible fact of a world external to itself. Its grasp of this fact is accompanied by the recognition of the mother's Otherness. What was once part of the subject is now an object split off from the self—a lost part of the self. This self-division is captured in the figure of castration. Janie's speaking repeats for Joe the moment of loss of the original object. Like the maternal object who was once part of the self, the phallus may go the way of the mother. Acts of symbolization and representation are said to substitute for the lost object, the object without which the subject is never complete. Symbolic acts and representations are attempts to restore and control, figuratively, the lost object. The subject lives always in a state of desire expressed through the impulse to unification and universalization. Plato's insistence on the virtue of the One may be read as an instantiation of this impulse.

Because this quest for wholeness begins with an account of male experience, namely the little boy's apprehension of his mother's missing penis, the tale depends on total and intractable difference and distance between subject and object. Matters are different for females for whom such radical difference and distance from the original object does not obtain. Since symbolization and representation privilege the male experience, women engaging in these activities become both subject and object. Women are simultaneously themselves and different from themselves. As themselves they are objects and not subjects. As subjects they are not themselves. Theirs is a double consciousness. Hurston's double-voiced narrative strategy represents this double consciousness. The narrative and its tale represent Janie's development of consciousness and identity as she acquires boundaries.

Early in *Their Eyes Were Watching God*, Janie sees a group photograph in which she is included. She fails to recognize herself. She has not yet distinguished inside from outside, and the text mimics this condition. Her quest for identity, for self-knowledge, proceeds through a narrative structure, mimetic in the first-person narration, but ultimately transformative through the device of Pheoby, who is also transformed through the telling. This is the neglected alternative. The world contains not only subjects and objects, selves and others, but fields which mediate their relations. Janie must become neither pure subject nor pure object; her telling of her story teaches her the difference between the two and teaches her that she is both.

Pheoby becomes Janie's pupil, and through the act of telling her story to Pheoby, Janie consolidates her identity as she is now among those who tell stories. Janie exists because Teacake existed, *and* because Pheoby is there to hear Janie's story. Janie is aware of her self-division, of her inside and her outside, of where she belongs and what she is, and of what is owing to whom. Her identity is coextensive with her speaking, and it is important that she is speaking to *someone* about *something*.

Janie tells her own story, and she is Pheoby's teacher. At the conclusion of her story, Janie says

Ah know all dem sitters-and-talkers goin' tuh worry they guts into fiddle strings till dey find out whut we been talkin' 'bout. Dat's all right, Pheoby, tell 'em. Dey goin' tuh make 'miration 'cause mah love didn't work lak they love, if dey ever had any. Then you must tell 'em dat love ain't something lak uh grindstone dat's de same thing everywhere and do de same thing tuh everything it touch. Love is lak de sea. It's a movin' thing, but still and all, it takes it shape from de shore it meets, and it's different with every shore. (p. 284)

To which Pheoby replies: "Lawd!...Ah done growed ten feet higher from jus' listenin' tuh you, Janie. Ah ain't satisfied wid mahself no mo'. Ah means tuh make Sam take me fishin' wid him after this. Nobody better not criticize you in mah hearin'" (p. 284).

They separate after Janie tells Pheoby not to be hard on them, Pheoby to go home to her Sam, and Janie to mount the stairs to her bedroom, and her solitude. But the solitude is a full one, full of thoughts and images of Teacake, who will live as long as Janie has thoughts. This comes perilously near to a version of idealism: "I think, therefore Teacake exists." And yet Hurston avoids that collapse, and it is the figure of Pheoby returning to her fretful Sam that pulls us back from the brink. This is Pheoby who is now "ten feet higher," and who knows what no one else knows. She knows Janie's inside, and she knows Janie's outside, although not immediately. Her knowledge is mediated, by the story and by her relationship with Janie. But Janie's story is her access, and her knowledge of Janie gives her the power of speech. Sam will take her fishing from now on.

Perhaps because I am a teacher I read this text as citing a version of a pedagogical relationship. Henry Louis Gates (1988) notes that Pheoby is a wonderful student. Wouldn't we all like to hear our students say that listening to us has made them feel ten feet higher? And Janie is a good teacher. Neither Janie nor Pheoby withholds, and neither intrudes. Theirs is a reciprocal desire. Janie's is for that "oldest of human longings—self-revelation," and Pheoby's is "to feel and hear through Janie." Pheoby's presence in this text enables it to enact connection as well as the self-division implicit in telling. There is a listener, and she has a purpose in listening. There is a speaker, and she has a purpose in speaking. These purposes converge in the desire to reintegrate Janie into the community. Pheoby's task is to take Janie's story to the curious townspeople who stand prepared to ostracize her. The third-person narration provides readers with information unavailable to Janie, thereby enlarging our understanding of self and other, of connection and separation, of solitude and community, and of the relationship and distances among them. Janie brings us near, and the omniscient narrator provides the distance we require to understand our own relationship to the text.

But how does Pheoby *know* that Janie is telling the truth? And how do we if the distance between self and other, and subject and object, is as great as it appears to be? We and Pheoby do not know. Or at least we do not know in any way that would satisfy Descartes. It is a matter of trust. Because we believe Janie, we believe what she says. We "feel and hear through Janie." But what we feel and hear is not identical with anything that Janie has felt or heard or saw. Janie's story is mediated by our own histories, and these histories enable us to feel and hear with Janie. We identify with Janie; this does not require that we be identical with Janie. Our own identities are, however, wholly contingent on the identifications we make. I identify with Janie, but I am not Janie. I am myself because I identify with Janie. We are not *only* different; we are connected—a knowledge repressed in all of the persistent myths which guide our thinking about selfhood. Identity depends on both differentiation and identification (a form of connection).

The world contains more than two things. This is fortunate for children and their mothers both. It is not clear to me, however, that gaining one's self and gaining the world entails loss. We do not have to choose between presymbolic merging and running off to the wilderness to live on locusts. The condition of self-division is not self-evidently a tragic state of affairs. It may simply be the condition that enables us, in our multiplicity, to enter human culture because we can make a compact with humanity. This is not a question of knowledge, but it is a question of education, which has as its aim the formation of identity and the forging of cultural connections.

Like art, our teaching serves as a passage between the world and the solitary intelligence. When we teach, we teach something, a fact astonishingly often neglected. The connections that might define relationships between teachers and their students, and between all of us and all of the others who populate our lives, do not repeat the presymbolic connection with the mother, although they do contain traces of the awareness of that state. Madeleine Grumet's work (1988, 1990) in curriculum theory investigates and clarifies the implications of this condition for our teaching. She argues that the classroom may provide a transitional space for students and ourselves in which we negotiate our own histories of differentiation and identification through the medium of the text. The presence of the text, the third term in the relational triangle, allows potential space for transformation. In addressing the opposing poles of mimesis and transformation in curriculum and teaching, Grumet acknowledges the child's mimetic relationship with its mother arguing the necessity of this mimetic moment in order to transform those original relations "within which we came to form." But mimesis eventually gives way to identification, as we alternate between the poles of differentiation and identification, between the claims of selfhood and the claims of our communities. She says:

> Daily experience continually moves through the phases of
> mimesis and transformation as we move between intentional

and reflexive thought. Nevertheless, as Jackson has pointed out, teaching too often clings to one approach or another, dichotomizing what is continuous in human experience....It is impossible to think about teaching without thinking about a relation to the object to be known. It is impossible to think about the object to be known outside the human relationships that designate it as meaningful in our world. (1990, 104)

Grumet, like Zora Neale Hurston in foregrounding Janie's narrative, gives priority, temporal priority, to mimesis. But she argues that human development depends on our departing the mimetic space along a new itinerary which will transform ourselves and the world.

Like our brothers, so many of us who would be ourselves suffer mimetophobia. We run screaming for the woods and mountains repressing as our brothers do more easily the claims of attachment. Doing so as teachers we help to reproduce the relations we would transform. What is repressed in the unconscious always returns. What we fear is what we get; we lose the world to our differences as we struggle to assimilate it to ourselves as once we were assimilated to our mothers.

The educational process must help us to reclaim the traces of our earliest connections, in order to help us to understand who we are and who we could be and in order to transform our infantile rage and dependency. Our voices are multiple, not singular. They echo with the tones and nuances of all the stories we have been told. The solitary singer sings to no one.

In "The Education of Women as Philosophers," Elisabeth Young-Bruehl (1987) questions the way that we think about thinking and the way that we have learned to think of ourselves as thinkers. She argues that a fundamental mistake in our thinking takes thinking as an activity of *selves*—singular, unitary. I think, therefore, I am. Invoking Freud's distinction between primary unconscious and secondary mental processes, Young-Bruehl urges us to abandon our commitment to mental monism, a commitment found in Plato's Republic of the mind with its rule of the one, for a commitment to new sort of *polis* of the mind—a democracy of the mind in which all mental processes are in conversation. Thinking is both mimetic and transformative.

In 1984 I went with my husband for the first time to Hungary. My husband had been granted a Fulbright Fellowship to work for six months on his translations of Hungarian poetry. I took leave of absence from my university and anticipated the luxury of uninterrupted days of thinking and writing. I think I wrote only two essays during the entire time, despite spending hours each day in front of the manual typewriter I had hauled across the Atlantic and half a continent.

I knew no one in Hungary besides my husband's colleagues. Nor did I then understand or speak any Hungarian. Once my husband left for his office in the morning, I was left to myself for the entire day. I like to walk. Because I live in the country, I like walking in cities especially. Usually I went out in the mornings, walked in the island park or shopped downtown or in our neighborhood, stopped in one of the many cafes for a coffee or a lemonade. And spoke to no one. At that time very few Hungarians spoke any foreign language. I felt invisible. I also understood, for the first time in my life, what it is to be stupid. I learned how much I rely on talk and on contact with others for my work. Invisible people don't write. Only in letters to my friends at home was I able to write. When I am alone with myself, I am myself and the sum of my connections and my separations. I am myself because I have identified and because I have been identified. Were this not so, there would be no one at home.

References

Bronte, C. (1867). *Jane Eyre*. New York: Carleton.

———. (1853). *Villette*. London: Smith, Elder and Co.

Cavell, S. (1979). *The claim of reason*. New York: Oxford University Press.

Freud, S. (1933). *New introductory lectures on psychoanalysis*. (W. J. H. Sprott, trans.) New York: W. W. Norton.

Gates, H. L. (1988). *The signifying monkey*. New York: Oxford University Press.

Grumet, M. (1988). *Bitter milk*. Amherst: University of Massachusetts Press.

———. (1990). On daffodils that come before the swallows dare. In *Qualitative inquiry in education: The continuing debate*, edited by Eliot Eisner and Alan Peshkin, 101–20. New York: Teachers College Press.

Holy Bible (King James Translation).

Hurston, Z. N. (1978). *Their eyes were watching god*. Urbana: University of Illinois Press.

Johnson, B. (1987). *A world of difference*. Baltimore: The Johns Hopkins Press.

Lessing, D. (1973). *The golden notebook*. New York: Bantam Books.

Pagano, J. (1990). *Exiles and communities: Teaching in the patriarchal wilderness*. Albany: SUNY Press.

Wallace, M. (1990). *Invisibility blues.* New York: Verso.

Williams, R. (1961). *The long revolution: An analysis of the democratic, industrial, and cultural changes transforming our society.* New York: Columbia University Press.

Woolf, V. (1929). *A room of one's own.* New York: Harcourt, Brace and Co.

Young-Bruehl, E. (1987). The education of women as philosophers. *Signs* 12 (2): 207–21.

Notes

1. See also essays in R. Fleming and M. Payne (eds.). (1989). *The sense of Stanley Cavell.* Lewisberg, N.Y.: Bucknell University Press.

Chapter 6

Claiming the Tenured Body

Elizabeth Ellsworth

> To take control of a particular discourse is as close as one gets to
> controlling the depiction of one's life.
>
> —Brenda Marshall

I wrote this chapter last summer in two days,
sitting at a tiny table
in the breeze and light
from an open window
in a very old library
near the ocean.

At the time, I thought of this chapter as autobiography,
as educational criticism (that is, cultural and literary criticism
applied to education),
and as a way of healing my passion for learning
by doing whatever it took
to enjoy and recognize some of myself
in the act of academic writing.

While this chapter still represents each of these for me, as I reread
it, I do so from within another set of interests and concerns. And
I want to frame its appearance in this book in a way that
foregrounds some of those interests and concerns.

I offer this chapter as an attempt to engage in situated inquiry
and situated writing in education. By this I mean that in this
chapter, I work within the question: What does it mean to be
writing from specific social and cultural positionings at a
particular historical moment for the purpose of unmasking the
interested nature of claims to universal truth?

Here, I write from my own social and cultural positionings about
the getting of tenure, even as those positionings shift, contradict,
and multiply from situation to situation.

I write about the particular power relations,
meanings,
practices,
pleasures,
and desires that surrounded my getting tenure
at a major research university
from particular, unstable positionings within
race,
class,
gender,
ideology,
sexuality.

By writing in this situated way, I am placed, as Patricia Williams
says it, "in a snarl of social tensions and crossed boundaries." I am
writing from a place (scholar, tenured) still not intended for me.

I am writing from positionings within and between gender,
sexuality, and ideology
that are unspeakable and incomprehensible
within the cultural and social paradigms that currently structure
universities.

And I am writing not at all to "fill" these silences
(since that is neither possible nor desirable),
but rather,
to "aggravate their historical significance"—
that is, to understand the historical, social, and political
meanings and consequences of such silences
in and for
education and educators.

Proposal for this chapter, written May 1991:

This paper explores the relation of solitude and the body to the process of getting tenure. It is autobiographical and focuses on the centrality of solitude in recovering my body and sense of self as a woman after getting tenure. Autobiographical stories are interwoven with an analysis of the institutions of higher education and tenure in the United States—specifically, the institutional construction of "solitude" at the university level, and the gendered meanings given to solitude and academic work.

Words that I copied and taped onto the walls of my bedroom, Summer 1991:

> There are so many stories more beautiful than answers—Mary Oliver, "Snake"

> We are learning by heart what has never been taught—Audre Lorde, "Call"

From the document entitled "Statement of Criteria and Evidence for Recommendations Regarding Tenure: Faculty Division of the Social Studies, University of Wisconsin–Madison, September 1990":

> The tenure candidate should have demonstrated the ability to conduct research that reflects original scholarship.

From the Oxford English Dictionary:

> Original: "not derivative or dependent. Proceeding immediately from its source, not arising from or depending on any other thing of the kind. A source. A cause. A fixed point from which measurement commences."

To get tenure, then, I "should have" presented myself as an independent source of new knowledge...as the single (sole) author of a clearly identifiable line of inquiry that was uniquely my own. I "should have" presented myself as the cause, the source, the one who originated a new line of concepts and theories. The One. I alone have had these concepts and theories. I had these concepts and theories alone. New knowledge should have come from me, the One.

> Alone: "all + one. Wholly one. Quite one."

[Holy One?]

> One: "essential, one by himself. Having no equal. Unique. Sole example. To leave to their own efforts. Exclusively. No one else in the same predicament. Solitary."

> Solitary: "one who retires into, or lives in, solitude from...for religious motives."

To get tenure, I should stand alone, I should be solitary. That is, I should have "retired into, or lived in, solitude from," so that my thoughts would be mine alone, so that by retiring from others, I would confront myself alone, my one Self and the ways of thinking that are mine alone.

Knowledge comes from one. The One. From God. In monasteries, seats of knowledge in Anglo-European cultures, one became a solitary for religious motives—to become One with the Source of Truth.

To get tenure, I should have presented myself as one who "retired-in-solitude-from" in the tradition of monks. To retire into or live in solitude implies a choice. Yet I have never chosen to write as a sole author the "articles, reviews, manuscripts, papers, books, monographs, chapters, or bulletins" required to get tenure. I experienced the solitary spaces of my writing and thinking as isolation.

> Solitude: "absence of life or stir."

To get tenure, I should have demonstrated "competence in research, conceptualization, theorization, synthesization, criticism, analysis, clarification." I should have retired from my body.

> Solitary: "a game to be played by one person."

> Isolation: "to cause to stand alone. Abstracted from its normal context for study. Isolated from normal social interaction. Quarantine."

My concepts and theories should not be contaminated by those of others. They should be sterile. To get tenure, I should assist the review committees in isolating my mind from its normal contexts (such as my body and my social interactions...from the stirrings of life and community) for study.

Yet I am a feminist whose daily life of study, interpersonal relationships, political actions, pleasures and play draws from and contributes to lesbian identities and cultures. My experiences of the things I research (pedagogy, curriculum, media, the social construction of meaning and knowledge) are always shaped by the ways I negotiate my own identities and social positionings as a white, middle-class, gentile, able-bodied woman and lesbian in Madison, in the United States. "My" research has always been grounded in the cultural expressions, ideas and conceptual frameworks that circulate and compete within (my own and other) women's communities. I experience the most productive, exciting, sustaining, rewarding, meaningful, and intellectually challenging moments of my academic life as I write, think, read, and argue *with* other women, feminists, lesbians.

Yet my work should be original, not arising from or depending on any other thing of the kind, not arising from or depending on any other woman, lesbian of the kind.

There is an old pasture close to the farmhouse that I live in (but out of sight and sound). I had saved six straight, ten-foot-long beams out from the bundles of slab wood that we cut into 18-inch lengths for burning in the wood stove. In April, I tied the beams, one by one, to the hitch on the beat-up orange John Deere garden tractor, and dragged them to the top of the pasture. I lined them up in the place I had begun to go to last October, where I sat on a straw mat intending to read or write, but mostly found myself listening to the wind that sounded like the sea and watching the leaves turn red or yellow at the end of each day of the new semester. Everything stirred and breathed.

By April, I knew I wanted to spend much time in that place. I stacked the beams like Lincoln logs to make a low and level foundation under the eight-foot by eight-foot floor of bare cedar boards that I wanted there. I pounded nails to the thunder, lightening, rain, mud, sun, and wind that flew through the pasture all within the same half hour's time—urgent and enthusiastic visitations by each of the four elements to this tiny platform retreat.

I began a large sketch book journal there. The first pages are filled with tightly focused interrogations of myself about the academy. I had begun original research of and into myself in the academy. How to be there? Why to be there? How to relate to it in ways that support my life and my social and political identities as a woman, a lesbian, a "radical" "scholar." These were now questions of life and death.

Building the platform retreat was a desperate act for me, fraught with fear—my first physical activity since the five days of almost nonstop heart palpitations in March. I didn't know whether lifting and dragging beams would bring them back. I knew what had finally made them go away...not going into school for ten days after seven years of never taking a sick day, seven years of running the tenure track; crying more in ten days than I had in the last thirty-eight years altogether; seeing, for the first time, the March birds that had been coming to the feeder all along; and deciding, without question, that I would not kill myself—literally or symbolically—to get tenure.

What made the palpitations go away was a profound reordering of my priorities. *My* breath, *my* heart and *my* heart's desires, would now come first. Building the platform retreat was the first physical manifestation of this shift, casting a space in the world where I would go to hear my breath and my heart. Where I would choose to retire in solitude—a very different form and meaning of solitude than the isolation expected by the tenure track. I sat alone with my journal, in the sun, with pens, pencils, a box of craypas, and asked: What versions of myself-in-the-academy were literally and symbolically killing me— and what versions of my-self-in-the-academy might sustain my life and support my passion for learning and teaching?

I re-encounter these questions every morning that I get up to go to school. Engaging with them is a continuous assertion of my will to change in the face of fear, deeply grooved patterns of being, and deeply invested senses of self. Willing myself to change has been a body-wrenching process entailing much more than playing word games with definitions of myself and the academy. One year after I built the platform, I wrote about what this will to change felt like in my body as I sat on the platform and screamed words into my journal.

> I mean to gnaw
> through
> the shreds
> of muscle and skin
> that keep me
> tied
> to parts of my self
> clenched in rusted teeth
> of traps
> set long ago
> to hold me
> against this north facing slope
> which has never welcomed
> or trusted
> the sultry breaths that sometimes
> crest the hill
> carrying scented whispers
> of what else
> might be
>
> I mean to bite
> through
> the last string
> of muscle and skin
> trail blood
> to the top of this frozen ridge
> and cross over

to the other side
where I will grow
new limbs
suited
for bearing
the fierce and gentle
givings and receivings
of my first spring

Based on a Journal Entry: April 28, 1989:

<u>The Academy Constructed (The Calling)</u>

<u>Romantic</u> narratives that lure(d) me to and fix(ed) my identity within the academy:

The academy offers a life of the mind, a context in which to think, learn, teach.

Solitude, introspection, detachment, contemplation are ok, expected, rewarded.

Teaching and research is important work, it is work that has intrinsic worth and absolute value—linked to civilization, progress, beauty, knowledge, enlightenment.

This job offers freedom of thought, discovery.

The academy is good—engaging with all that is best—the human struggle to know oneself, the world, God.

The academy challenges its students and teachers to do our very best, develop our capabilities, our unique gifts, our power.

The academy offers a life valued by others—respected, sought after, modeled after, learned from, remembered.

The academy makes a difference in students' lives by initiating them into a life of the mind, and helping them to realize their own unique skills and voices, to explore the world.

<u>Political</u> narratives that lure(d) me to and fix(ed) my identity within the academy (Second Calling):

This is a powerful institution that directly affects lives—it confers credentials, legitimacy.

It is a site of struggles for equal opportunity.

It is an institution worth fighting for/within as a political/feminist activist. Historically, it is an institutional context out of which social change has been forged and social activists sent forth.

It is a site for doing some kinds of political work that aren't being/can't be done anywhere else.

People become politicized here, higher education changes their lives.

The academy is a source of public and private resources for social change efforts that go unsupported elsewhere.

The academy is a place of meaning construction and use, a site for collective work, alliance building, *collective* construction of knowledges, communication across differences.

It is an institution that at least pays lip-service to (and therefore often must actually work in support of) values such as equality, justice, freedom, etc.

It is a place that encourages the envisioning of alternatives, and new terms of social organization and social relations.

The Academy De-Constructed

What I've learned through living out these constructions in my body and in my sense of self as an academic:
    The academy offers a life of the mind—yes—*and* it must be made to be a place for the body as well. Or at least I must find ways of being present in my body when I'm there and I must find ways of giving my body even more sustaining and welcoming places elsewhere in life where I can go to

nurture, heal, and feel
such as this platform
a place of solitude.

    The academy has value—yes—and that value is not absolute, intrinsic. What value it "has" is historically situated, contextually specific, socially constructed. Yes—the academy can challenge me to do my best...and "best" must be defined in the here and now, my "best" changes with each moment and each effort. Yes—the academy offers *relative* "freedom" of thought and action, self-determination, and always within constraints. It offers work valued not because of intrinsic worth—rather, because of the ways it has been able to make things happen in particular historical moments that others find to be valuable, useful, helpful.

Yes, the academy "empowers" people with credentials, legitimacy, etc., and often for the "wrong" reasons and outcomes. It may be worth fighting for/within, but not from the position of the Professor constructed as The One with The Answers, the Savior of the institution or the Savior of students. Rather, it may be worth fighting to construct spaces in the academy where the professor's voice is positioned as one among many legitimate and knowledgeable voices.

It *has* been the site for social change, political work, envisioning alternatives—but within limits. The academy is not the source/seat of revolution. It does offer resources for personal and political work, and the nature of those resources often shape and constrain the kinds of work teachers and students do. People do become politicized here, change their lives, and the academy is not for everyone, it's not here to "save" everyone.

It is a site for collaborative efforts and alliance building, and the institution is structured against this—it actively resists this—alliances and possibilities of collaborative work must be won anew each time. It pays lip-service to values of freedom, justice, equality, and this lip-service is a source of leverage to change things—and the terms in which equality, etc., are often cast also robs energy from more unsettling alternatives and definitions.

The academy does offer a place from which to envision alternatives, and it is not always the place where longed-for alternatives can be lived out—even in my classroom. Or even in my own out? in? out? in? lesbian body as I attend faculty meetings, write articles, deliver papers, chair committees.

Instead of trying to be The One with The Answers that the academy wants me to be, can I see my work there as partial, contingent, necessarily incomplete? Can I relate to the academy as just one site of my life's work, as one source among many of my multiple selves?

The Academy Re-Constructed

First steps in rewriting and resituating my selves, breath, heart within these constructions in ways that are life sustaining and support my social and political identities:

I have to get a life—spiritual, physical, mental—outside of work in the academy. I want to stop thinking that the energy I put into the academy is "better" spent (that is, more worthy, more politically or absolutely meaningful) than energy I put, for example, into reading fiction and writing poetry. Think about political work some more. What counts as "political?" Is doing tarot political? Is going to the Michigan Women's Music Festival political? Is reading fiction and poetry political? Is creating a "life lived fully"—i.e., with awareness, mindfulness, strength, passion—a selfish yuppie bullshit cop out? Can I be "political" some of the time? Is political work and commitment an all or nothing stance? To what extent are rigid and authoritarian "politically correct" definitions of "what is Political?" an ego savior trip indulged in by those of us who consider ourselves to be "political?"

Maybe these questions aren't about The Political. But about constructing politicals. That is, different sites and ways of creatively disrupting the barriers and boundaries of class, gender, race, sexuality, religion, age, ability, size—that injure our passions for learning, that restrain our abilities to respond to ourselves, the world, each other— that constrain response-ability. I want to create with others multiple sites and ways of living out my commitments to disrupting these barriers—one kind of political in the academy, another in women's communities, another in a letter to a friend. With others, I want to do contextual analyses—semester to semester—to figure out what needs to be done here and now, what's possible and appropriate—what are the constraints. Remember the academy is *one* site of "political" struggle, not *the* site. Remember, the academy is *not* the place for everyone, it/I don't have "The Answers" for everyone. With others, I want to define academic projects through a balance of collective and personal passions, talents, interests, and imperatives. Realize the institution works against this balance and against collective efforts. Realize there may be more appropriate places than the academy for following some personal passions, talents, interests and imperatives. Work to change the institution—but only as a part of a collective effort—not as The One with The Answers. Have my own sense of self-esteem come from many places, not just from work—which only leaves me easy prey for the academy's agendas and definitions of who I am or should be. Send some of my energy elsewhere in life. Find solitude, introspection, contemplation else*where*, and pursue it not only in the service of my academic work—but for myself, women's communities, for participating meaningfully in creative self-representations of lesbians and other marginalized groups.

Find "intrinsic worth" and "immanent values" elsewhere—in the spirit—the earth—my relationships with others. Be valued by others for honesty, for taking action out of what is true for me in the moment—as much as I can tell from my body, heart, mind, spirit, *not* for being The One with The (Original) Answers. Support my capabilities and power of self by growing across *many* places.

August 8, 1991: Alone in the Library

When I think about how solitude has enabled me to heal, reclaim, and reconstruct my now tenured body—I don't want to try to explain it. So maybe I can describe it.

In solitude: I feel my own body—my body is not assuming the pain, longings, desires, fears of others. I hear my own breath. I hear one of my voices…one that is not my academic voice, my feminist voice, my professor voice, my friend voice, my lesbian voice, my lover voice. A voice that is different from each of these…that often questions, decenters, disturbs and rewrites these others. A voice that I have constructed and known only in and through solitude.

In solitude, I laugh when I meet, face-to-face my own obsessions, sped-up-ness, the ways I lock into one of my selves for too long, or across too many different sites, inappropriately, ineffectively, in unhealthful ways.

I cry when I feel how far I have been from the voice I hear only when I am alone…the body I feel only when I'm alone.

I cannot "get enough" of solitude. It will always be something I need from time to time. It will always be the source of the sound of my breath. It will always be the construction site for a self that can be forged out of the rhythms, sensations, thoughts, emotions, fears, and longings that come present only when I willingly retire into solitude.

It is this additional, different self forged in solitude that gives me someplace else to stand in relation to the academy and refuse to present myself there as "The One." I see my academic self differently when I am within places and moments of solitude. That academic self becomes one among my many selves—not "the One Self." The academy becomes one place among many. The cedar platform in the pasture becomes the construction site for knowings that are different from the academy's…often challenging to or unsettling to the academy's.

When I'm alone and something happens—when, for example, I read a book…hear a hawk whoosh into the pasture…or feel myself drawn to an action or decision—I am temporarily spared the readings and constructions that would be made of me and my actions by others and by institutions. I can respond to such moments of things-happening-in-solitude in ways that remain temporarily unfixed by others (such as my mother, my best friend, lesbians in Madison, my colleagues). Responses from the self I construct through solitude can be playful and tentative. And this self is constantly changing in response both to time alone and to time with others. She is never the same from time to time of solitude. After years when each time I walked onto campus, each word I wrote, each conference paper I read, each interaction with other tenure-tracked colleagues—fixed, straight-jacketed me according to others' agendas, interests, fears, standards, desires, and needs—solitude has become the place where I can temporarily and contingently unfix and allow my many selves to float. A place where I can luxuriously and deliciously trace through my words, feelings, heart, and spirit the effects that various responses, selves, and meanings might have for me. A place where I can temporarily ignore the narratives others might be wanting or expecting me to live out.

In Spring, 1991, I joined a women's writing group as one of my first steps toward reclaiming my writing self after getting tenure. I wrote these words to introduce myself to them, and tell them why I was there:

fears and dreams of a recovering academic lesbian

I want to write words that burn the page behind them
fling spit across the room
slap the ground
I want to write reports from the cusp of change with words
that remain agile as the curve shifts fast

I want to write words that lift a peach-colored moon above my bed
words that touch watercolors to a wet page
words that leave a woman wanting to meet me

I want to write medicine words that others can use again and again
as balm salve disinfectant smelling salts
words that join me and you at the belly
unmistakable words

I want to write words that I recognize

Author's Note

Michele Besant, Joyce Dehli, Mary Moran, and Margaret Nash have given me thoughtful and useful comments on a draft of this chapter. Over the past year, they have helped me to see, feel, and hear my words—not just think them. I want to thank them for inviting me into their writer's group, and for creating a context of support and critique that has made it possible for me to even imagine writing a chapter such as this.

Chapter 7

When We're Together, I Feel So Alone: Solitude in the Midst of a Crowd

Beth Rushing

I date my recognition of solitude to an experience I had a few years ago. I went to graduate school in North Carolina, but spent four months in Canada doing fieldwork for my dissertation. For part of that time, I collected data in the Canadian national archives—a task that required only minimal human interaction. The women who got the archives materials took the slips of paper describing what I wanted, and put those books, files, microfilm, or whatever on a shelf in a room for me to pick up. They didn't really need to talk to me, and besides, French seemed to be their first language (it wasn't mine). I was living at the Ottawa YMCA, where I knew no one and came into contact with almost no one. I ate breakfast in the Y cafeteria among freshly showered people who had just finished their exercise rituals and were on their way to work; we didn't interact. When the archives were closed on the weekends I walked around Ottawa, went to public events (a polka festival, an arts fair), museums, a big shopping mall, bookstores. I had no friends or colleagues there, and was perfectly content with this situation.

At first I didn't really recognize my feelings as solitude, until a seemingly trivial thing happened that changed my entire perspective on human social interaction. After a few days in Ottawa, I had a routine: waking, breakfasting with the exercisers, walking to the archives, spending the day reading and writing, getting dinner on the way back to the Y, eating in my room, then reading and writing more in the evening before sleep. One evening, after I had been doing this for maybe two weeks, I stopped in a small market to get some things to eat for dinner. I put my food on the counter for the clerk to add it all up, and was rummaging around for the right money when she asked me a question or commented about something; I can't remember the details well, but I was shocked to be in a nonroutine conversation. What I do recall is that a reply to whatever the clerk said required a creative effort, putting together words that were outside my thought processes at the moment. All I could manage was to mumble something in response, pay for my food, and get out of there as fast as possible. Once outside, I felt a tremendous sense of relief, but also a little strange, like something was wrong with me. I felt stupid. I had lost the ability to converse, or at least to converse effortlessly.

Now I can describe it like this: You're floating on your back in water, and you hear what's going on around you, but in those muffled voices like adults have in Charlie Brown specials on television, and you're glad because you're closing your eyes, weightless, about to fall asleep or into a trance because it feels so good to be alone with your thoughts, and then you get hit with a beach ball, and now you've got water in your nose and you want to scream at the kid who threw the ball, but you can't find the right words because you've been thinking about something else entirely and didn't anticipate needing those screaming words.

The way I remember this solitude in Ottawa is as a feeling: not quite a physical sensation, but definitely more than a psychological condition. My reaction to the store clerk seemed so bizarre, so out of character for me that I had to think about it, to puzzle it out. And since then (it's been about six years), I've thought a lot about what the feeling and my reaction to it meant. I've come to define what I experienced in Ottawa as being a corollary to solitude. That kind of self-immersion does not always accompany solitude, but I believe it is most likely to occur when one is alone amidst a crowd because the crowd makes you so much more aware of your solitude. Furthermore, I suggest that such solitude is frequently experienced as an almost tangible feeling, as I have described above.

While the feeling I've described was quite positive, there are times when solitude is not desirable—many or most of us want and need human connection, and our society has parlayed this need for personal contact into a multimillion dollar industry (whether the need or the industry came first is outside my topic, but certainly an interesting question). However, solitude is vital to many people's lives. There are some things, perhaps many things that either cannot be accomplished without solitude or are enhanced by the presence of solitude. Solitude, then, is to be desired at least some of the time.

Now, how is solitude to be achieved? Most of the time, the term evokes images of wilderness, miles from the nearest civilization or human settlement. That is a way to achieve solitude, but it is not the only way. Indeed, the Ottawa solitude I've described here is quite distinct from the wilderness kind. In Ottawa, solitude happened for me in the midst of large numbers of people, even in the context of occasional interpersonal contact. Since then I've come to realize the ease with which solitude can be attained: it happens frequently, and particularly in heavily populated places.

One thing that initially attracted me to sociology is the way that the sociological perspective sensitizes one to the myriad ways that the people around you, both individually and collectively, help shape your behaviors, beliefs, and what you think of yourself. In my attempts to make some sociological sense of the Ottawa solitude I experienced, I turned to Georg Simmel, a German sociologist whose insights into social interaction are often intriguing and thought-provoking.

Simmel wrote that while we might expect the dyad to be the basic element of social interaction, in actuality isolated individuals can be seen as fundamentally social actors. Elaborating on this point, he argued that "[t]he feeling of isolation is rarely as decisive and intense when one actually finds oneself physically alone, as when one is a stranger, without relations, among many physically close persons, at a 'party,' on a train, or in the traffic of a large city" (1964, 119).

Whether physical solitude or psychosocial solitude is the most intense is not particularly important, though it is likely that we are all more aware of solitude if our surroundings constantly serve as a reminder of our solitude, thus heightening the sensation. Returning to my loss of conversational ability as an example, it is entirely unlikely that I would have even discovered the nature and extent of my solitude had I been physically alone. It takes an other (or others) to highlight this kind of solitude, to make one aware of its existence. For me, it took the clerk in the market, who was probably simply being friendly, to make me realize the degree to which I had been alone with my thoughts.

Solitude doesn't require such complete immersion into oneself that results in loss of ability to converse; it can be achieved in a shorter amount of time and in different settings. Many common situations can create or enhance solitude: riding the bus, walking down the street, eating alone in a restaurant, waiting for a train. In each of these situations and others like them, human social interaction is normatively proscribed: our culture discourages all but minimal verbal or eye contact between strangers in public social settings. We simply are not expected to strike up conversations with the people who share the bus or other public places with us. Societal conventions limiting public interaction with strangers (what sociologist Erving Goffman has termed "civil inattention") thus facilitate the achievement of solitude in a crowd. As a consequence, urban life is entirely consistent with and conducive of psychosocial solitude.

In an essay on "The Metropolis and Mental Life," Simmel (1964b) addresses another aspect of solitude amidst a crowd by suggesting that people living in cities build up, as a necessity, a defense against incoming sensory overload. Simmel terms this defense a "reserve," and notes that one psychological manifestation of this reserve is "not only indifference but, more often than we are aware, it is a slight aversion, a mutual strangeness and repulsion" (pp. 415–16). In our solitude, then, we are repelled by the presence of others, finding solitude preferable to the alternatives. We attempt to maintain the situation of solitude, focusing on internal states that are heightened by the presence of others. Solitude in such situations enables us to insulate ourselves from the slights and indifferences of everyday life: we protect ourselves by not allowing others in. In this way, solitude is like a fortress against others, and its construction leads to an aversion toward those others.[1] Although solitude in a crowd does not generally elicit extreme aversions, it does generate a feeling of detachment. Simmel argues that this detachment or reserve "grants to the individual a kind and an amount of personal freedom which has no analogy whatsoever under other conditions" (p. 416). Here is where Simmel fails to comprehend a vital aspect of urban solitude.

Like so many other experiences in this world, the solitude potential of urban life is not the same for women and men. Indeed, while solitude is possible on the subway or the street, the full experience of that solitude is mitigated by women's requirements for assurance of our safety. We simply cannot routinely immerse ourselves in our thoughts, when the realities of safe passage in urban life suggest otherwise. Walking down the street might enable one to become engrossed in thought, but in many places, for that walk to be accomplished safely, women must be vigilant to their/our surroundings. This essentially limits the experience of solitude for women in some urban settings.

Even when safety is not an issue, the ability of women to have solitude in a crowd is hampered by other gender-related factors. For instance, women routinely encounter harassment in the form of whistles, leers, or comments on our appearance as we move about in public. Even when such harassment is not perceived to be threatening (many of my female students interpret it as a compliment), it does invade our solitude. And who hasn't had the experience of contentedly dining or sitting alone, only to be joined by someone, typically male, who offers to "keep you company"? Solo women are presumed to be unhappy with that situation, and there seems to be no shortage of men who are willing to step in to help.

Solitude in a crowd requires a particular set of circumstances: one of the foremost is that the people around you must cooperate. The crowd—whoever they are—must obey the social norms that dictate polite inattention, norms that are different for men and women. These gendered norms also make solitude virtually impossible for women to achieve at home/in their families, at least within the context of the two-adult heterosexual household. As countless studies of men and women at home have noted, women bear the brunt of responsibility for day-to-day home life. Because this "second shift"[2] is a reality for most contemporary women in families, solitude at home remains out of reach unless it is a result of physical isolation ("Calgon, take me away..."). Men, on the other hand, can and frequently do achieve solitude even in the middle of a bustling family life: they read the paper, zone out in front of the television set, and snooze on the sofa. This solitude is possible for men because women's work makes it possible. Not intentionally, of course, but as a consequence of the gendered way that housework is allocated. Although women are expected to be attentive to the needs of family members, men are relatively free to achieve solitude. While the baby cries.

While dyadic relationships are probably not crowds in the usual sense in which the term is used, we can talk of couples in the same way as we have been talking about larger crowdlike groups. Simmel argues that even within intimate social relations such as marriage, solitude has "positive sociological significance" (p. 120). At first glance, this assertion might seem counterintuitive to some: solitude might be thought to be antithetical to intimacy. Indeed, the desire for solitude within a close relationship might be threatening, though it need not be.

One of the advantages of solitude is the space and time it provides for introspection, for self-assessment and thought. Some intimate relationships cannot stand up to such scrutiny, but many can, and many even require it. Thus, solitude is an important component of intimate relationships in that it helps the individuals who comprise the relationship to come together as more complete individuals, enriching the relationship. This is the sentiment that is expressed in the marriage ceremony statement "our love must have spaces." Unfortunately, however, such space has historically been more a part of men's marital experience rather than women's. Families, then, are one kind of crowd that may allow for solitude, but not for all the adult family members. Like public urban places, the solitude opportunities in private families are different for men and women. However, individual efforts at changing gendered experience have a greater chance of success in the family setting than in the larger, urban setting.

Why should solitude be so attractive? Simmel wrote about solitude as a state of freedom, liberating us from the normal day-to-day experience of informal control by others. It's easy to see how physical solitude can do this: if no one else is around, you are at liberty to do as you please. But how can solitude in a crowd be liberating in this way? One part of the answer to this question is that it isn't: solitude in a crowd cannot provide the same kind of freedom that physical solitude does. In a crowd, one is typically not free to completely ignore social conventions regarding public behavior. At the same time, a crowd does provide a certain amount of invisibility or anonymity that, in turn, generates greater latitude for behavior. Note that this anonymity may not be available in all types of crowds—families, for instance, do not offer anonymity, but they do offer private, backstage allowances for what might be otherwise unconventional behaviors.

When I reflect on writing this essay, it is interesting to me that some of my most productive and satisfying sessions of writing took place not when I was closed in my office, but when I was around others. Pieces of this essay were written in restaurants, hotel lobbies, airplanes, and in other similarly public places. Sometimes I had to leave my office to feel sufficiently inspired to continue putting these thoughts on paper. Writing in public has been important to me for a number of years, perhaps a version of writing exhibitionism. While I'm not sure I can explain the origins of this desire to write in public places, I believe that the solitude that I feel when surrounded by others contributes to the pleasure of that experience.

In many respects, solitude in the midst of a crowd is considered to be unacceptable, antisocial, dysfunctional. Being with others and feeling alone appear to be antithetical. This is probably due to people's discomfort with what may appear to be a rejection of them, a failure to need them. But solitude in a crowd is not really a rejection of the crowd as much as it is an affirmation of the self—a space within which we can connect with our thoughts and beliefs.

References

Simmel, G. (1964a). The isolated individual and the dyad. In *The sociology of Georg Simmel*, edited by K. H. Wolff, 119. Glencoe, Ill.: The Free Press.

———. (1964b). The metropolis and mental life. In *The sociology of Georg Simmel*, edited by K. H. Wolff, 415–16. Glencoe, Ill.: The Free Press.

Notes

1. This is similar to some popular notions about people who are physical isolates (hermits), who are presumed to be unwilling and unable to engage in normal social interaction. I think that frequently we consider that inability to be a cause of the solitude, whereas I would argue that such an inability to interact "normally" might be also considered to be a consequence of solitude.

2. The term "second shift" is used by Arlie Hochschild to refer to the housework and child care that employed people must complete after their "first shift" of paid labor. Women are primarily repsonsible for this second shift. See Arlie Russell Hochschild, *The Second Shift* (Viking Penguin, 1989).

Chapter 8

Borders of Solitude

Tuija Pulkkinen

A remarkable chapter in the discourse of philosophy describes the characteristics attributed to the great philosophers. This discourse creates philosophy as an extremely solitary occupation. The life of a philosopher, in these characterizations, is constituted in opposition to life in a family. The solitary male figures in the fables of philosophy leave family and go boldly where no man has gone before, to the final frontiers of knowledge.

The figure of Socrates is born in its opposition to the figure of Ksantippa and her world. The character of Kant is known to be a bachelor. His life—just as Spinoza's who is portrayed sitting in his small candlelit chamber without comforts—is described in a mode of asceticism and in direct opposition to the excesses of family life. Wittgenstein climbs the solitary mountains like Nietzsche, who is plagued by his mother and sister. Marx sits in the British Library to avoid the excessive demands of his family.

In the realm of describing the philosopher's life, family is the Other. This does not mean, as it first would seem, that family cannot be combined with philosophizing. On the contrary, just because it is the Other of philosophy, family is essential to philosophy.

By the concept of family, I do not only mean the legal or sociological institution of family or only the nuclear family based on heterosexuality. I rather use the concept in the wide meaning, resembling the usage which G. W. F. Hegel gives to it in his philosophy of right. He opposed it to the concept of civil society which is governed by pursuit of one's own interest. The concept of family is characterized by the inability to separate one's own interest from that of the other members of the family. Thus I am using family to mean any relationship where love, care and unselfish intentions are present and time-saving economy is not practiced.

This far, nearly all of the characters in the story of philosophy have been male, and the story, of course, has not only been written but also lived. What happens when the philosopher is a woman? My concern here is the concern of the numerous women who have, for some reason or other, plunged into the sea of thought and started to swim along with their bearded companions, first failing and then refusing to recognize their gender-specific place in the game.

The time is postmodernity, the place is feminism. The topic is the solitude that this stance involves, the solitude it demands and the solitude to which it condemns women in the combinations of thought and love and care. The message is that the first and second waves of feminism need to be combined with postmodern thought in order to enter into the dialectics of solitude and connection, and the dialectics of solitude and loneliness, where the topic invites us.

My Experience

For me philosophy was in the beginning a most private enjoyment. As a teenager I enjoyed the trips to the library and the solitary moments in my room. My family was not academic; my friends for the most part not interested in the same things as I was. I did not share my new language with anybody. Philosophy belonged to me; the family was comfortably the Other.

Later, the primary function of philosophy for me was sacred entertainment. It meant moments of deep concentration, sheer energy, tickling puzzlement, clear perception, tragic and hilarious collapses of previously held views, unexpected connections of thought, ecstasy of abstraction. All in solitude.

But in my lower middle-class family the television was always on, people shouted, and the uninterrupted sequence of family meals was never turned off. To emphasize my chosen Other, I climbed the stairs of the library of my hometown in order to find solitude; there I could be by myself with my thoughts.

Solitude and the sharing of thought is a class-specific issue. In my surroundings thinking was considered, well-meaningly, as a potential social disadvantage and thus dangerous or at least suspect. Solitude had to be fought for, and there was not much sharing of thoughts. On the other hand, I know families with roots in the academy, where thoughts are exchanged and love is combined with a shared need for solitude at times. But even in these families, the border between philosophy and family is gender-specific. The tension between the two always seems to intensify when the thinker needing solitude is a woman.

As much as being a thinker, my experience is being a woman, being part of the culture of women. To be encultured as a woman instead of a man in modern Western culture leads to the development of gendered abilities such as sensibility, the ability to put oneself in the place of others, and a type of relativism in everyday life. Women, clearly, have in modern Western cultures been the specialists of love and care, the main guardians of "the family."

When family and philosophy meet, we enter the field of feminism. On this field, the first wave of feminism denies my womanhood, while the second wave denies my experience of philosophy. At the moment it is time to welcome the third wave of feminism, which deconstructs both womanhood and experience.

The Waves of Feminism

I choose to use the present tense when discussing the waves of feminism; I do so because I believe that they should not be characterized as historical phenomena, but as living dimensions of feminist culture and politics. The waves I describe are present in contemporary feminism.

The first wave of feminism fights for the solitary room. Simone de Beauvoir wanted to show that women could philosophize if only they were given the same chances, if only they were not burdened by family, if only they were given solitude. Women were not by definition social creatures who had a natural inclination for caring and connection and who would hate to be alone.

From a postmodern perspective, the first wave appears very modern. It builds on the idea of unveiling the "person" under the womanish garment, just as modernism was to unveil the pure form and color under the garment of excessive styles in the history of art. The movement of the first wave is to peel off the unnecessary and get to the purified core. Here it meets with philosophy's modern journey to the purported final frontiers. Such a purifying impulse is gone in the postmodern. The postmodern thinker knows that there is no core to be revealed; under the surface that is peeled off, there is another surface. Our cultural coding knows no final frontiers.

When the first wave of feminism tries to squeeze the female-inscribed body into male frames, it has to deny women who philosophize sexuality, care, and family. The second wave of feminism responds rigorously to this denial. The female world is to be defended, and it has to be taken seriously. For the second wave there is no common goal of neutral personhood; the female world *is* different.

The claim of the second wave can be made in an essentialist mode or by referring to a women's different praxis. Or it can be interpreted as a strategic, political move. Whatever the metaphysical ground, the common denominator of different versions of the second wave is that it stabilizes the coding: men are connected to reason, theory, abstraction, dominance, and violence; women to empathy, care, love, connection, aesthetics, and experience. The code prescribes: men and philosophy, women and family.

If I am to listen to my experience as I am told to because I am a woman, and I therefore recall my experience of philosophizing, there seems to be something that does not match. Women do not enjoy abstract thinking, I am told. So, either I am not a woman or my experience is not a real experience. This quandary leads to the heart of postmodern issues of feminism. The third wave of feminism not only deconstructs the oneness of the political actor "woman" into class, race, nation, tribe, time and place; it also deconstructs the categories of "female" and "experience."

The female/male distinction as a foundation and final frontier is questioned in the work of Judith Butler (1990) when she makes gender a "trouble." For Butler "there is no gender identity behind the expressions of gender; that identity is performatively constituted by the very 'expressions' that are said to be its results" (p. 25).

Likewise, the foundational character of experience has been made problematic and seen as constituted in discourse. Teresa de Lauretis (1984) deals with experience "as a *process* by which, for all social beings, subjectivity is constructed" (p. 159). Joan Scott (1991), working on experience as evidence in history, proposes an approach which does not take experience as the origin of explanation but as that which we want to explain. She wants to "focus on processes of identity production, insisting on the 'discursive nature' of 'experience' and on the politics of its construction."

One of the most important elements of the postmodern for me has been the idea of productive borders. When in the world of knowledge you arrive at a frontier, what you meet is not the final limit, ground, foundation or truth; rather, what you meet is difference. And the border, as the place of difference, does not only separate, but also constitutes the two that it lies between. The border is productive of difference. So instead of saying that women and men are different, we say that there is an operative border—male/female—in the culture, a border which makes us fall into one or the other. And instead of finding out what we really experience, we should try to look at differentiating structures that make us call something experience and something else not.[1]

Butler makes gender identities, constituted in a system of productive borders, appear fluid. Similarly, Scott treats experience as moments of play in productive borders. Both writers work within feminist discourse. I would even say that it is not surprising that the agenda for postmodern philosophizing is feminism. Postmodern theory produces the effect of dispersal; it relativizes and sets up a productive movement that does not allow fixed positions. Women's culture in Western societies points in the direction of postmodern multivocality.

According to postmodern lines of thought, when talking about solitude and connection, philosophy and family, we should try to locate the differentiating borders and their constant productive movement on the conceptual stage.

Solitude and Connectedness

The first wave of feminism fights for the solitary space for women. Because philosophy is largely a solitary occupation, the possibility for women to philosophize is closely tied to the issues of the division of housework, childcare, and active energy invested in social relations between genders. The fight of the first wave is far from over; in fact, it is being fought all the time. But in this fight women do not have to give up their sexuality, care, and pleasure in order to philosophize.

The second wave of feminism has created a new political culture of women based on connectedness and conscious female ethnocentrism. It is very important for women to emerge as "we" at certain moments. This second wave, like the first, has not broken. If the third wave questions the existence of "we" and connectedness as the final solution, this does not mean going back to the solitary chamber of the philosopher. Rather, it suggests the dialectics of solitude and connectedness.

In "my experience" I climbed the stairs up to the city library in order to be by myself with my thoughts. Actually I was never there just by myself. I was there together with books. The black spots on white paper mediated the whole system of intellectual culture to me. I was not by myself; I was in a constant state of coming into being—in a creative confrontation with the Western philosophical culture. It was not so much *my* thoughts that gave me pleasure, but rather that I entered a discourse which created my pleasure. In this retelling of "my experience" the locus of happening shifts from the self to the flexible borders of the self. I was surrounded by two thousand years of signs. I was coded, inscribed; the context of "I" was building up. The stake of solitude without noises intensifies the connectedness to signs.

Philosophy is a tradition, a collection of stories and concepts and ways of putting them together. It is a vocabulary, as Richard Rorty would say, or a language-game, as Wittgenstein would say. As the latter pointed out, you can join in this form of togetherness, but you can never have a language-game of your own. There is no private language and there is no private philosophy. Another way to say this is that philosophers are a tribe, and my sitting up in the library was part of the initiation rituals.

This gives us new insight into the worries of the first wave of feminism. Paradoxically, women who were thought to be too connected to others ever to be solitary philosophers actually were not philosophers because they were not sufficiently connected to others, because they were excluded from this particular philosophical form of connectedness.

The myth of a solitary philosopher who works all on his own is demythified by the conceptual linkage of all philosophy in order for it to be philosophy. There is no philosopher in the candlelight alone with her/his thoughts because these are actually thoughts *in* the discourse that creates her/his being as a philosopher.

Solitude and Loneliness

Still, philosophy when it is actually practiced is a solitary occupation and a philosopher needs to be alone. If connectedness is one of the borderlines of solitude, then loneliness is another.

Solitude and loneliness are the same state with a different accent. At the outset the two states look similar, simply being alone, but there is a remarkable difference. Solitude is a positive state that is produced by the borders of "family." Connectedness is essential to solitude. The difference between the two is a dynamic locus of philosophy. Loneliness is a negative state where there is no difference, but only a night where all cats are black. The dynamic locus of philosophy shrinks into nothingness and negativity.

Philosophy as an activity for women today is gender-specifically connected to loneliness. The male philosopher, because he is a solitary hero, often attracts love and care. There is an existing system of signs that enables him to engage in relationships of productive borders.

Female thinkers are still more easily pushed to the shadows of loneliness and into a space of no distinction. Women are, because of extensive hopes for their contribution in love, care, and connection, forced to oscillate inevitably between the state of loneliness and intrusion. A step out of privacy towards connection may become fatal in terms of the need of solitude. Female philosophers still very seldom find the same admiration and comfort in family life as their male colleagues without sacrifices in their professional life.

In the life of a philosophizing woman all too often people enter her room without invitation, or no one visits. And when no one visits, her attributes start to diminish because others with opposing attributes are not present. A thinker needs solitude but a thinker also needs connection; the myth of a solitary philosopher has come to an end with women's entry into the discourse. The invisible love and work behind the seemingly solitary male philosophers simply becomes visible when there are women in need of the same comforts.

Women are more often hurting themselves at the border of philosophy and family and are more sensitive to this area. It is less easy for a woman than for a man to occupy a position of philosophical agency and create its Other inside the "family." Women are still left lonely because of their philosophizing, but what is at stake is not an absolute loneliness of a philosopher but loneliness which is relative to the context of women at this particular moment.

The border between philosophy and family, essential to philosophy, does not have to be fixed to gendered personalities as it has been this far. Postmodern thought deconstructs subjectivity in its transcendental and epistemological form, but it also influences our thinking of personality in an everyday context. Kathy Ferguson's notion of "mobile subjectivities" could be used to designate states of persons at the borderline of philosophy/family. Here we would find family and solitude not in a strict division of labor between fixed personalities, but in shifting positions at different times and different constellations. There is no need to keep a personality fixed to one or the other of the patterns of "philosopher," "woman," "man," "mother," "father," "friend," "lover," "parent"; all these resting places in mobility might involve more or less solitude at times.

Theory Against Philosophy

Part of my experience involves an emotional contradiction between philosophy and the antitheory attitude of second-wave feminism.

There is an angle for connection in the postmodern which becomes visible, for example, when Jean-François Lyotard describes the mode of his book *Differend* as "philosophical, and not theoretical,...to the extent that its stakes are in discovering its rules rather than in supposing their knowledge as a principle" (p. xiv). Theory, in his use of the term, means creating a metalanguage that constitutes the grammar of an object-language, whereas philosophy "denies itself the possibility of settling, on the basis of its own rules, the differends it examines" (p. xiv).

This distinction offers a point of entry into the current discussion on the relationship between feminism and postmodern thought where the political effectiveness of feminism is opposed to the relativizing stance of the postmodern paganism. If the feminist politics are directed against theory, domination, and planning, we have nothing to fear from postmodern thought. In fact, just the opposite.

If we want women's historical culture to have some impact in politics, that would be to avoid making things clear-cut or making a theory, and instead to keep things in movement, ambiguous, sensitive to differences and different points of view.

Feminism has feared that postmodernism deprives it of political and individual moral agency. What is important to see here is that our awareness of the constituting processes of subjectivity and agency do not make agency disappear. Judging morally does not disappear in postmodernity. What it may cause to disappear is the comforting feeling of being part of something larger, the semireligious sensation of taking part in a mission.

The postmodern in general secularizes. Existentialism told us that God is dead, that we have to make our moral decisions alone, and that is why we have angst. Postmodernism takes a step further when it tells the same: God is dead and we have to decide by ourselves. But the atmosphere changes...the general attitude in postmodernism is not angst but affirmation, joy and play. Secularizing does not mean that action disappears; in fact, just the contrary. Secularization means heightened responsibility of an individual for her actions because there is nothing behind or beyond on which one can rely in the questions of culpability. The comforting structures of a progressive movement are at the same time structures of power, and the awareness of these structures makes us more able to act, to fight injustices.

A postmodern denaturalizing gesture, like the one that is done to the idea of a solitary philosopher in this essay, does not diminish the value of the practice involved or end it. Consciousness of philosophy as a particular tradition does not make a philosopher less a philosopher just as consciousness of the institutional character of art and abandoning the romantic myth of the genius artist does not make a postmodern artist less productive as an artist.[2]

Relativizing the solitude connected with philosophy and the connectedness of women makes the relationship between women and philosophy more likely. Being a philosopher can be combined with being a woman of flesh and blood, with love and care, and with solitude.

I suppose I must tell the end of the story. My experience goes on. The life after the original family who comfortably created the necessary Other for philosophy, has been a series of moves at the borderline of identity of a philosopher and its Other: trying to find the Other, finding the Other, being the Other, and trying to avoid being the Other. And the story of being a philosopher and a woman goes on, in solitude.

References

Butler, J. (1990). *Gender trouble: Feminism and the subversion of identity*. New York: Routledge.

de Laurentis, T. (1984). *Alice doesn't: Feminism, semiotics, and cinema*. Bloomington, Ind.: Indiana University Press.

Ferguson, K. (N.d.). Mobile subjectivities. In *Reversal and its discontents: The man question*. Berkeley: University of California Press. Forthcoming.

Hegel, G. W. F. (1967). Hegel's philosophy of right (T. M. Knox, trans.). New York: Oxford University Press. (Originally published 1821.)

Lyotard, J.-F. (1988). The differend: Phrases in dispute. *Theory and history of literature: Vol. 46* (G. Van den abbeele, trans.). Minneapolis: University of Minnesota Press.

Scott, J. (1991). The evidence of experience. *Critical Inquiry* 17 (4): 773–97.

Notes

1. A beautiful example of this is Jonathan Culler's writing on authentic tourist experience in the article "The Semiotics of Tourism" in *Framing the Sigh: Criticism and its Institutions* (Norman: University of Oklahoma Press, 1988) where he writes: "The paradox, the dilemma of authenticity, is that to be experienced as authentic it must be marked as authentic, but when it is marked as authentic it is mediated, a sign of itself, and hence lacks the authenticity of what is truly unspoiled, untouched by mediating cultural codes" (p. 164.)

2. On denaturalizing critique in postmodern art and on its political contents, see Linda Hutcheon, *The politics of postmodernism* (London and New York: Routledge, 1989).

PART II
Solitude and Culture

Chapter 9

A Unicorn's Memoirs: Solitude and the Life of Teaching and Learning

Kal Alston

Carol Gilligan, in her book *In A Different Voice* (1982), forcefully challenged the model of moral reasoning and justice ethics that had provided the framework for research in moral development. Her argument, based on empirical studies of women in simulated and real-life situations of moral indeterminacy, was both provocative and complex. However, much of the complexity was elided in work on women that followed. The take-home lesson was simplified to one in which the morally successful man envisioned himself as standing on top of a mountain, autonomous and rational, and the morally successful woman was at the center of relational webs, connected and affective. Justice ethics, with its long tradition,[1] was opposed to care ethics.[2] In some cases this opposition was simply a difference, an acknowledgment that the modernist view of individuality is only one possible view of human life; in other cases the criticism extended beyond the modern intellectual tradition's univocality to suggest that this more feminized mode of encountering the world is superior to the other tradition. In either case, these philosophies of success/relationship were cast as separate and oppositional worldviews.

The posing of this "other," feminized mode of identity and discourse provides actual women with several interesting possibilities. One could argue that modernism with its competitive, hierarchical values constitutes something of a wrong turn—accidental or highly conscious or patriarchically inevitable (depending on one's commitments to sociobiology or social history or Freud). In this case the assertion of this new (old) discourse serves as a critique and a call for a return to a natural, premodern way of being and knowing. On another view, this alternative discourse serves as a parallel, balancing corrective to the alienating, disconnective effects of the heretofore privileged discourse that has been public, male, and dominant. The private, relational feminized context has served in silent counterpoint to the public domain, and to value each will allow individuals to shed their illusions that either discourse can suffice.

Obviously these two takes on the possibility of multiple spheres are not the only ones. Nevertheless something like these structures of belief undergird much of the discourse on gender, both in the marketplace and in the academy, and it is situated in these locations that questions about solitude arise. What kind of reading can we give to solitude in context of lives of connectedness or lives of individual achievement? What brand of solitude, if any, has social, political, and/or personal value for women, for any particular woman, for a woman engaged in a life of teaching and learning? In this essay I will look at three instances of solitude and the multiplicity of meanings and value in those instances. The stories overlap in places because they are all my stories, and life is not very neat.

Solitude and Politics OR Sisterhood Is Powerful

I came of age in the 1970s. My age cohort was born on the tail end of that demographic humpwhale, the Baby Boom. Our politics were shaped in and by the now-familiar litany of events starting with the assassination of JFK and ending with Nixon's resignation and the "end" of the Vietnam War. I remember the public tears of assassinations, the War, Kent State; the outrage of bra-burning in Atlantic City and of Stonewall; and the celebration of *Roe v. Wade* and of landing on the moon. It was a time. I suppose everybody says that, but my peers and I wanted desperately to be counted in the Sixties generation, because of its revolutionary rhetoric and mood, even though it was only our older brothers and sisters who were actually in on the action.

I was in ninth grade in 1972. That year is significant, even though I didn't know it, because of events in my own life and because Dartmouth College admitted female students for the first time that year (an event of which I was blissfully ignorant). That year was the first time that my friends and I started to talk about feminist issues (women's lib, as it was fondly referred to in those days). Granted, our dedication to the cause was pretty sporadic; in general we were more involved in such earth-shattering debates as whether Deb or Brenda would be crowned Queen of Hearts and whether we wanted to go to the Heart dance. In some ways we were just thirteen-year-old girls, like thousands of middle/upper-middle class girls in the suburbs in post-WWII

America. We were listening to Steve Miller instead of Glenn Miller, but for much of those days we were unconflicted—talking about boys and trying to get the maximum freedom possible from our parents.

In the spring of 1973, two things happened that challenged that complacence. First, Ros R. told me that she wasn't going to compete as hard academically anymore because boys didn't like smart girls. She and I had long been recognized as two of the smartest girls in our grade, and we were chums as well as friendly competitors. I found her declaration so odd—I remember my surprise that day in science lab at a table with a polished black surface. She had given it some serious thought clearly, but I thought she was mistaken: in the first place Alan S. wasn't worth it in my book, and in the second place my brains seemed to be valuable currency with all the men I knew, like my father and teachers. I hadn't really thought about it, but I did not want to believe that she was right; I did not want the cost of being "smart" to be too high because I didn't think I could stop being smart. (Of course, while Ros stepped up the charm school motif and turned down the heat on academic assertion, she didn't stop being smart either. She went to a first-rate university and graduate school, and when last I heard she married well to boot.)

These revelations made me somewhat nervous. Obviously, I was out of touch with the zeitgeist. First, half of the girls in the gifted program one year behind me had gone into regular college-prep because they were worried about their social lives, and now Ros was defecting. I had never before internalized this conflict between academic/work and life/romance. My own mother was very smart (not, to my adolescent mind, possessed of the towering intellect of my adored father, but she could hold her own) and worked without seeming detriment to the family or her marriage. With her life as a tacit exemplar and my induction as my father's intellectual sparring partner at the dinner table, this idea of bifurcated success was baffling. Having always been verbally precocious, I was used to getting approval from adults around me and respect from my classmates for my diligence. Ros's declaration was my first inkling that womanhood might make different, difficult demands.

The second event of that ninth-grade year was being selected as a spokesperson for the pro-choice side of a social studies class debate. To tell the truth, I don't remember much of the arguments we used; I do remember winning (no doubt for my rhetorical force and eloquence). But what stuck with me was that women's liberation was about more than whether the Miss America Pageant was sexist; this

was life-and-death serious. I don't know what side of the issue Ann
Marie B. ended up on in her adult life, but I do know that that day she
faced a classmate (me) full of certainty that I had right on my side. I
have since developed arguments for the choice position that are
nuanced and philosophically sophisticated in comparison to the simply passionate cant of twenty years ago. But this was an introduction
to the world of politics, of the defense of one's most closely held personal beliefs in the public arena.

By 1976, Dartmouth College had graduated its first class of four-
year female students. I arrived on campus that year, academically confident and socially anxious. I knew that my class had a ratio of three
men to one woman. I can't say I minded much, prospectively; I, *sans*
math anxiety, could figure out that that ratio meant better dating odds.
I also believed that men were, on the whole, smarter than women—in
the same way that they are generally taller. That is, I believed that the
ratio in my freshman class followed some sort of natural distribution
of brains. There were smart women, women who were smarter than
men—exceptions like my mother, my friends and me. And so what
could be better than being in school where all of these smart people
were going to study hard and become friends? I had groaned with dis-
gust to read the supplement to my high school yearbook: fully 95% of
the girls when asked to project ten or twenty years into the future had
predicted being married to their high school boyfriends with somewhere between two and six children. Only one girl had public aspirations; she predicted that she'd be a United States senator. It was, however, widely rumored that she was a lesbian (not a term of much
affection on the Main Line in 1976). So here I was among the exceptional men and women, ones who were determined to make a difference. It never occurred to me that "choice" might mean choosing
domesticity over academic, vocational success. I still didn't much
believe that there was a conflict.

There are a thousand stories I could tell. Let me however simply
comment that life at Dartmouth made me a serious feminist. This, for
me, went beyond belief in equal pay for equal work. I was witnessing
life on a battlefront. I saw the things that men do to women when
threatened (date rape, gang rape, "lighthearted" humiliation in dorms
and dining halls, academic sabotage), and I saw the things that women
do to themselves (treating women from women's colleges as if they
were typhus carriers, becoming bulemic and anorexic, humbling themselves academically and socially to fit in and get dates in a time when
dating a Dartmouth "cohog" was punishable by fraternity excommu-

nication). Some of it I only observed and some of it I experienced, but I bore much of the worst of it alone. In spite of the fact that I made some lifelong friends—male and female—in college, I believed that certain things were better kept private. And so it was not until I was twenty-two years old and working at my first job that I admitted out loud most of my pains and realized that these experiences were not just mine or my best friends. As Mary C. said to me, "Feminism is the realization that you are not alone, that you are not crazy." These were not idiosyncratic events, not even totally idiosyncratic to Dartmouth (only perhaps more intense).

So I began the 1980s with a sense that feminism offered me and other women the opportunity to make sense of our lives. Once you came to understand that you were not alone, nothing was too onerous to bear. Our lives were not going to be only about cooking and child-bearing; we were going to be filing briefs, prescribing medicines, and going to graduate school. Some of us were going to live women-centered lives; some of us were going to take lots of lovers (pre-AIDS) or marry a hip, sensitized fellow. None of us would be alone. Children, lovers, spouses, and above all our friends/sisters would see to that. Those homebound devalued relations of female duos like Lucy and Ethel were a thing of the past; we were part of each other's personal resources and public support. All that we had whispered in kitchens was now to be taken seriously as public discourse; after all, wasn't the personal political?

Those two revelations almost ten years earlier were in full flower: there were costs to being in our transitional generation; having it all was going to be expensive psychically, physically, politically, economically. And the stakes were potentially quite high. Our older sisters had declared themselves liberated, but they hadn't passed on the battle plan. How were we supposed to work to support a spouse through medical school if we were in law school? Whose thesis should get typed first and by whom? Who will watch the baby? The division between private and public life had come tumbling down, but it was unclear how the redistributions of public and private duties would work out at the end of the day.

In the midst of such confusion, it is not surprising that women began to hold up the standard from Virginia Woolf's book that "a woman must have money and a room of her own if she is to [do great things]" (1929, 4). Solitude and independence were the things denied us in the past as we took ourselves seriously only as mothers, wives, sisters, daughters, and other helpmates. Now we were going to be free

to be and do for ourselves. This is, of course, where the *politics* of solitude comes in. There was a time when the solution to oppressive
domesticity was viewed as being a simple matter of leaving it behind.
But, baby, it's cold outside. "When I said I vanted to be alone, I didn't
mean this alone." And wasn't this like the French Revolution, trading
one bad scene for another? There were costs to being alone as well as
to the connections. But how to loosen the bonds without destroying
them; after all our ability to nurture and connect is part of what
brought us together as sisters. Recognizing that we are not alone is
what enabled us to seek a place for ourselves, separately. So we are left
trying to have meaningful relationships without stepping on our
needs as individuals—a modernist dilemma. Can we put our hearts
into the project of solitude—time and space in which we are not
accountable to others—without taking our hearts away from those we
need and who need us? Having brought the private into the realm of
public discourse, can we take pieces of that privacy back for ourselves?

The balancing act required of us is to be autonomous, each thinking her own thoughts, in the midst of learning how to be political, to
live in concert. The political requirements of feminism, a public discourse, have consequences for our beliefs about potential conflicts
regarding our responsibilities—to each other, to the future, and to ourselves. Solitude in this context becomes not only potentially frighten-
ing personally but dangerous to others who depend on our physical,
emotional, and intellectual presence.

Solitude and Aesthetics—Marginality and the Construction of Identity

The move toward solitude for many women entails a balancing act—
whether her concerns are practical (How am I supposed to get time
and space alone in the midst of the demands of my significant others?)
or political (Am I supposed to feel bad because it feels so good to be
disconnected, dis-affective, de-webbed in my solitude?) or philosophical (Exactly how close is solitude to autonomy, and if I give in to a
desire for solitude am I giving up my ethic of care?). It may on the surface seems insignificant—a few minutes here and there—who could
begrudge anyone that? But to be alone without being compelled to
take anyone seriously other than oneself can easily feel like a betrayal
of one's obligations to others. At the same time the prospect may feel
like a threat to one's self. Learning to be in solitude without fear or
compunction or longing may take some work on the self.

I am a solitary person. I live alone, by which I do not simply mean that I reside alone (although I do) but that my days are not marked, in the main, by the call of other voices. Nor do I mean that I am a misanthrope or a recluse or a friendless waif. I have many friends (in every conceivable nuance of that word), true and good people whom I can rely upon in times of trouble, with whom I can share times of joy, or with whom I can grab a pizza. Although at the age of thirty I found myself an orphan, I have two siblings with whom I have reasonable relationships (given geography, history, and dispositions). So to say I live alone, to me, connotes a set of life choices that have significance beyond the daily manifestations of being physically alone or not. I mean that my social and moral obligations to others arise in the context of a prior and highly significant relation to my self—a context and work that I take seriously every day. I like to think that this examination—this work if you will—is less psychological or mystical than it is aesthetic.

I learned to read when I was three years old. For years the parental struggles included keeping "inappropriate" reading material from my clutches and separating me and my book long enough for me to wash the dishes/go outside and play/go to sleep. As for many bookish children, reading provided me a separate, private world away from the possibility of physical danger and social slights. In my babyish way, at a very young age I intuited the safety that a solitude bounded by books could provide.

I always felt that my parents should have understood that need better than they did. They had moved our family from Greensboro, North Carolina (where our next door neighbor was a sit-inner at the Woolworth's counter and my father worked with King and others in the Convention of the South), to a previously all-white neighborhood in Pennsylvania in 1964. The kids' big thrill was having three bathrooms; my parents were however involved in prelitigation conferences with the Fair Housing League. They were primarily interested in living in a nice house and sending us to good public schools, but they were cognizant of the fact that the decision to move into this town, this neighborhood, was more than personal.

These were days in which my brother and I would run shrieking through the house for our parents if we saw a "Negro" on the television. There was nascent movement in terms of race to be seen, but it was a case of exceptional individuals or of fields (like entertainment or sports) in which the Negro's presence contributed to the profit margin.

We moved to town too late for me to go to kindergarten at the school down the street. Ever after, because I was placed in the Academically Talented Program, I was always bussed away from neighborhood schools. I also was in a self-contained classroom with the same eighteen students for six years. In retrospect, I believe that that year-to-year sameness combined with my enjoyment of school overall provided a safe space for me. I made fast friends with the children in my class who lived in my neighborhood. Occasionally I would go after school to play at the house of a little girl who lived on the next street. One day Patty A. told me that I couldn't come to her house anymore (although she could come to mine) because her mother had had complaints from the neighbors. Our own neighbors had built a fence to keep our balls (and us) out of their yards. My mother explained these events and all of the name-calling and the rest as ignorance; we should feel sorry for these people who would not open their worlds (homes and hearts) to us.

I looked out on the world and for the most part, until I went to college (ironically) I found no faces that looked like mine. I had friends in school and church whom I loved and who loved me. I recognized, although not consciously, that while in many ways I was just like them—we shared interests, tastes, attitudes, and secrets—I was slightly apart. I was of them and not of them all at the same time. As we got older and moved to junior high and high school, I could see that more clearly. I recognized that although in many instances I was one of the gang, I always also represented something. I provided my fellows with an opportunity to test their prejudices; they could look to me and say that they knew a Black person and that I was a friend or not. I was a symbol of how well the Civil Rights Movement had gone. I was the product of two highly educated professional parents; my siblings and I were bright, personable, polite children. We were, you should pardon the expression, the paradigmatic "credit to our race" who made good the case for integration and the shedding of racism.

I was aware at a mostly subliminal level of my symbolic weight, but in the main I was interested in being myself—of finding myself. I recognized that, because of my parents' choices, my life was more complex than, for example, my cousins who grew up in the south, wherein they went to integrated schools but only mixed socially with other Black people. Like my school chums, my relatives could not quite understand me. How could I like this or that white person, trust him/her? They could never put themselves in my position and realize that I didn't look at Kenny or Jessica as white but as people with whom I shared the public experiences of my growing up.

I chose the friends that I had (as they chose me), and in the years of late adolescence I began to understand that there were choices to be made about the shape of my social and personal commitments. Charles Willie (1981, 15) suggests that cultures require the presence of "people who live in but also between and beyond the races of humankind." The creative power of that presence is in the affirmative choice to reside in the margins rather than being "marginalized." That is, rather than being exiled away from the center of action, these out-riders use their positions in, between, and beyond to resist and subvert the taken for granted relations of the world.

Willie acknowledges, and Foucault (1983) assents, that to make this kind of project of one's life is challenging, daunting, and dynamic. Every person does work regarding identity in one way or another, and my story is no different in the general principle than that of any other adolescent. Most of us are occupied with the formation of selves and the situating of those selves in social relations. We not only want to find ourselves as individuals but to find our places in families, occupations, age cohorts, friendship webs and the like. Those engaged in activities of ethical self-formation find that the rules of morality are primarily constituted for sociality. In the practice of our relations to others we find out what kind of persons we are. We can relate ourselves to the groups that claim us and that we claim; familial, racial, ethnic, gender, sexual, physical, religious, and other identities make claims on us that we may answer or not in a multiplicity of ways.

In my own idiosyncratic choice to reside more fully in the margins, there was a concurrent choice to make use of the aesthetic qualities of solitude. To recognize that we all, in some ways, live alone yet to claim that solitude neither as a refuge from the conflicts of sociality nor as a necessary evil in a world of individuals becomes a highly creative project. Rather than what happens to you when no one else is around or a goal in the midst of the demands of others, solitude here becomes the arena in which one plays out a life deliberately and consciously on the margins. The aesthetic quality of life and of solitude reside in moments of heightened awareness in which one's relation to the world is somehow made crystalline. Dewey speaks of "the combination of movement and culmination, of breaks and reunions" that manifest that "the experience of a living creature is capable of aesthetic quality" (1917, 17). Consequently, the aesthetic quality of solitude does not result in isolation, but in ongoing appreciation and increasing apprehension of experience, inside and outside of solitude.

I once remarked to a friend in graduate school that I felt like a unicorn, rare and interesting but also separate and alone. It was a day when I suppose life in, between, and beyond seemed more burdensome than dynamic. My friend's observation was, like Willie's, an incitement to look at my position as one of creative potential. I took him seriously, and that encounter allowed me consciously to confront myself and to affirm my work/life of solitude with refreshed energy.

Solitude has become whole-some for me—a space in which confrontation, transformation, and affirmation are possible. In the midst of my multiple identities and communities, I move from my self, which is alone, into the world I make with others. Solitude enables me to feel unity with other women when I see their pain at sexual violence as *our* pain; to know, firsthand, the frustration of other African-Americans as we struggle with the schizoid race un/consciousness of our culture; to feel at one with Jews across time and space as the Kol Nidre is chanted at the High Holy Days. The solitude of a life on the margins provides the space in which I can be a home to myself, without seeing that home as solitary confinement.

Solitude and Work:
A Life of Teaching and Learning

In the academy, solitude takes on still other shades of importance and meaning. Being successful here requires that one demonstrate one's scholarly competence and the capacity to be both a good teacher and a colleague. It has long been my contention, even before I became a professor myself, that in some ways tenure decisions come down to whether one's senior colleagues can visualize meeting one over the coffee machine ten or twenty years down the road. In some cases, the deliberation has to do with whether they believe that you and your work will bring intellectual/academic credit to the department. In other cases it may have more to do with how well you draw students to the department or whether you fit with the vision the department has of itself as a collegial, political, or social entity. By this I mean that life in academia has a palpable inter/subjective quality that suffuses the proceedings. Solitude in this life has an ironic duality.

After finishing my coursework and exams in graduate school, I chose to live about 150 miles from Chicago. My advisor found this somewhat worrisome because he feared that I might get sidetracked away from the inspiration and support of my cohort. His fears were both founded and unfounded. I found that I did miss the interaction of people who were interested in the same ideas that I was. I also understood that dissertation writing was a solitary pursuit. While I continued through phone calls and visits to connect (gratefully) with my fellows, the actual work was done alone in libraries and at the computer. After all, dissertations are to mark one's (individual) contribution to the field, so I was told.

Post-dissertation, then, one is to begin the lifelong task of marking one's place in the "field" through one's writing, speaking, and associations with other like-minded (or perhaps not) academics. We are also, if we stay in the academy, to mark out places in our departments, schools, colleges, and universities. This requires another set of balancing capacities: on the one hand career maintenance requires that we write, publish and promote ourselves as individuals; on the other hand the collaborative urge asserts itself loudly and clearly for many of us. We live, professionally, in the midst of other persons, colleagues and students, with ideas and insights that form the ground of discussion, debate, rivalry, and the formation of knowledge itself. I sometimes feel that I could go from office to office on my campus and never tire of talking and thinking with my fellows. I know that as edifying as that might be, promotion and tenure committees are interested in concrete demonstration of my individual efforts and contributions. In my discipline, in any event (unlike the sciences, for example), collaboration has an element of risk, at least until I have "proven" myself as a scholar.

Teaching has its own set of complexities. Aside from teaching assistantships in grad school, before I became a professor my teaching experience was mostly in theater. I have taught every age group from elementary school through college in a variety of settings. Theater is unambiguously collaborative; that is, even as a teacher or director, one has no illusions that the project at hand could be completed without the participation and cooperation of all. I bring those predilections and strong beliefs with me now into philosophy of education classes. Teaching as a practice requires that I, the practitioner, consider carefully my ethical commitments to the practice itself, as well as to myself and to my students. Teaching takes place in the context of institutions, and other broad practices, and these institutions provide boundaries and traditions for practices. Part of the traditions contemporary graduate students have inherited include inculcation into norms of competition and professional distance—not only from their fellows, but from their teachers. I am to them, even when relations are at their best, the giver of evaluation, the holder of their fates, separate and not quite of them. Consequently, in the part of my job that I enjoy most, that I see as least availing of solitude, I sometimes feel most alone.

Both teaching and scholarship provide a rich culture of possibility for collaborative work, and many people recognize that richness and take part in it. That participation for graduate students and more junior faculty can be satisfying; yet it produces a sense of dis-ease at times. Like children scarfing cookies from the cookie jar, we are as yet unsure that the pleasures of thinking, talking, working, and writing together won't get us in trouble down the line.

There are, however, moments, encounters, relationships in which I find great joy and the communion. For myself I see no small amount of irony in finding a career in learning and teaching. Both of my parents were educators, and growing up with a mother who was a teacher convinced me that it was not the life for me. For a very long time I resisted looking to education as a place for myself. Now I see the naturalness of the fit. All of the contradictions and tensions of any particular job or setting notwithstanding, I see this as a life in which my life of solitude and the importance of relations with others can find fulfillment. The path I have been hewing on the margins connects with the satisfactions of taking ideas about education and social practices in general very seriously. The complexity of my own life commingles with the complexity and dynamism of a professional life which is multifaceted and multileveled. One's capacity to be on one's own is challenged as are one's commitments and relationships with others by the demands of the multivariant tasks. Here I have a room of my own—with connecting doors to my students, colleagues, discipline and intellectual traditions.

Epilogue

I chose to write this essay in a highly personal voice because I find it extremely difficult to speak for women (writ large) regarding solitude or any other subject. I have observed many of my peers struggling to get time and space that is their own in the midst of the demands of marriages, families, and other constraints. The conflicts and the constant aligning of priorities affects the lives of all the women I know, in every profession and at every age. I have an everyday look up close at women in academia. These women struggle daily with allocating their time to students, committees, organizations, families, allegiances and affections on behalf of themselves and others. For many of them solitude stands up against those demands, and they make choices that make sense for their lives.

I would not presume to speak in more than general terms about the nature of those choices because I am certain that every story has its own weight and importance. This volume will go some way to raising solitude to the level of explicit inquiry—questions, discussions, and more questions. I originally wanted to subtitle this piece "A Survival Manual." I changed my mind because I do not mean to suggest that my memories and strategies can do more than light one small corner of the potentially wide world of discourse.

Solitude, for me, constitutes occasions of self-reflection, self-confrontation, that encourage me in my encounters in the world. I have tried to share some of those occasions here to suggest some of the ways that my life circumstances have both pushed me and enabled me to take myself seriously not only as connected to history, traditions, and communities, but as a woman for whom solitude has become a window onto the worlds in, between, and beyond which I live.

References

Dewey, J. (1934). *Art as experience.* New York: Putnum and Sons.

Foucault, M. (1983). On the genealogy of ethics: An overview of work in progress. In *Michel Foucault: Beyond structuralism and hermeneutics,* edited by J. L. Dreyfus and P. Rabinow, 229–37. Chicago: University of Chicago Press.

Gilligan, C. (1982). *In a different voice.* Cambridge: Harvard University Press.

Willie, C. V. (1981). *The ivory and ebony towers: Race relations and higher education.* Lexington, Mass.: D. C. Heath and Co.

Woolf, V. (1929). *A room of one's own.* New York: Harcourt Brace and World.

Notes

1. On the developmental side, see Lawrence Kohlberg's stage theory; on the philosophical side, see John Rawls.

2. For example, Nel Noddings, *Caring: A Feminine Approach to Ethics and Moral Education* (Berkeley: University of California Press, 1984).

Chapter 10

One-Way Mirrors, Alchemy, and Plentitude

Glorianne M. Leck

The guy on the talk show was railing on and on about how anybody who could see Madonna or lesbians as contributing to society was obviously not someone who should be teaching teachers. "I don't know. But, I tell you, frankly, I wouldn't want this Glorianne Leck to be teaching my daughter anything. I don't know. But, I think you need to make sure, if you have students going to the university or if you have children coming up who may attend the university, especially when it's a university right here in your town, you almost, I would think, have a right or a responsibility to lodge a complaint about this to the Board of Trustees, or to someone, uh, the President of the University or the Board of Trustees." And I heard him go on to say that people like me are a threat to the family and our presence in politics and universities is what is making this world such a mess.

There it was that feeling, again. Someone had taken my words from an editorial I had written, scrambled them in his head, spit them out of his mouth with his venom and now he was trying to stir up violence against me as I become an object for his violent homophobic feelings. That familiar feeling—alone with no protection, fending for myself—came sliding up into my throat. First the fear, then a kind of paralysis, the kind a wild doe must feel when power wheel pick-up trucks focus their spotlights on her. The paralysis, the silence, the wait.

I wait, knowing that my paralysis will dissipate, the talk show host will stop his attack, the spotlights will move off of me and I will take a deep breath and reclaim my sense of being in control of myself. I'm fifty years old now and am nearly able to assure myself that the wave of fear will break. I try to assure myself that harsh words or criticism will not necessarily be followed by violence. As I direct and persuade these initial sensations, they peak and a gigantic wave spreads the relief sensation throughout my body. There in that immersion I grieve and let go of moments of my violent childhood, reassure my adulthood and use my sense of shared humanity to reestablish and find balance. In that centeredness I again feel a kind of peace, that strength of being in and with, while identifiably separate and somewhat unique.

I'm fifty years old now. When I was two and a half I had what Herbert Spiegelberg (1961) has since called an "I am me" experience. I've named that early recollection my existential birth. The occasion was, for me, a way of digging in my heels, a way of resisting force. Thus, it was both a proclamation and an effort to preserve, to canonize a knowable identity with which I could survive. It seems now that it was a political/philosophical move to establish an image, a self-concept, an objectified self. The response came bubbling out of a cauldron of resistance to false accusation, to negative objectification, to expected violence, to paralyzing fear. This construct of identity was fueled by a reflective use of intelligence and some still less understood (by me) biological incentive to survive.

I was a very young child when I got involved in this alchemy. Now I reflect on that significant act of choosing a way-of-being, for what must have been at best a vaguely constructed idea created within a cultural time frame of past, present, and future; and childhood, adulthood, and transcendence. It was then that I constructed my first known concept of solitude: the location where I could construct a transcendent state that allowed me to identify myself, be a self, and make sense of a world of violence, conflict, and unclear messages.

Embodying a Euro-Caucasian gene pool and peasant values, diet, and attitudes, the "me" resided within and was nurtured by a large-bodied, very strong and able female child. In first grade the class photo showed this large child standing a half of a head taller than her teacher. The high school yearbook photos showed this substantive adolescent appearing uncomfortable in a dress, high heels ("fuck me" pumps) and (although we can't see it) a girdle. The photo is marked by the appearance of strain as she tried to keep her knees together in a "ladylike" position. There was always an awkwardness in these "ladylike" roles—I liked the roundness and nurturing of woman, but "lady" eluded me.

My inner photo showed me as this: nurturing, reflective, athletic, articulate, a success in school and more interested in the affections of the girls than the boys. The reworking and the further construction of the linear "me" was marked in my memory by the gestalts and transformations that I earned and learned in moments of risk and feelings I allowed myself when in retreat. Often the retreat was a protective solitude that would bolster my sense of belief in my own self-worth. But there were other times when, as an adolescent, I could find no retreat. The loneliness, the objectification, and the fear were frozen in the presence of violence.

When I was eight we moved to a tavern on the edge of a small town. My folks became the tavernkeepers. Our kitchen was our living room, the sick room, where we brushed our teeth, did our homework; it was also the public kitchen for the restaurant. The public toilets were also our toilets. We hauled out a portable shower on Saturday night so family members could each have our weekly cleansing.

The tavern was where the action was, and it was home to a large extended family. Mother was in and out of the bar and the kitchen as her work required. Customers came and went in the kitchen just as they did in the bar. We always had company. I did have a bedroom of my own by the time I was ten. On several occasions I woke in my bedroom with some character standing next to my bed who had wandered up the stairs into what was called "the upstairs living quarters." I had to depend on myself for safety.

Every day was a holiday. Someone always had a birthday, a new baby, an engagement, an anniversary, a new job or a religious ritual to celebrate. Festivity, humor, activity, sports, drunkenness, fighting, sex and everybody's troubles were a part of everyday existence. I was raised in this extended community. I was used to having many people around all the time. Conflict, sexual imposition, and violence were lurking close by in every conversation and every activity. My father's sensitivity to the tensions around him became the barometer for my safety. When he could no longer deal with the tensions, his violence rose to the surface, and I would be the one who he would hit.

Being alone was dramatic and counterpoint to the daily bustle. Being alone meant being out of the way of the immediate risk of violence. In my room, alone, I kept a daily diary. I talked to myself. I reassured myself amidst the background noise of a tavern juke box that went from noon to two A.M., seven days a week.

My bedroom walls were cluttered with movie star pictures. I collected baseball cards. My bedroom then, like my house now, was a bustling environment filled with photos and books and artifacts that provided me with a sense of connectedness with community.

By sixth grade I knew I had as much sexual attraction and desire for girls as I did for boys. Of course, in rural America in 1952 I hadn't learned the name of or the consequences for that secret. What I knew were the sensations and that it must be kept a secret. I lived and breathed McCarthyism in Wisconsin in the fifties. I also knew about heterosex, violence and death. I was street smart in a country tavern way, and I was politically keen as I protected my minority status. I felt less at risk with girls than I did with boys.

Adolescence was too much for the "me" to bear alone in such a demanding and threatening world. The bustling lifestyle created so many feelings, demands, and pressures. At fourteen I returned to the cauldron and deconstructed, then reconstructed until I had brewed myself another kind of solitude. This one was spiritual, contemplative. This time I ordained a companion. I concocted a large, all-knowing, invisible friend and borrowed it from what others were calling "God." It was like having Santa Claus all year around. My god was a strong, kind, masculine, protective, paternalistic Christian-type god who provided a constant presence. I no longer had aloneness in my solitude. I struggled with everything without benefit of my previously centered self. I ran all my life through the approval of this other being, and could therefore justify anything I chose to do in the name of god's approval. I rationalized all my actions with him and sought those answers and that approval from outside myself. I wrestled with roulette Bible, impulses as inspirations, prayer as promise, and sex with boys as love.

With the exception of learning to trust boys, I achieved at everything I did. I won the school elections and the debate and good citizenship awards. I threw a baseball with such accuracy and power that the pitcher from the local semi-pro baseball team used to work out with me. Glen Glenetski always said, "Glorianne, it's a crime that they won't let a girl like you play major league baseball." He was, in my mind, an exception, a man against the grain of the men's culture.

Bothered by the lack of recognition from my parents and their friends, I moved further and further away from the community of tavern life. I spent all my nonsleeping time at school and at church. In 1958 I resisted my father's insistence that I go to work in the shoe factory and that I quit high school in my junior year. With considerable effort on the part of a minister and my teachers, I was allowed to work for my room and board and to stay at home to finish high school.

After graduation I emancipated myself from the small town, took my god, some NDEA loans and a $300.00 scholarship and went off to attend the University of Wisconsin. I had not yet been at the university even a month when my Greek and Roman culture professor, Walter Agard, asked us to read Plato's *Republic*. That work, that experience stirred the cauldron again. As I began to read I knew this was the most important book I had ever read. I warned my college roommate not to be concerned about my absence, that I was going off to read Plato for a few days.

I found a quiet corner in an unused bathroom stall in the basement of the dorm next to the laundry room. I read Plato for two or three days. I didn't sleep, I didn't eat, I didn't experience any dailiness in my life. Words became tools, and I felt less rigidly confined to "me" and more assured of having some value and some connection in a greater scheme of human things. I came out of that experience with a different view—not so self-conscious under the gaze of others, not hiding inside looking out and being in control, not acting and controlling in order to put my spin on others' view of me. I felt myself merge into some tradition of learning and exploring. There was something new, unusual, intense, fertile and comfortable about being in the flow of a shared tradition of discourse. Here I felt the pleasures of feeling elevated from the day to day. But elitism was alienating, too, as it called for joining with those who struggled to understand *others* without acknowledging or living with the internal problem of *being* an *other*.

In February of the following year I listened to a pronouncement by my philosophy of religion professor, A. Campbell Garnett: "Now let's be clear about one thing. There is no god apart from what we create as a god. God is a human creation. We as human beings create the world in which we choose to live." It made perfect sense to me and caused me to consider why I, like many others, had constructed a god and a religious faith as companions in my life. Taking responsibility for that construction and considering now, with less desperation, that there might be many constructions and many options in the way we see ourselves interacting with the world, I felt an immediate reduction of my pain and my fear of others. However, in this experience I again felt the full weight of my individual responsibility for constructing who and or what I was.

I was again focusing on being alone without adult or outside authority to protect me. With that awareness of being totally responsible for myself came another wash of old fear, paralysis, the wait, and then the self-encouragement, the exploding wave and the euphoria of release from the control of others. Bolstered by a rich university environment, good literature, theater, political involvement and particularly by the writings of Simone de Beauvoir and Albert Camus, my solitude became not just a release after loneliness, but the home of my centeredness. Like the peace after the pain of a migraine headache subsides, like the sleep after lovemaking, like the relaxing of the body after the thunder finally responds to the lightning bolt, I learned that loneliness can be a passageway, but not the *only* way to come home to a more abstract shared being, with safety and rest.

I was learning that loneliness is a reaction *and* a choice. I had begun my thinking on solitude by binding it to loneliness; I saw solitude as a contrast to community, to distraction, to the demands of others. I came to solitude through loneliness that I had first learned in childhood in my experiences with physical and verbal violence. When I would control or find release from the fears that cultivated that loneliness I would assert my notion of solitude. Solitude became a good, safe place to be.

Even as my sharing of viewpoint with existential philosophers enriched my sense of self-confidence and choice, there remained that constant and nagging problem of not yielding to heterosexual norms and being constantly in the presence of and threatened by prejudice and hatred toward lesbians. At some point after encountering multiple acts of homophobic violence along with the constant daily presence of having my life and my love being made invisible, I was able to find some personal affirmation in Hannah Arendt's construct of "the human condition." I felt a shared meaning with her words and I felt most at home with a concept of people if not with institutions. I identified with others who experienced the oppression wrought by religious bigotry and patriarchal hierarchies. Because I grew up with violence, homophobia, sexism, racism, class and religious prejudices constantly jarring me out of my sense of safety in community, I learned that I felt the most in common when I was *in the street* and not in the institutionally sanctioned professing communities.

The street was where everyone had a secret, an albatross, a good cause or a good case of "what the hell's the use." It was more comfortable being with communities of poverty, race and resistance—in the civil rights movement, in feminism, in lesbianism, in lesbian and gay rights politics, in environmental and antiwar political movements. Here acceptance of individuals was more commonly pronounced. From 1970 until 1990 I lived an alternative lifestyle in a cooperative community. There I found diversity and acceptance in a shared constructed space we called our home. In that community and home we could be political and personal.

From the principle of symbiotics and in the learning of the "personal is political" in feminist politics, I transformed my sense of the meaning of solitude to yet another configuration. I recognized solitude as a construct that I borrowed from the hegemony of dualistic language symbols and a line metaphor. It had been a place, a state from which I could recover after retreat from confusion, violence, and shame. Solitude on closer examination now appeared simply to be a retort to a lack of plentitude. Places I had gone before for solitude—my favorite fishing hole, long rides in my car, my books, religious sanctuaries—suddenly became alive with the richness of the meanings and the shared notion of retreat and recreation. When going into a Gothic church, I no longer felt alone with a construct of a god. I felt in the presence of, and a small part of the many who go to a church to swallow the pain, the shame, the loneliness, the abuse, and the shared mourning for the lack of plentitude in our lives. Being safe became a political act of merging, not withdrawing.

The radio announcer takes another call and this time they aren't bashing me but they are making pronouncements on Clarence Thomas's nomination to the Supreme Court. I think of Clarence Thomas and how different our paths are from pain, poverty and minority. The talk show host is objectifying him, and I feel scared for both of us and angry at the institutions that maneuver us. Thomas's face is always scared and it always sweats. I saw when he accepted the nomination, and I felt deeply as I watched and identified with his fear, his sweating and choking-up as he thanked his grandparents for driving him to be better than everyone around him. I felt my own history and the fear of isolation, I remembered again the pressures of that resounding message, "You're no good unless you're better than the rest." I heard the call for strength, solitude, isolation, competition and protection.

It was being a "woman identified woman" (Koedt and Firestone 1971, 81–84) in a community of men's rituals of masculinization that scared me, beat me, repulsed me and fostered my sense of not being worthy of being a contributing member of their community. And likewise it was women-serving-men rituals of feminization that saddened me, bored me, repulsed me, and made me feel not worthy to be a contributing member of their community. It was the constant emphasis on heterosexual rituals like dating, engagement and marriage that left me feeling out of place and out of line. It was Euro-ethnic racial attitudes and rituals that left me feeling that I wished I hadn't been born with race or physical features. It was violence against workers that left me feeling angry about the inequity of distribution of material goods in a society arranged by class. It was knowing the violence against children that engaged me in the work of liberating perspectives of choice for children.

During some times in my life solitude was a respite, at other times it was self-indulgent, but it almost always felt safe, yet safe in the way a prisoner feels in jail. Now I recognize solitude not so much as a safe place, but more significantly as a place where I go to heal after a defeat. Those early constructs of solitude speak to me of memories of giving up, not standing up, and most of all of living in isolation and in fear.

It was deconstructing the being "out of line" metaphor that showed me a way to transform my shame and self-loathing. This helped me to identify with others who were similarly ensconced in "out of line" metaphors, and allowed me to recognize in others what makes one sweat and choke and display fear when the system falsely promises to let you in. It was after the sweating and crying that I have known the sweet joy of solitude as individuality, privacy, and creative reflection.

And now I reach again for the philosopher's stone. I can see that deconstructing the concept of solitude as a final or safe resting place was and is critical to my sanity, connectedness, and the alchemy of my movement toward locations of plentitude.

References

Arendt, H. (1959). *The human condition*. Garden City, N.Y.: Doubleday Anchor.

Koedt, A., and S. Firestone. (1971). The woman identified woman. *Notes from the third year: Women's liberation*, 81–84. P.O. Box AA, Chelsea Station, New York, NY 10011.

Spiegelberg, H. (1961). On the "I-am-me" experience in childhood and adolescence. *Psychologia* 4 (3): 135–46.

Chapter 11

Inner Life, Outer World:
Women and Solitude in India

Darshan Perusek

...and how *I asked*
was it with you *so long ago?*

—Michelle Murray,
"Poem of Two"

I spent the summer of 1990 with my sister Deshi in her small two-bedroom apartment in Indraprastha College, a Delhi University–affiliated campus for women. The campus, fortunately, is a kind of verdant haven in what is, in summer, a very dusty and brown city. Across from the front veranda of the apartment are old, deep-green mango trees which are home to an incredibly argumentative and noisy bunch of crows who stay up all night debating God alone knows what crow-issues and, when they come to an impasse, fly over the apartment to the ancient peepul[1] tree across the back veranda, its thick foliage home to a colony of equally noisy parrots who streak across the sky morning and evening and vigorously contest the crows' intrusion into their space. The back of the huge desert cooler[2] is occupied by a pair of pigeons who have raised generations of baby pigeons in its spacious interior and who have decided that the water hose which runs along the outside wall from the faucet in the bathroom to the cooler is their own personal swing. The result is that the hose breaks away from the cooler and the water runs into the open window of the apartment downstairs, prompting an agonized cry of distress from its inmates; Deshi rises like a shot and scrambles to turn off the water to the accompaniment of "Damn those pigeons!" And always morning and night, the shrill cries of the peacocks who, my friend Ranga told me with quiet resignation, have made a maternity home of her garden and

117

strongly resent her intruding to pick the tomatoes and hot peppers she had planted and raised to fruition.

The inside of the apartment all summer long was equally alive with human faces and voices: the aroma of simmering curries and fragrant *basmati* rice from the cooking in the kitchen; the eternal whistle of the tea kettle; the comings and goings of vendors selling fruits and vegetables; of Kela, the cleaning lady; Bahu, the cook; Ameet, her twelve-year-old nephew; of Ramchand, the laundry man; Kushal, the plumber; Hassan, the electrician....Since most of my family and friends live in Delhi, Deshi's small apartment was the rendezvous for all kinds of happy reunions, with sometimes as many as ten of us sisters and nieces and nephews nestled together at a time on mattresses on the floor at night, and more cousins and friends dropping by during the day. With each fresh arrival, another round of tea, another batch of rice and vegetables.

When I returned at the end of summer to my quiet, tranquil little house on the prairie in Wisconsin, I was due back at school in four days. I had the house all to myself, except for my daughter who, like me, has her own room here, and we retreated, each into her own private space, to prepare for our return to school, she to learn, I to teach and learn. I was alone; I had all the quiet I needed to reflect and think, but I felt in my solitude, no "trance of pleasure," the kind that Virginia Woolf talks about when she was alone in the country, away from London and visitors (1954, 318). In truth, my spirit protested against the quiet and the tranquility; it felt crushed by the silence, oppressed by the empty spaces inside the house and outside, desolate in the absence of human faces. Outside, yes, there was, later in the fall, the honking in the sky of those intrepid travelers, the Canada geese, as they flew across the autumn sky on their way to distant lands. But love them as I do, they were just that, travelers, not friends who made their home around where I was. And I heard no knock at the half-open door late at night of friends calling as they entered, "It's too hot to go to bed. How about a cup of tea and some poetry?" The doors here were all shut, the homes all fortresses, proclaiming to friends and strangers alike the sanctity of private space.

As I brooded in the silence of this alien solitude on the ungracious aspects of closed doors, both literal and metaphorical, I found myself reflecting on the contrasting image of the home in Nehru's sister Vijaya Lakshmi Pandit's description of life in the Nehru family home. The family house, she recalls, belonged to everybody and relatives could come at any time and stay as long as they wished; it was, as she says, their unquestioned right to do so: "A tonga³ piled high with luggage would drive up to the porch and a number of relatives would settle down in whichever room happened to be vacant, and if there was no room, it did not really matter because the western concept of a room of one's own did not exist. Mattresses were put down on the floor in winter and string cots on the veranda in summer. Everybody was perfectly happy" (1979, 30–31).

Life in the home of Attia Hosain, Mrs. Pandit's Muslim contemporary, seems to have been no different, although women in her home, unlike in that of the westernized Nehrus, observed purda⁴ and kept to the zenana⁵ section of the house. Thus, when Laila, the narrator in Hosain's autobiographical novel *Sunlight on the Broken Column* (1964), looks back at life in Ashiana (the name of her home), it is crowded both with the ghosts of her ancestors, the first of whom five hundred years ago "had fought his way across the northern mountains through the Khyber Pass to the refuge of green valleys many marches south" (p. 39), and with the living presence of relatives and friends, whose combined presence, she says, made it a house "of feasts and music and laughter and plenty" (p. 40). After the death of Baba Jan, her grandfather and patriarch of the family, Laila returns for his burial to her ancestral home in the village of Hasanpur, where once again the boundaries between the outside world and the inside are blurred: "The house was crowded not only with relatives from Hasanpur itself, but from neighboring villages. They surrounded my aunts who sat on the large takht⁶ in the high arched, deep veranda. Village women squatted in the courtyard and their children sat by them silently or stood and stared without playfulness....A woman nursed her baby, her coarse shirt pulled away from her heavy breast and the ragged dopatta⁷ barely covering her" (p. 95).

In terms of class, my family had none of the wealth, power, and status of the ruling class families of Mrs. Pandit and Attia Hosain, but the life they describe is, in spirit, what I knew as a child, as it would be to most Indians. My paternal great grandfather was a treasurer in the court of a minor princeling in the Punjab and, as such, must have seen how the rich lived. It was, perhaps, his acquaintance with this life that led him to divert some of the gold he was in charge of in his own direction by hiding it in cans of butter. Unfortunately his wife, who was something of a simpleton, marvelled at this miracle and announced it aloud in the neighborhood, where upon his irate lord fired my great-grandfather and the family fortune went into decline. My grandfather, who seemed to have inherited his mother's naiveté, didn't do much by way of productive labor and spent his days instead singing bhajans (devotional songs) to his favorite god Shiva, leaving it to my grandmother to manage the secular affairs of the family by running an informal financial operation lending money to small entrepreneurs (fruit and vegetable sellers, etc.). It was left to my father to pull the family up once more, and he did this by taking advantage of the new opportunities opened up by education in the British colonial administration. When he graduated from D.A.V. (Dayanand Anglo-Vedic) College in Lahore at the age of twenty-two, he entered, as they say in India, "government service" as a clerk, from which service he retired in Poona in 1952 at the age of fifty-five as assistant accountant.

I am not sure, but it must have been sometime in his teens that he came under the influence of the Arya Samaj, a Hindu reformist and nationalist movement started by Swami Dayanand Saraswati, a Brahmin from the western region of Kathiawar, the home of Mahatma Gandhi. To the new professional class in the Punjab, this movement provided, as Prakash Tandon, son of a prominent Punjabi family, writes in his autobiography, "a western social reorientation combined with simple Vedic belief and ritual" (1961, 33). This simplicity my father always observed in his religious practices. The walls in our house were, for example, free of the familiar pictures of Rama and Krishna found in traditional Hindu homes; instead, affixed on the wall in the living room was a portrait of the Swami meditating, eyes closed, in the lotus *asana*, naked but for a loin cloth. The Arya Samaj, since independence in 1947, has over the years lost the progressive element of anticolonial nationalism which marked it in its early days, but these elements were still strong when we were children. As a consequence, instead of stories celebrating the *pativratya dharma* of women (the worship of and devotion to husband) and, worse, ritualistic practices which perpetuated and reinforced the Hindu patriarchal ideology of the inferiority and "innate corruption" of women, what we heard from our father were inspiring stories of the Vedic age, when women were treated with love and respect, and learned women like Gargi and Maitreye engaged in philosophic debates with their male counterparts. The impact of these stories on shaping the identities of us, his daughters, was really important.

My memories of growing up as a girl in India are therefore largely happy, and at the heart of these memories is a concept of home radically different from what the home represents in the West. The Indian home, unlike the home in Western bourgeois democracies, is not a "man's castle" within the walls of which the individual retreats toward the end of the working day and raises the drawbridge; it is, as in Mrs. Pandit's description, more of a communal space where the flow of human traffic from without is virtually unrestricted and, within the home itself, no individual member of the family has any clearly demarcated space, no door on which to hang the sign "Do not enter." One of my memories of my dual life as a child—Indian culture at home, English education at school—is reading how David Copperfield was ordered to go to his room and having as little a notion of what this meant as I had of a "host of golden daffodils" dancing in the sun, or of swallows twittering in the barn.

My parents did have a room where they slept, where I assume they must have had some measure of privacy at night, since my two youngest sisters were conceived and born in that room, but in the day, we seven children had free access to it, just as we had to the other two rooms and the kitchen. At night, my three brothers slept in one room, we four sisters in the other, on mattresses on the floor or on *charpoys* (string cots), two to each mattress and charpoy. None of us had any separate area to do homework or study for exams; the rule was to find any corner that happened at the moment to be temporarily unoccupied and settle down there with books, until the sound of footsteps on the staircase announced a visitor and it was time for one of us to go to the kitchen to make tea, while the others scattered like a flock of birds to find new, unoccupied corners.

It did not matter how inconvenient the timing of the visit; the rights of the guest overrode any individual or familial contingencies of the moment. Symbolic of these rights was a jar of pastries or cookies my mother would set aside on a tall shelf in my parents' bedroom for "aaya gaya" (i.e., guests; literally, for those who arrive and leave). Since this was also the only unofficially designated "changing room" where we dressed to go out or change into our home clothes, it was perfectly legitimate to close the door to it for the duration, provided you kept up a continuous chant of "Don't come in, I'm changing!"

But even here, there was no guarantee of privacy because there was no knowing when some brother or sister, oblivious to the chant, would crash in through the closed door, but most of all my father, who was given to wandering around the house doing equally loud chanting of his own of verses from his beloved Vedas and Upanishads, which is why Deshi's and my brilliant use of the chant to dip into the jar for a quick steal did not work very long, what with having to share the spoils with a delighted sibling or being hauled off by our incorruptible father to receive a sharp slap on the wrist from our angry mother.

We must have each found ways of retreating into ourselves in the midst of this constant tide of life with its unceasing tumults and turmoils: here, a passionate argument over whose turn it was to make tea or cook; there a fist-fight over some real or imagined insult or betrayal; in this corner a noisy game of snakes and ladders, in that full-throated but tuneless singing. We must have, because all seven of us were in school and had to study for exams; five of us went on to graduate and medical schools. We must have, or else all of us would have, like lemmings, left *en mass* to perish in the closest body of water.

Having grown up with this idea of home, solitude for me has little to do with the need for privacy and personal space. I fully subscribe at an intellectual level to this need; after all, my feminist consciousness has been nurtured by Virginia Woolf and Simone de Beauvoir. But not emotionally, because it was not until much later, as an adult, that I became fully conscious of the solitude of countless numbers of Indian women within the walls of the very home which for me had been a place of nurturance and loving intimacies.

Not until much later, for instance, did I understand fully the solitude of the widows I saw in my childhood clad in red saris, whose shaved heads and unadorned faces and bodies declared to the world their status as outcasts from the fortunate community of their "suhagin" (married) sisters. Not until much later did I understand the solitude of Aajibai (grandmother), an old, bent woman who lived in a crumbling outhouse adjoining a small handloom factory near our house, whom I found dead one day when I brought her the tea and chapatti (bread) my mother would have us take every morning. Dead, I realized, in the solitude of poverty. And not till much much later did I even begin to comprehend the depths of despair that must have driven that woman who still haunts my memory, whom I saw in flames one bright sunny day from the roof where we would climb to watch festive wedding processions, running down the street with her arms lifted high above her head, her mouth an eerie scream that shattered the quiet of the day.

Like the Punjab of the Arya Samaj, the Poona of my childhood, too, was the center of anticolonial and social reform movements, a major concern of which latter was the status of women. But there was nothing in my life at home (and even less in my life at school, where our education consisted of the glories of the Elizabethan age and the military genius of "empire builders" like Clive and Hastings) to take heed of the winds of change that were unsettling the colonial order and, equally important, penetrating to a degree the rigid patriarchal structure of the traditional Hindu extended family. I was unaware, for instance, that Poona was the home of Maharishi Karve (1858–1962), the famous social reformer who scandalized Brahmin orthodoxy by marrying Anandibai, a child widow, and who founded in 1896 the Hindu Widows' Home in Hingne, near Poona, where Anandibai's sister Parvatibai, herself a widow, was to find both home and livelihood as teacher. And Poona was also, I now know, the home of Pandita Ramabai's educational center for widows, which was even more significant in a way than Karve's in that it was founded and run by a woman in what was then largely a male-led reform movement.

Pandita Ramabai (1858–1922), daughter of an unconventional Brahmin father who believed his wife and daughter should also learn the sacred Sanskrit texts forbidden to women, later converted to Christianity, but this early education by her father had an unexpected result in that it revealed to her both the hateful and irrational antiwoman sentiments of so-called ancient "sages" like Manu and Atri (ca. seventh century A.D.) and gave her the tools to do battle with their contemporary counterparts. In no other country, Ramabai was to observe bitterly in what has since become a classic in the annals of Indian feminist historiography, *The High-Caste Hindu Women* (1888), was the mother at the approach of childbirth so laden with anxiety as in India, "where in most cases her hope of winning her husband to herself hangs solely on her bearing sons" (p. 8). She tells the story of a friend of hers in Calcutta who had been warned by her husband not to give birth to a first girl and informed her, when she did, that if she persisted in this crime, "she should be superseded by another wife, have coarse clothes to wear and scanty food to eat, should have no ornaments, save those which are necessary to show the existence of a husband, and she should be made the drudge of the whole household" (p. 9).

Things had changed for the better by the early decades of this century, but it was common in my mother's generation around this period for a daughter's birth to be received with gloom; especially so if there had been all daughters before and no son, in which case the infant girl last on the scene was sure to face neglect and even ill treatment. My Aunt Kaushalya, a distant kinswoman, used to tell us with no particular hurt or sense of grievance, that when she was born, the fourth or fifth daughter in a son-less family, her poor mother was so ashamed that she put her in a basket by the cowshed, hoping she would die. But kindly neighbors, moved by the sight of the helpless infant, would as they walked by squeeze a little milk out of a dropper into the tiny mouth. The baby, having survived against all odds into a healthy child, was finally taken back into the embrace of the family. And my own dear friend and contemporary Rina tells me that when her mother was expecting her, her father, having turned his wish for a son into a conviction that so it would be this time, had musicians lined up at the door to announce with joyful noise the arrival of a male heir. When his expectations were cruelly dashed into the ground by the report of a baby girl, he walked away in silence and sent the already paid musicians away!

The dread of having daughters Pandita Ramabai observed among the high-caste Hindu women of women a hundred years ago continues to pervade the lives of their sisters from other castes and classes to this day, especially of peasant women, who are valued the more as they bear sons who will till the land with their fathers. The results of a survey conducted in 1982 in a village in the Punjab for *Manushi*, a women's journal, showed among other things that women's preference for boys over girls was overwhelming, despite their personal belief that daughters would be better for them because they would be more emotionally supportive and help them more than sons would. The writers report that the respondents' dread of giving birth to daughters was based on four main reasons: (1) their own life as women, and very often what they saw of their mothers' lives, gave them an aversion to produce another sufferer like themselves; (2) their own life was made more miserable and degraded every time they failed to produce a son; (3) many of them did not see their daughters as having any better chance in life; (4) as distinct from the mother's own interest, the family as an economic unit saw these daughters as a burden because of dowry responsibilities and limited employment opportunities for women (Horowitz and Kishwar 1984, 87).

From the south, in the meanwhile, sociologist Vanaja Dhruvarajan reports that the ideology of *pativratya dharma* continues to retain its tenacious grip on the lives of women, both high-caste and low. What this ideology means in terms of women's self-identity and their place in the home can be surmised from the following composite of the "good wife" Dhruvarajan put together on the basis of what she was told by the men and women of the village of Musali, where she herself was born and lived until the age of thirteen.

> A woman should realize that a man marries to continue his family line by getting sons....She [the wife] should never think that she has an existence apart from her husband....A Pativratya always eats what is left after her husband has eaten. Even if she was happy in her parents' home she should not

think of it in her husband's house....Obeying the command of one's husband without question is a mark of virtue and good conduct. She should never be inquisitive. She should never be arrogant....A Pativratya will be happy to die before her husband....A Pativratya burns herself in the funeral pyre of her husband as it is not worth living after her husband's death.... She believes *Pati pratyaksha devatha* (Husband is the living God). (pp. 26–27)

The women she met, Dhruvarajan notes, were conditioned not only to live up to these expectations but to so internalize them that they wholly accepted their inferior status without protest and, in fact, acted as willing and even brutal agents of this ideology in relation to their female wards (daughters, daughters-in-law), who they made sure never strayed outside its parameters.[8]

She describes how this conditioning is reinforced in songs and folklore in which the villains are usually the mother-in-law and sisters-in-law, who complain about the unfaithfulness of the wife, her lack of respect for her elders, her revealing family secrets to neighbors, or of her being just plain lazy. While the women in-laws do the complaining in the songs, it is the husband who does the punishing, at times reluctantly, to teach the wife her place. And the punishment? Beating, kicking, starvation, and isolation, among other things. Many women, Dhruvarajan says, explained to her that the first few years of married lives, until they bore a son, were "a living hell," when their main concern was to make their existence in the new home bearable by finding ways to escape beatings from their husbands, getting enough to eat, reducing the number of chores so that they were not completely exhausted by night, and getting enough sleep to enable them to carry on the next day. Sleep itself, however, was a hard-to-be-found luxury, because the husband had to have his sexual enjoyment, and being a good sexual partner to her husband was, after all, a wife's "sacred duty" (pp. 82–83).

Regarding this so-called "sacred duty," an old woman, married at the age of seven in the early part of this century (that makes her my mother's contemporary), casually mentioned in an interview with another researcher that she had noticed her husband's fine white teeth only when, on his deathbed, he beckoned to her to come closer. Upon being asked, hadn't she borne him children, hadn't she ever kissed him, she admitted matter of factly that children she had borne him, but kiss? Who kissed in those days, she asked? And sex? Sex was a small unpleasant matter at night in a dingy corner room, something she knew she had to put up with, since she had been taught that "just as the scorpion liked to sting with its poisonous tail, so sometimes do men. A good wife [she had learned] always bore with the 'sting'" (Lakshmi 1984, 5–6). And yet the male villagers Dhruvarajan talked to saw no contradiction in pointing to a woman's sexuality as one of the most serious impediments in a man's spiritual journey. The impediment, they believed, did not have to arise out of anything a woman did; her very presence is corrupting, since it is well known that sexual desire leads a man astray, and a woman, being the very embodiment of sex, could not help but be a temptation. Dhruvarajan was reminded by them of the words of the saint Sarvajna on this matter: "Where are the men," the saint asks, "that can look at women, ripe fruits or gold and not desire them?" (p. 27).

No wonder, then, that the two dominant themes of songs women sing should be the harshness of life in the husband's home and the loss of the sweet joys of the parents' home. "The feeling of solitude," Octavio Paz observes in *The Labyrinth of Solitude*, "which is a nostalgic longing for the body from which we were cast out, is a longing for a place" (p. 208). That place, in women's folklore and songs, is the parental home, which, notwithstanding the fact that they are initially unwelcome, is still the only place where they remember being loved and cared for, and to which after being married they cannot return except for brief visits, and that only so long as the mother is there to welcome her. After the mother's death, the doors of even that home are closed, since who can know the loneliness of life among strangers except the mother, who herself had known its bitter taste? "No one can be happy after marriage, at in-laws place," a woman said in the *Manushi* survey when asked to name the two or three things that made her happy (Horowitz and Kishwar 1984, 100). And one of Dhruvarajan's respondents said, in words that echo a sentiment familiar to women all over the country; "Women do not have a home of their own. They always live in someone else's house, work for someone else" (Dhruvarajan 1988, 81).

As I pause to read what I have written, there come drifting into my mind the words of a Punjabi folksong that women sing at the wedding of a girl, in which the girl begs her father not to send her away from home:

> We are a flock of birds, O Father,
> We will fly away one day.
> Our journey is long, O Father,
> who knows where we are bound.

I am a long way from where I was born; I had not thought when I was a child that this is where I would be. And it is good where I am, I think, as I sit on the steps leading out to the backyard. It is my home now, and it's a green home and a goodly one. The doors around me look out upon the world with their stony gaze, but the world itself is lovely and spacious. I look at the finches on my bird feeder in the yard, and turn to listen to the cry of the blue jay in the maple tree. (I love blue jays as much for their boorish manners as for their color; they bring me back the crows in the mango tree.) I take back what I said earlier about my return last summer from Delhi: it wasn't the silence or space that crushed me; what crushed me was my distance from my family and friends. Silence itself is healing, the sense of space liberating. What truly crushes us, what truly makes us homeless and alone, is the silence in which our deepest needs and longings go unheard. That is the solitude of the women of Musali, and of their sisters elsewhere.

I still don't like locked doors, those symbols of the privatized family; behind them, I know, lurks solitude of another kind.[9] But it would be good, I think, if the women of Musali had doors they could lock against their oppressors. It would be good if, inside their homes, they could mark off some space they could call their own.

My mother must have needed that space, I know, space to grow into and beyond to embrace the life outside it. My own life would have been very different if her spirit had not hungered for a larger life. Tillie Olsen wrote in *Silences* of the sense of constriction, of waste, of the unattainable. My mother must have felt that, must have felt the constriction, felt the way life cramped her. Married at fifteen, eleven pregnancies. "No more," she said, after the second, and went to get an abortion, but Miss Sharp, the missionary nurse she went to, sent her back home with a stern sermon on the wickedness of taking life. "No more," my mother still said, and went to the field to get wild *dhatura* (a poisonous plant) and pushed it inside her; the dead fetus had to be removed from her near-poisoned body bit by bit. And so she let her body bear children till menopause, when she breathed a sigh of relief and said, "Thank God it's over at last!" True, she fulfilled her obligations as a wife and mother, she did what she had to, but she did it, I remember, with the utmost economy, with as much effort as was necessary, no more. Motherhood had no fascination for her; she didn't dislike us, her children, but neither did she see us as the reason for her existence. Like Rebecca Harding's Audrey in *Earthen Pitchers*, my mother lived in the home she was supposed to, but she lived in it as if she had "her own home and her own people elsewhere and will be gone to them presently" (cited in Olsen 1965, 105).

She is gone now, but I remember one night talking with her, Deshi, and my younger sisters, and Deshi asked her, "What did you dream of doing when you were young?" "What dream?" she asked, surprised. "I knew I would be married and raise children." "Well, this life is over," Deshi said, "what about your next life?" Her answer came in a flash, without a moment's thought: "I will start learning as soon as I am in the womb, and become a professor."

Doors. She needed one to thrust her uncle out, my mother did, when she wanted to go to the high school in a neighboring town, her own town having none, and her father agreed, but her uncle exploded, "What? Send a young unmarried girl away from home? Are you out of your senses, brother?" And she never went, but she saw to it that her own daughters did go to school, and here I am. Because of my mother. "She was given too small a stage to play her life in," my brother said after she died. True. She, and so many more.

There was available to my mother's generation the larger stage of the anticolonial struggle in the first half of the twentieth century when women, responding to the call of Gandhi and other nationalist leaders, came out of the seclusion of their homes into the streets and on the public platform. But on this larger stage itself, they were given no script for a new future; rather, the same old one all over again, of the nurturing wife and mother. Only this time, it was in a new idiom and a new context, as "mothers" of the nascent nation. Gandhi himself, while offering women a new dimension to their lives, was careful not to seem to encourage them to abandon their familial roles; in fact, he refused to allow a woman to enter politics without prior permission of her husband or guardian.[10]

In any case, my mother was no rebel, or if she was, she kept her insurrection concealed. The only outward signs of it, now that I think back, were the hour-long comas she would sink into unexpectedly, her eyes shut, her fists clenched, her entire body rigid. Her doctor used to call this a "hysterical fit"; I now see it was her body's way of shutting down when it could stand the strain of living no more. Prakash Tandon, from whose autobiography I quoted earlier, remembers his own mother's similar "strange habit"; she seldom complained or lost her temper, he says, "but when she could stand things no longer, she would quietly go to bed without anyone knowing it, and lie there in a faint, sometimes for several hours" (Tandon 1961, 37). The family, in the meanwhile, just like ours, would go about their affairs in a normal way and wait for her to open her eyes, which she would hours later to pick up her work as if nothing had happened. "She did not," her son recalls, "like to be asked how she felt" (p. 37).

How could my mother rebel? The very dreams we dream, our very visions of the possible, are limited by the horizons of the actual world in which we live, and hers was the feudal/patriarchal world of duties and obligations. "My child, there are certain rules of conduct that must be observed in this world without question," Laila's Aunt Abida in Hosain's *Broken Column* (1961) reminds her impetuous niece who, by intervening in her uncle's physical chastisement of the servant girl Nandi, had shown him "disrespect": "You have a great responsibility. You must never forget the traditions of your family no matter to what outside influences you may be exposed....Never forget the family into which you were born" (p. 38).

This was the world my mother knew, not the enlightenment world of Mary Wollstonecraft, or the socialist world of Rosa Luxemburg. And of her own world, she was taught, what could one say but that it was not easy? Not easy for anyone, but especially not easy for women. That's what she, in turn, told us, her two older daughters, when we walked away from circumstances in our lives that no longer seemed livable. But like Marge Piercy (1985) to her mother, I say to mine:

> My dear, what you said was one thing
> But what you sang was another, sweetly
> Subversive and dark as blackberries
> And I became the daughter of your dreams. (pp. 31–32)

"Her nightmares, more likely," I hear Deshi say, laughing. That's what she herself would have said. In fact, did say when Deshi divorced her husband and, later, I. "Did he abandon you?" she asked Deshi, angry. "Did he go out with other women? Did you think of what everyone will say?" But she herself told my father once that she wished him well, but that one life with him was quite enough, which to my father, raised as he was in a culture where devoted wives prayed to be remarried to their present husbands life after life to come, was nothing short of heresy, as monstrous an outrage as an actual divorce. And where else, I remind Deshi, did we learn our first lessons in justice and equality than from Mother, who, contrary to the custom in traditional households where age and gender determined allocation of goods and services (who was fed first and in what measure and kind—male head of the family before all others, other males before all females, older females before younger), made no such distinctions but gave us each the same portion, from my father down to my littlest sister. And remember that time, I ask Deshi, when she came to your apartment which you hadn't cleaned or dusted for over a week, and you expected to be lectured on your derelictions as a housewife, and all Mother said was, "This is what I would have liked."

True, I think, she and how many more, as my daughter calls from the kitchen with a familiar question, "The kettle is boiling. Won't you come in for tea?" and I walk back into the house where she waits for me, smiling, in a pool of light.

Afterword

This has been a difficult piece to write, torn as I was between the need to render the truth about my own largely happy experience growing up as a girl/woman in India, and my keen awareness that for countless numbers of my fellow-women, this experience is, at best, marred by open or subtle indignities and humiliations, at worst a tale of unmitigated horror and suffering. This awareness was itself complicated by my fear lest, in dwelling too much on what are very real oppressive conditions for women in India, I present them as mere victims of class and gender and deny them any role in the shaping of their own lives.

I am all too conscious of the tendency of privileged women academics to take what Australian sociologist Jane Haggis (1990) describes as a "peculiar relish" in finding extreme examples of the subjection of women in the Third World: genital mutilation, for example, in Muslim Sudan, and sati in Hindu India. It needs to be recognized, Haggis correctly cautions, that women, like the once-colonized countries of which they are part, are not passive victims of domination, but that they participate, albeit in ultimately dominated forms, in molding the process of domination and in setting limits to its shape and forms.[11]

If my account betrays any of this "peculiar relish," I must apologize; I did not intend it to. But one can only tell one story at a time, and this story became, as I went along, one of man's inhumanity to woman. In telling the story of women's role in the Telengana People's Struggle (1948–51), when peasants engaged in armed resistance against the feudal oppression of the Nizam and the Hindu landlords in Hyderabad state, Kannabiran and Lalitha (1989, 196) explain a similar dilemma they faced: "One concern that constantly surfaces for us is that, in attempting to analyze the political dimensions of [their] isolation and vulnerability, we do not erase the creativity, the commitment, or the will that women brought into the struggle." My account has, I'm afraid, downplayed that creativity. To pay homage to it, I must wait for another time.

As for the place of solitude in my own life, as I grow older I find myself often thinking of some remote Himalayan peak where, like the ancient Indian sages, I will sit in stillness in the last years of my life and commune with the Infinite. But that's just a notion I play with. In truth, I have never cared for those misogynist sages, and my need for communing is more with people I love and care about than with the all-encompassing Brahman. So I will find my solitude, my stillness and silence, right here where I live, in my home, in the very center of the web where the lives of so many of us women are consumed: the kitchen.

In fact, when I moved to Wisconsin three years ago from Ohio, where I had lived the poverty-stricken life of a graduate student, for a full-time teaching position, I was able to rent a house where I had room enough for a separate study. My friend Leonard presented me with a beautiful oak desk and a shiny new lamp; I took off to buy myself some brand new bookshelves and a comfortable chair. The study looks beautiful, except I don't work there. I have gradually sneaked everything I need back to the kitchen table, which is where I have worked all my life. I felt an exile in my study, banished from the sights and sounds of life, condemned to an intolerable solitude. The pages on which I write are sometimes marked with tea stains and the yellow of turmeric. But I don't care. I'm back where I feel at home. In my kitchen.

References

Dhruvarajan, V. (1988). *Hindu women and the power of ideology*. Westport, Conn.: Bergin and Garvey.

Haggis, J. (1990) The feminist research process: Defining a topic. In *Feminist praxis: Research, theory and epistemology in feminist sociology*, edited by L. Stanley, 67–79. New York: Routledge.

Horowitz, B., and M. Kishwar. (1984). Family life: The unequal deal. In *In search of answers: Indian women's voices from Manushi*, edited by M. Kishwar and R. Vanita, 69–103. London: Zed Books.

Hosain, A. (1961). *Sunlight on a broken column*. New York: Penguin Books.

Jeffery, P. (1979). *Frogs in a well: Indian women in Purdah*. London: Zed Press.

Kannabiran, V., and K. Lalitha. (1989). That magic time: Women in the Telengana People's Struggle. In *Recasting women: Essays in colonial history*, edited by K. Sangarai and S. Vaid, 180–203. Delhi: Kali for Women.

Lakshmi, C. S. (1984). *The face behind the mask: Women in Tamil literature*. Delhi: Vikas.

Olsen, T. (1965). *Silences*. New York: Delacorte Press.

Pandit, V. L. (1979). *The scope of happiness*. New York: Crown Publishers.

Paz, O. (1961). *The labyrinth of solitude: Life and thought in Mexico*, trans by Lysander Kemp, New York: Grove Press. (Originally published 1950).

Piercy, M. (1985). *My mother's body*. New York: Knopf.

Ramabai, P. (1976). *The high-caste Hindu women*. London: George Bell and Sons. Hyperion reprint edition. (Originally published 1888.)

Sangari, K. and S. Vaid (1989). *Recasting women: Essays in colonial history*. Delhi: Kali for Women.

Tandon, P. (1961). *Punjabi Century, 1857–1947*. New York: Harcourt, Brace, and World.

Woolf, V. (1953). *A writer's diary: Being extracts from the diary of Virginia Woolf*, edited by L. Woolf, New York: Harcourt, Brace and Company.

Zaretsky, E. (1986). *Capitalism, the family, and personal life*. New York: Harper and Row. (Originally published by Harper and Row, 1976.)

Notes

1. A large, shady tree with heart-shaped leaves.

2. An air cooling appliance lined with fragrant straw and fitted with a fan which blows water-cooled air into the room.

3. A horse-drawn carriage.

4. Literally, from a Persian word meaning "curtain"; in a wider sense, concealment of women by a veil, and separation of the physical and social space of men and women.

5. The space within the home marked off from the *merdana*, the area reserved for men.

6. A wooden divan.

7. A long scarf draped around the upper part of the body and head.

8. To understand the nature and scope of this participation, see Patricia Jeffery's (1979) *Frogs in a Well: Indian Women in Purdah*, especially "The Two Faces of Purdah," pp. 165–75. For Hindu women, see Dhruvarajan's (1989) *Hindu Women and the Power of Ideology*. Both writers bring to bear on their subjects a combination of virtues rare in academic writing: intelligence, sensitivity, and—most wonderful of all—lucidity.

9. On this topic, see Eli Zaretsky's (1986) fine analysis of individualism and subjectivity.

10. See Lakshmi (1984), 25.

11. See Jane Haggis (1990), 69.

Chapter 12

The Solitary Reader Revisited:
Dialogues on a Working-Class Girlhood

Elyse Eidman-Aadahl

When I was young in the suburbs, I used to tramp the open woods of the watershed near my housing development. I tracked squirrels and spied on deer. I climbed trees, fed box turtles, and skipped rocks. Best of all, I discovered a secret hideaway: a huge ravine where two dead trees arched overhead and where honeysuckle leafed in the spandrels each spring creating a deep, dark mystery. Set well back from the worn paths used by fishermen to drag their row boats to the reservoir, this ravine became my secret hideaway, a place to think and dream, to scribble in a journal about the persons I was trying to become. This private place is as vivid to me now twenty years later as any part of my childhood.

As I read, I find kindred spirits everywhere. In *On Becoming Lost: A Naturalist's Search for Meaning* (1990), an adult Cathy Johnson draws sustenance from childhood memories of glorious isolation in the woods:

> The Missouri Ozarks where I spent spring, summer, and fall as a child are lovely—in a poignant way. They are lovely as well to my inward eyes, the eyes of memory and imagination. I see, still, those green mountains, empty, blue-veiled, silent except for the scream of a hawk or bobcat. With part of me, I see the secret rivers wash a deserted gravel bar with water pure as a glacial stream. Once, when I was young and wandered a deserted stream I found a fly fisherman's hand-tied lure caught up in a tree at water's edge and started with surprise as if I'd been touched, snorted like a deer in alarm: someone had been here before me. It seemed strange, then. (p. 82)

Later I discovered Maryalice Marshall, a psychologist, who recalled her need for solitude as a teenager in terms much like mine:

In my mid-teens, I purposefully sought periods of solitude. I had favorite places to go, usually outdoors, which were conducive to self-reflection and my everpresent search for life's meaning. One special setting was located in a large, private park within walking distance from my house. On top of the gentle slope, covered with trees and overlooking a small lake, existed a "natural church." Several logs were spread around a majestic wooden cross. A totem pole stood behind the "pew," and a tiny log cabin was at the foot of the hill. This became a place of enchantment for me, a place where I could go to meet myself. I would sit or wander aimlessly, reflecting upon my hopes, dreams, struggles, and conflicts. I would leave feeling serene, replenished, and balanced. (In Kottler 1990, 25)

Solitude, Adolescence, and Schools

Serene, replenished, and balanced: words we as adults rarely associate with adolescence. Indeed, these are the romantic, wistful words of a privileged woman remembering. Nonetheless, I've been thinking about connection, solitude, and adolescence a lot lately and wonder where young women find their versions of my watershed, Johnson's Missouri hillsides, or Marshall's natural church. They are, I'm sure, unlikely to find them in school. In my work as a high school teacher and now as a teacher educator, I and my students live in institutions that seem to offer neither meaningful connection between self and other nor the solitude requisite to forge a connection with self. Feminist theory crackles like electricity between the poles of connection and autonomy, solitude and community, yet educational practice finds it difficult to create authentic and fulfilling versions of either.

In thinking about this, as in many things, I am tutored by my students. I learned from Diana, a young teacher candidate, how she perceived painful experiences of "forced connection" during her own schooling. The instant "intellectual intimacy" required by group work troubled her as it seemed to demand a peculiarly unauthentic self, malleable and superficial, if one were to move in and out of relationships hour by hour, activity by activity. I learned from Kathy, an aspiring English teacher, of the mechanized conviviality of cooperative learning activities that she remembered. (My friend, Wendy Saul, recently put it: "Can you imagine what Emily Dickenson would have done with cooperative learning?") While still believing cooperation and community are vital, she is convinced that "we students were never encouraged to cooperate on anything deeply important to us, nor were we given the time to discover if anything *was* deeply important to us outside of parties and shopping and sex." I learned from Charmise that she joined the stage and light crew as a high school student for one single reason: to be allowed to hide out in the lighting booth in the auditorium. "Sometimes," she told me, "all I needed was a period here and there to pull myself together." Then she added: "The problem was you always had to be somewhere next period ready to run through the lesson." In schools there are few opportunities for self-selected withdrawals, for temporary time-outs.

I hear a similar questioning of the forced march of school activities in Lucy Calkins' (1991) rethinking of writers' workshop:

> Not long ago, I said that our job in the writing workshop was to be like the circus men who run about keeping plates spinning on the ends of sticks. But in many writing workshops, the plates are spinning. The writing folders are filling. The teacher keeps it going: "Why not read it to a friend?" "You could add a line." "Would you like to tell me more?" "Why not fix it up?" "I'd copy it over." Rehearse, draft, revise, edit. The plates are spinning. Rehearse, draft, revise, edit....The plates are spinning, but are they going anywhere?" (p. 2)

How different, Calkins notes, is this frenetic activity from the image of the absorbed young writer alone in her room that poet Richard Wilbur describes:

> I pause in the stairwell, hearing
> From her shut door a commotion of type-writer-keys
> Like a chain hauled over a gunwale.

> Young as she is, the stuff
> Of her life is a great cargo, and some of it heavy:
> I wish her a lucky passage. (quoted in Calkins 1991, 3)

These voices suggest some of the contradictions of teaching in many contemporary public schools—even good ones—where all is surveillance, yet so many students are lost along the way, where the rhetoric of individualism is enacted through batch processing, where we teachers work to march students through a day of forced intimacies and discontinuous bits of knowledge. No wonder that for so many students the school day is merely an interruption in their plans for themselves, squeezing out the time when they might otherwise discover if anything is deeply important to them outside of parties and shopping and sex and perhaps, to use academic knowledge as part of that discovery.

Revisiting "The Solitary Reader":
Voices at the Margins

These stories are not quite the same as those my white working-class high school students told in the classroom research project I profiled in "The Solitary Reader" (Eidman-Aadahl 1988).[1] But they are stories which have motivated me to revisit the students I wrote about then and the ideas we created together. In that earlier article, I described how I and my high school basic writing classes conducted research into our experiences as readers and writers through processes of observation, self-analysis, and story-telling. When we first waded through our collected journals and depositions, replayed the audiotapes of group discussions and interviews that became the basis for "The Solitary Reader," I was struck with the powerful case these students—male and female— made for literacy in its social dimensions, their desire for connection and solidarity, their resentfulness that so much of their schooling drove them apart from their friends or encouraged them to aspire to leave their families and communities if they were to adopt the middle-class lifestyles the high school labeled as successful. I noted then that "their model of reading was 'one child, one book,' silent, sedentary, leading to nothing more than the consumption of the book itself" (p. 167). For them, the uses schools made of literacy as an *isolating* and *controlling* technology were foremost, and I wrote about our research into alternative conceptions of literacy from the perspective of a teacher who wanted to limit the isolation I contributed to in my own teaching (Finkelstein 1979, 114–40). Now I must question whether like the circus men Calkins describes, I was really looking for ways to keep the plates spinning.

So I returned to the "data" of our work together to wonder what in my eagerness I overlooked. What I found were the insistent voices of six young women in my two study classes whose insights restore some measure of balance to the literacy story we wrote together. Through their voices, I have been helped to rethink both solitude and connection, and how literacy work in schools operates to support and constrain both.

New Voices in a New Context

Throughout the data for "The Solitary Reader" some of the young women argued the importance of reading as an opportunity for "time out." There was the voice of Clare, a cheerful and assertive student who wanted nothing more than to be left alone with a book in the cubby behind my rolling bookcase. Once she asked if she could keep a small personal library on one of the shelves. Of course, I replied, but why wouldn't she want to take her books home with her? "I can never read at home," she answered blithely, "'cause I'm always being interrupted."

Jenny similarly came to treasure the opportunities our classroom research project offered her to escape, temporarily, her fellow students. For two weeks she worked alone in the library, books stacked around her like walls (according to our media specialist) never talking to anyone till the period was over. Later she remarked in her journal: "I really needed those two weeks in the library. I worked hard, and all by myself, and I feel good about what I learned to do. Thanks for keeping everyone out of my way."

Demands, obligations, constraints, or in Tillie Olsen's words "interruptions, not continuity" (1972, 37); when I looked again I saw that these themes marked many conversations I had with my white working-class female students. There simply were very few times, at home or at school, when they could "work hard, and all by myself" or when someone could be counted on for "keeping everyone out of my way." The solitude I treasured as a young woman was less the gift of space—space to roam undisturbed in the woods—than the gift of time, time to be uninterrupted.[2]

For both men and women, contemporary schools are not places where students often experience the gift of time, time to be uninterrupted. Jackson (1968), writing of elementary schools, noted the simple fact that much of what they were about was learning to live in "crowds." Learning occurs in groups in most schools, and much of our conventional notions of teaching involve coordinating the activities, pace, and interests of many people so that the class "works" according to expectations. Teachers and students alike find themselves interrupted by organizational contingencies, matching their pace to the demands of others, and spending most of their time waiting for something to happen. To be "successful" in school terms means learning to adapt to such environments.

Compounding issues of time and space, the environment coerces a forced gregariousness. Jackson writes that "students are there (in school) whether they want to be or not, and the work on which they are expected to concentrate often is not of their own choosing. Thus the pull to communicate with others is somewhat stronger in the classroom than in other crowded situations" (Jackson 1968, 17). Robert

Everhart (1983) traces this theme through a series of studies of junior and senior high schools which document how the "pull to communicate" that Jackson noted as "a trend in its nascent stages, has become dominant by the time the student reaches high school, for herein the students have created a complex, separate, and well-articulated network in which to carry out that communication" (p. 7). As students move through the batch-processing of secondary school they learn to give minimal attention to the fits and starts of their academic days, releasing themselves instead into a peer culture where they experience some measure of "authentic," as Larkin (1979) characterizes it, involvement and where they can exert some measure of control.[3]

The pressure to participate in this culture was strongly felt by *all* my high school students, but was lived differently by women and men. As my white working-class girls came to high school, they often experienced a diminishment of the power and control they held in middle-school peer culture where, as Clare recalled it, "the girls ruled the school." Social activities in high school revolved around boys: their sports, their work, their interests and desires. Furthermore, the young women in my study classes were not members of the prestigious social groups where girls were likely to assume school-sponsored positions in extracurricular activities.

These dimensions of their social lives explain a significant difference between my female and male students as they reflected on their own literacy and their lives as readers and writers. For the young men in my classroom, their experiences of "in school" and of "out of school" were quite distinct.[4] Outside school they were often wage earners—some of them bringing home a significant income in family-owned businesses or in less legitimate activities. Outside school they controlled their peer groups and led relatively unrestricted lives in their families. Inside school, however, they experienced a diminution of authority and a loss of freedom which they resisted. For the young women, neither school nor home nor peer group offered many opportunities for authority or control. The interruptions, the distractedness, the constant "pull to communicate" in schools were not much different from the interruptions they tolerated at home or pressures to please they experienced in their peer group. Indeed, as Clare and Jenny demonstrate, school was a sphere which *might* be manipulated to offer what other spheres do not: solitude, personally controlled time and space. In school, Clare and Jenny could claim their right as a "student" to the kind of environment necessary for them to do productive work. The identity and circumstances offered by reading and writing, for those young women who could overcome the taunts of their peers or the pressures of family, actually became a haven. To explore this further, I turn now to conversations I held with four of my students through their dialogue journals.

Clare and Salina: Solitude and Homework

"Solitude" is not necessarily the same as physical separation and should not be confused with loneliness. Kottler (1990) defines solitude as "that state of self-possession when we are in touch with ourselves and temporarily unaffected by others' needs and wants" (p. 2). In short, we are not interrupted.

Although they rarely complained overtly about the expectations their families, friends, or boyfriends held for their household help and emotional comfort, my female students did complain of "interruptions," of a general distractedness that haunted their attempts to think; a distractedness Clare associated with adult womanhood and the specter of housekeeping:

> I guess I'm growing up now, and it's kind of sick. Now, when I go into my room and Stella [my sister] has crapped all over it and the dishes are piled up because mom's working, and my brothers are running around messing everything up IT REALLY MAKES ME CRAZY! I try to concentrate on something or do my homework, but I can't 'cause I keep thinking about everything that has to be done. I never used to care much about how things looked, you know, 'cause I was just a kid. But now I do care and it's like I'm more like my mother. So I guess I'm ready to be out and on my own.

"Everything that had to be done" was the everything associated with the second shift of unpaid labor at home after paid labor somewhere else. These young women *all* were members of large families with working mothers or guardians and no money to purchase the labor of other women—maids or babysitters—to help with the chores of maintaining a family in a changing economy. They felt responsible at home, *and* they felt the need to prepare themselves for employment after graduation. Their mothers, their aunts, their older sisters were exhausted. They saw themselves becoming exhausted too. However, the importance and centrality of the "second shift" to home life impressed them, making it peculiarly attractive.

Salina and I discussed this in her dialogue journal over the course of several entries.

Salina: I'm behind on my work because I'm helping Mom more around the house. She's been working at Weis and doesn't get home till late. And I'm always babysitting my brothers and sisters. Do you have children?

Me: No I don't. That makes a big difference. Did your mother just start working at Weis? Write to me about what's going on.

Salina: My mother has been working for a few months....I need to find a job too. I have to help out at home. There's not enough time for everything. That's why I can't do my writing at home.

Babysitting drives me crazy, but I don't mind. I think I'd like to have children right away. Children need their mothers. What mothers do for children is important. My mother worked hard for us kids. Now she's working hard at Weis and I don't think they appreciate her at all. Not by what she says.

Me: People play many important roles in each other's lives. Children aren't the only option. You have everything to gain by waiting, Salina.

Salina: I'm just writing and thinking out loud. I don't want to really have kids now without a job. I think being a mother is the most important thing there is. Lots of girls don't realize how important it is.

Attending high school in the mid-1980s, my students were surrounded by an official rhetoric chastising women for abandoning their "true office" of mother. They also came from families where, particularly in the 1980s, women's work was a necessity rather than an option. They had been affected by what Jessica Benjamin (1988) describes as the reenchantment of motherhood. This made for tension and guilt. For example, Clare spoke of how she experienced being an angel-in-the-house (my words, not hers) and her feelings of guilt when she took time just for herself. "I do a lot at home to help out. But it's not that my family actually orders me to stop or anything, it's just that I feel that they want me to come do something else, that they miss me or resent me. Is that stupid? During reading time, reading is what I'm supposed to be doing so I don't feel guilty."

Salina and Clare reminded me of the Smithton women, a group of women devoted to reading romance novels described in Janice Radway's *Reading the Romance* (1984). They too experienced tensions between the conception of a women's role they and/or their families held and their desire for the personal space romance reading came to represent. Informants explained to Radway that they were "troubled about the propriety of indulging in such an obviously pleasurable activity. Their doubts are often cultivated into a full-grown feeling of guilt by husbands and children who object to this activity because it draws the women's attention away from the immediate family circle" (pp. 89–90). However, it was this unrelenting demand for attention, for the draining emotional work of reproducing the family which made reading such a necessary escape for the women. The Smithton women stressed the privacy of reading and how reading allowed them to focus their attentions in a way their lives did not. Reading, according to the Smithton women, allowed them to escape not their family *per se* but the emotionally and physically draining tasks of attending to their family—a task which was specifically theirs (pp. 91–92).

Clare and Salina also saw family nurturance as appropriately feminine, both burdensome and attractive, necessary but impossible. Both believed that women were naturally more nurturant than men, and both surrounded the idea of "motherhood" with a romanticism at odds with their perceptions of their mothers' real lives. Despite their mothers' visible stress as they attempted to raise their families and sustain a family wage in a challenging economy, it was the ideal of motherhood that these young women held on to. The more they perceived the "public world" of paid employment as demeaning, lacking in fulfillment and respect, the more their imaginations retreated wistfully to an image of the full-time mother that no longer suited the family's circumstances.

Jessica Benjamin (1988), using Weber's concept of "reenchantment," calls this, as mentioned above, the "reenchantment of motherhood." Referring to the hard marketing of "traditional family values" which marked media and politics during the 1980s, she argues that:

> The contemporary celebrations of motherhood are a classic example of reenchantment, which is the attempt to replace a lost relationship with an ideal....Thus as the concrete forms of maternal care and recognition diminish, their loss is repaired by the symbolic evocation of motherhood. The symbolism of ideal motherhood actually obscures the waning of the sociable domestic world that originally supported it. The isolation of the nuclear family household in the post-war era and the reduction of its social ties with the outside world (which are now largely ties of consumption) deprived the mother of her

own holding environment—the web of kin and neighborhood relationships that supported, advised, and nurtured her. (pp. 206–7)

Clare and Salina entered adolescence at a time when both the loss of that domestic world and its powerful reenchantment were palpable. Being "realistic" (as Salina described it), they were both enrolled in a range of business classes which they hoped would provide them the skills to land an entry-level clerical position somewhere. Being "just nuts over little children" (as Clare described herself), they were also eager to become someone's angel-in-the-house. But watching their own mothers, they clearly saw that although mothers reproduce (support, sustain, nurture) the family, no one reproduces the mother. They assumed an "adult" role in their own families by offering to reproduce motherhood. In ironic ways, they counted on school to reproduce them. Central to that recovery was solitude, even if found in a reading cubby, the library, or between the pages of a book. Where would they find it in the future?

Robin, Danielle: Reading to Escape?

Oliver Morgan defines solitude as something more than the circumstances of physical isolation. Instead, he views solitude as a particular mental state, one which is almost always chosen. In contradistinction to isolation, alienation, withdrawal, even silence, the person in solitude "may be in a state of stillness and quiet, [yet] solitude is characterized by active contemplation. It is a condition of attentiveness and presence in the moment that facilitates an emergence of integration and wholeness" (cited in Kottler 1990, 18). For Morgan, solitude is never passive or escapist; it is a state of deepest engagement with the world around us.

The possibility of this type of contemplation is what Cathy Johnson (1990) finds in the woods around her Missouri home:

For me, these Missouri woods are an antidote. *Woods* is only a metaphor, a microcosm of nature; it doesn't matter if there is a single tree about. Alone in the Sand Hills, at the beach, above the timberline would do as well, if these places were my own. There is simply too much going on outside—most of it unexpected—to allow too much concentration on who I am, what labels I wear, what I should be doing or thinking. I simply am. I am present. I am present to what is going on around me, outside me. And not very much concerned with my own precious self, thank you. (p. 58)

The active engagement with self, with project, with purpose that solitude promotes contributed to a feeling of personal efficacy for some of my young women students. Yet they experienced a tremendous conditioning at work against the idea of being alone. It was not only the family and its dependence on women's labor which militated their opportunities for solitude, it was also the relentless pressure of peer culture. Withdrawal from peer society, even briefly, was regarded as abnormal and suspicious by most of the students in the class.

Mihaly Csikszentmihalyi and Reed Larson, in *Being Adolescent* (1984), argue that

> in many cultures, being alone is feared, not because of physical dangers, but for more mysterious psychic threats that hatch and fester in solitude. The man who keeps to himself is suspected of sorcery. The woman who prefers to be alone is surely a witch....It is not just being alone that is dangerous, but any attempt to separate oneself, in thought as well as in body, from one's kin. The notion of individuation, the effort to differentiate oneself from the group, which is so central to the Western idea of personal identity, has been viewed with distrust in most human cultures. (p. 50)

This distrust surrounded the young women in my classes, Robin, Danielle, and Sherry, who enjoyed reading and who chose individual reading over other group activities. Their preferences, stated simply as desire for the pleasure that novel reading brought them, became central topics of discussion in our research project. Most of my students, male and female alike, judged the interest these girls expressed in reading as attempt to escape peer culture and, more insidiously, as evidence of maladjustment. The boys in the class were the most outspoken in their judgments—eager to label the Robin and Danielle as "weirdos" because of their craving for solitude, but it was the girls in the class who sustained and elaborated their judgments. While the boys shrugged Robin and Danielle off with a word or phrase, the girls wrote long journal entries imagining the motivations and the effects of an avid interest in private reading. In these entries they wondered whether these girls chose solitude out of fear of attachment or hostility toward people. It was virtually impossible for them to image solitude as an authentic pleasure.

In "The Solitary Reader" I discussed the effects of these judgments, but I failed to let Robin and Danielle speak for themselves. Both girls were keenly aware of how their behavior was interpreted, bristling at the judgments their peers expressed. Robin was a girl who rarely concerned herself with the fashions and fads of high school society. "Why does everyone care so much about what I wear and how I do my hair. Who cares?!!!" she wrote. Danielle, on the contrary, was viewed as pretty and fashionable, and therefore appropriately part of the party scene. "Shelly [her friend] thinks that I should go out more. But I go out when I want to go out. Sometimes after work I just want to go home because I'm tired and the idea that I should be out drinking till I puke just to prove I can is stupid. I'd rather just go home by myself, go to my room, put on some music and think. That's when I do a lot of reading—listening to music that is."

For both Robin and Danielle, solitary reading is simply something they enjoy. But their own pleasures did not match the expectations their friends had for what they ought to find pleasurable. It seemed so clear-cut to the majority of the class: Robin, who was not attractive, chose solitude as a consolation and Danielle, who was attractive, needed to be persuaded to give up private pleasures to fill the role expected of a high school party girl. Thinking about Danielle and Robin reminded me of how contrary to high school society women's solitude is, particularly as Cathy Johnson framed it. Perhaps more students need a chance to set aside "who I am, what labels I wear, what I should be doing or thinking...not very much concerned with my own precious self, thank you" (p. 58).

Wanda's Journal:
"Things will be different when I'm in charge"

And then there was Wanda, a senior who took my English class as her last remaining credit before graduating in our vo-tech's bricklaying program. Wanda let me keep her journal, a stiff-backed black and white composition book with smooth, translucent paper, because it delighted me so. I can recover some of my reactions to her thoughts through my own comments interspersed here and there where I found some white spaces among the tightly packed pages.

But there was an entry I read, but did not respond to: "Ms. Aadahl, you've got to read *The Solitary*. Cool book, really. It's about Jane Cahill who graduates at 17 and then goes lives by herself. What she does is raise rabbits and grow a garden. RG [reading group] wouldn't like it— or understand—but you would. Read it this summer."

I did not read *The Solitary* (Hall 1986) until this new look at my students' journals prompted me to hunt the book down in the library where Wanda had found it. This remarkable adolescent novel, and Wanda's cryptic references to it helped me see that the solitude my students (and myself as well) craved was neither the embracing of individuation and autonomy, which feminists have justly critiqued, nor a failure to adjust to the demands of sociality. Because it touches upon so many of the themes my students were discussing in their journals, I wondered what would have happened to our research together if I and my students had all read it together.

In Lynn Hall's novel, Jane Cahill is a young woman not so different from the students in my class: eager to leave home, unsure about how to support herself, believing college to be possible but not desirable. After graduation she leaves her aunt and uncle to homestead alone on the family farm. As she works to survive her first hard winter, she catalogues the dimensions of her solitude in terms familiar from my students' journals: time and control:

> For the first time in her memory she was independent of time. Seven o'clock, get up. Eight-thirty, be in her seat in her first class. Eleven-forty to twelve-ten, lunch period. Saturday, up early to get her part of the housecleaning done so she could go to her Saturday job. Sunday, go to Sunday School and church to placate Uncle Doyle....The bits of time that weren't demanded of her by others, Jane used to pull herself in herself in whatever solitude she could find, at the park or the library or wherever, to live in her dreams for escape. (p. 11)

The bits of time that Jane captured in fits and starts when she was at her uncle's house were now essentially hers to control. In fact, control was what she began to experience in all facets of her life—control that came initially from breaking bonds with those who had demanded her attention:

> The joy of her aloneness was growing daily more evident to Jane. The tiny luxuries of waking in the mornings, lying in bed until she'd had time to plan her day, eating what she wanted for every meal, within the limits of her budget, instead of wordlessly accepting whatever Marlyce fixed, eating when she was hungry, not when someone else decreed that it was mealtime, being in control of her day. That, she thought, was the key. Control. She had to listen to no one's noise but her

own. She worked hard, but she worked according to her own decisions, and for her own direct benefit. (p. 36)

Yet when the immediate joys of solitude fade, Jane fears the motivation for her solitude. "Am I hiding out here? Am I such a coward that I can't face life like everybody else?" she asks (p. 35). Like several of the students in my class, she cannot imagine a life for a woman alone. To clarify her thoughts, she evaluates different courses her life might take by picturing herself in the future. "Ten years from now, if I stay here, I'd probably have the rabbit business built up to some sort of livable income or else found some other way of keeping body and soul together without having to leave this place....If somebody did come along to marry I probably wouldn't want to because I'd be too used to living every minute for myself" (p. 35).

The possibility that she would not choose "conventional" family life conjures a host of women's stereotypes. Upon taking a cat from a friend, she wonders: "Am I going to turn into the classic neurotic old maid with her houseful of cats?" (p. 47). And she pursues a romance with a boy named Aaron to see whether she could have such a life. In a chapter that led Wanda to write in her reading journal, "Every girl in this class should read this," Jane and Aaron go on a date to a rabbit show so that Jane can continue to learn about the breeds that will become her livelihood. The date is, to quote Wanda, "typical, just typical." Aaron becomes bored and restless, despite Jane's interest in learning more about rabbit judging. She briefly wishes she had come alone so that she could manage her own time but then concludes: "When someone who looked like Aaron asked out someone who looked like her, it was crazy to wish it away. Shrugging, she said: 'I'm ready to go anytime you are'" (p. 69).

Over time, however, her experience with Aaron teaches her that traditional romantic roles—as extended through Aaron's expectations and sense of self—would demand too much of a sacrifice and offer paltry rewards. She puts aside nagging doubts about the need for romantic love, deciding she will choose it on her own terms or not at all, and she thinks about whether or not she will ever have children. Again, without foreclosing the possibility, she decides that she doesn't "need" that either. Most remarkably, however, it is when she comes to understand why a woman would want, however briefly, to escape the confines of home and marriage, when she releases herself from the myths of romantic fulfillment that occasionally nagged her, that she feels the greatest connection with her own mother and begins to understand the torturous events of her childhood. For the first time she writes to her mother in prison and asks her to write back. "I think twelve years is too long, don't you?" (p. 83).

It is in solitude that Jane discovers deep connections to family and friends, particularly Iva, a woman friend who has also chosen a solitary life. At Iva's store, Jane talks to Iva about the solitary life and urges her to respond to the fears and doubts that have arisen: does she mind growing old alone? does she miss romantic love? does she think herself selfish? doesn't she think that "[l]ike the song says about people who need people are the luckiest people in the world?" (p. 38). In response, Iva chuckles and snorts, answering each objection cleanly. Finally she concludes: "Well sir, if I was God and running the world, I'd try to make it so everybody, men and women, had to live alone for awhile, take care of themselves, support themselves, learn their own strengths, if you know what I mean" (p. 38).

The book closes with Jane creating a space for living within the tensions between autonomy and connection, solitude and fellowship. In an ending scene that Wanda described as "pretty deep" Jane plans a Christmas dinner for a growing circle of friends who offer her real recognition: Iva, neighbors, her aunt. She is conscious of her choices, aware that she is creating rituals and traditions that will be with her for many years to come, so she chooses traditions to comfort and please herself and to extend hospitality to others. Having decided to be "the solitary," Jane can find and express authentic connections with others. "It's not the ending I thought it would have," Wanda wrote in her journal, "but it's the right ending. Better than what I thought it would be."

Toward a New Balance

Last year, those-who-do-such-things bulldozed a wider path for the fishermen. The agricultural lands surrounding the watershed have been developed into housing tracks and shopping malls. Occasionally, on route to visit my parents, I've thought about revisiting my secret place. But I know I won't. I don't want to know if it's not there.

I haven't seen Wanda since her graduation day many years ago. But I felt a powerful connection to her journal as I reread it. The girl she was touched the girl I was. After reading *The Solitary*, Wanda wrote that "you could live all by yourself happily if you know you have friends." Later in her journal she asked me "Did you have a happy childhood?" I wrote back: "Well, it was full of the usual complement of challenges and traumas—times I thought the world was over for me—but looking back they were little things. I always felt pretty solid and well loved." In the margin next to my comment she scribbled: "Me too."

How can we conceive of schooling so that both connection and solitude can be experienced, so that mutual recognition among students and teachers, students and students, can thrive? I ended "The Solitary Reader" with a brief tip of the hat to young women like Clare, Jenny, Salina, and Wanda, writing: "Of course, the solitary reader does exist! We may want to show our students that they are not the only type of reader, but we don't want to destroy them entirely. Are there places—in the school, in the classroom, in the rhythm of the school day—where the child drawn to the cozy quiet the solitary reader craves can enjoy reading without facing the dilemma of engagement or withdrawal?" (p. 175).

It is, of course, more complicated than the dilemma of engagement or withdrawal—more like the *interrelationship* of engagement and withdrawal, connection and solitude, the price of thought. Solitude— as opposed to loneliness or isolation—stands in relationship to connection, to mutuality, to the web of human regard that sustains us. From the safety of meaningful connection to others, our minds can venture out. Freed, temporarily, from the interruptions and distractions around us, we think in new ways. It feels good. Cathy Johnson puts it well: "But there are those occasions when time seems to stop; the sun stills in the sky, we cease breathing, lost for an endless, timeless instant. Something so captures our attention that we are no longer simply ourselves, our busy, thinking, feeling, fussing selves, but become something other. It happens too seldom to take for granted, and yet it happens just often enough to call for an encore" (p. 116).

References

Benjamin, J. (1988). *The bonds of love*. New York: Pantheon Books.

Calkins, L. (1991). *Living between the lines*. Portsmouth, N.H.: Heinemann.

Csikszentmihalyi, M., and R. Larson. (1984). *Being adolescent*. New York: Basic Books.

Cusick, P. (1972). *Inside high school*. New York: Holt, Rinehart and Winston.

Eidman-Aadahl, E. (1988). The solitary reader: Exploring how lonely reading has to be. *The New Advocate* 1 (3): 165–76.

Everhart, R. (1983). *Reading, writing, and resistance: Adolescence and labor in a junior high school*. Boston: Routledge and Kegan Paul.

Finkelstein, B. (1979). Reading, writing, and the acquisition of identity in nineteenth-century primary schools. In *Regulated children/liberated children*, edited by B. Finkelstein, 114–40. New York: Psychohistory Press.

Hall, L. (1986). *The solitary.* New York: Charles Scribner's Sons.

Jackson, P. (1968). *Life in classrooms.* New York: Holt, Rinehart & Winston.

Johnson, C. (1990). *On becoming lost: A naturalist's search for meaning.* Salt Lake City: Peregrin Smith Books.

Kottler, J. (1990). *Private moments, secret selves: Enriching our time alone.* Los Angeles: Jeremy P. Tarcher, Inc.

Larkin, R. (1979). *Suburban youth in cultural crisis.* New York: Oxford.

Olsen, T. (1972). *Silences.* New York: Delacorte.

Radway, J. (1984). *Reading the romance.* Chapel Hill: University of North Carolina Press.

Willis, P. (1977). *Learning to labour: How working-class kids get working-class jobs.* Lexington, Mass.: D. C. Heath.

Notes

1. I have characterized the young women in this study as "working class" commensensically: each came from homes where the primary wage earners worked in factories or small manufacturing trades. In four of the families, secondary wage earners worked in "pink collar" or other low-skilled positions: cashiers, etc. One of the young women, Jenny, had a parent who attended, but did not complete college.

2. The issue of space and privacy was reformulated for me when I was in Japan, a crowded place by Euro-American standards. There I witnessed tremendous cultural support for the contemplation and solitude in the midst of others. Virtually every house or public place offered a series of small, soothing vistas: recesses which held a single bonsai or arches which framed a single spectacualr view. Routinely, men and women would stop to sit and contemplate the view while crowds of shoppers or family members made their way around them without hesitation or interrupting. The privacy symbolized by the German's love of high thick walls or the Britain's hedged garden or the American teenager's desire for her own bedroom was choreographed in Japan by the visible "cooperation of others" in the enactment of solitude.

3. For a sample of the U.S. literature, see Robert Everhart, *Reading, Writing, and Resistance: Adolescence and Labor in a Junior High School* (Boston: Routledge & Kegan Paul, 1983); Phillip Cusick, *Inside High School* (New York: Holt,

Rinehart & Winston, 1972); Ralph Larkin *Suburban Youth in Cultural Crisis* (New York: Oxford, 1979).

4. Paul Willis, in *Learning to Labour,* makes a persuasive case for the continuities between how the "lads" (nonconformist male working-class students) enacted resistance in the classroom and how they participated in shopfloor culture outside of school. My male students generally aspired to be skilled craftsmen and technicians, to work in family-owned machine shops and construction businesses. They invested themselves in their work seriously, rejecting school as limiting and "babyish" in its imitation of what they viewed as "real work."

Chapter 13

Speaking in Tongues: An African-American Woman in the World and the Academy

Beverly M. Gordon

Black women must speak in a plurality of voices as well as in a multiplicity of discourses. This discursive diversity, or simultaneity of discourse, I call "speaking in tongues."

—Henderson 1989

The phrase, "speaking in tongues" resonates within me—it exemplifies my life history as an African-American woman negotiating a career, motherhood, involvement in my community, while finding a personal space for myself. I speak in tongues to accommodate the plurality of these discourses as they intersect my life. I speak in the tongue of the academy to demonstrate affiliation and legitimation, and the understanding of its unique language, codes and meanings. In the African-American community, I speak in tongues that identify and affirm love, allegiance, and respect for the nature and uniqueness of the African diaspora situated in the Americas. At home, I speak as a mother of my three-year-old son with all the accompanying dreams and fears African-American mothers have for their sons. Finally, I speak to my own spirituality—my being and becoming as I live each day.

While W. E. B. DuBois' talk of dual consciousness (1903) is helpful for me, his words are incomplete. Intertwined with the issues of race and class are intergender and intragender issues that go beyond male-female relationships.[1] Whether dealing with White males or Black males, as well as those issues identified as being salient by and associated with White women's gender issues, these debates situate me on the fringe of the discourses. I am a fringe dweller speaking in tongues.[2] Such an existence can be solitary. My challenge is to find my place, to serve my constituency, and to be at peace with my spirit. Because I grew up as an only child, solitude and I are old friends. In fact, at certain moments solitude has been so comfortable that it has been transformed into a detrimental isolation. Solitude, which is being alone in the quiet of one's spirituality or inner self, is different from isolation, which is being lonely for a critical mass of people, particularly African-Americans, to sustain, encourage and collaborate with in academic endeavors.

The dawning awareness of the imposition of the role of "other" and not the taken for granted "we" living on the fringe of dominant and even secondary discourses in the academy, while being in and of the African-American community; reconciling my life's dissonance to find a peaceful space for my family; becoming comfortable with my own voice: these frame my thoughts on solitude addressed in this essay.

Invisibility in Everyday Life: Personal Reflections on Growing Up as a Little Colored Girl in America

Coming to terms with marginalization began early on in my own life history. Learning to reject the norm of invisibility and struggling against the lessening of my humanity occurred almost imperceptibly at first, but become clearer the older I became. I recall my response to the societal images around me. In the mid- to late-1950s in the dawning awareness of an elementary school girl, somehow I came to know that the television portrayed images of "regular people," yet strained to find images of regular people who looked just like me. After all, my family—my grandmother (Mama), great-grandmother, aunt and uncle, my mother and I—were, as Mama would say, regular "colored people." I lived in New Jersey with my grandmother, aunt and uncle in a house with fruit trees, white and concord grape vineyards, a rose trellis, and an old barn in the backyard, with the additional perk of my great-grandmother living only a few blocks away in a little suburban community town on the Jersey shore. My mother lived in Connecticut in a housing cooperative located on top of a hill surrounded by woods filled with rabbits, racoons, and blueberry patches. Except for my great-grandmother, all the adults worked full-time jobs. I went to school, did my homework, and sang in the St. James Episcopal church choir. We were normal, regular people.

However, what I observed in the dominant society were images of Buckwheat in the Little Rascals movies, "colored" men dancing with Shirley Temple or driving Jack Benny's car, and the infamous Kingfish. While there were Black women on the *Amos and Andy Show*, their domineering, condescending, and loud mannerisms did not reflect the colored women in my family or the families of my relatives or friends.

Even watching American Bandstand was little consolation. I knew there were colored people in Philadelphia because I had cousins there. I also knew colored entertainers could be on television because they were on the show, but where were the colored kids? Other images that had an impact on me during these formative years included watching Edward R. Murrow's documentary *Harvest of Shame* and feeling badly about colored migrant workers and their families who had to live in shacks. But as the dominant culture is not a monolith, I was able to glean within its crack an African-American presence.

In these early years I employed African-American culture, specifically music, literary works, and films to express my being. The Black aesthetic, part of the cultural knowledge I identify as African-American epistemology, generated from the Black experience in the Americas, resonates in me and captures and articulates my feelings and emotions. Juxtaposed to the apparent limited representation of African-Americans in the dominant culture, I clearly remember films about African-Americans such as *St. Louis Blues*, *Stormy Weather*, and *Porgy and Bess*. There were two particular movies, *Anna Lucaster* and *Carmen Jones*, that had beautiful colored women in them, as well as the play, *Simply Heavenly*, one of a series broadcast on the PBS station. It would be years later before I learned of the contributions to American literature made by Langston Hughes and many other gifted African-American writers, but the play engaged me because of its colored characters who looked just like me. Occasionally, other glimpses of the African-American aesthetic experience such as the briefly lived Nat King Cole Show made their way into the mainstream culture, but these were few and far between.

During these formative years perhaps the most important and impressionable images for me that reflected the African diaspora were in Harlem. When my mother took me there, I encountered a range of Black (in a generic sense) people, from the wealthy to the street folk, from the famous to the everyday people in a range of professions, occupations and businesses. I remember a huge billboard with the faces of many people of color that pronounced that people of color formed the majority population the world. While I do not remember the specific wording, this billboard was significant to me, because it affirmed my existence and humanity, while negating the *invisibility/nonentity* of Black people in the dominant culture. This was the first piece of mass culture that ever told me there were more "colored people" in the world than White people.

And then there was the Apollo Theater. In the Apollo I saw my first underground movie from South Africa in which Mariam Makeba sang. At the Apollo, I also experienced shows such as *The Mo' Town Review* and the James Brown show, where I dreamed of being one of the Shirelles or Martha Reeves and the Vandellas, just as my mother and aunt had dreamed of singing like Della Reese, Dinah Washington and Gloria Lynne. It was also in Harlem that I first encountered Malcolm X as he stood on a street corner preaching about Islam. As both a refuge and a competing reality for me, Harlem was an oasis for images of the African diaspora in the White cultural sands of the dominant society.

My elementary school had an integrated student population and two African-American female teachers. While I remember few overt ugly racial incidents during my early school years, there was a dawning awareness on my part that the older I got, my inclusion in the "we" of "we kids, we classmates, we neighbors" was becoming problematic. For example, in fourth grade I wrote out thirty valentines for Valentine's day and only received four; two of those came from the other two African-American girls. In fifth grade when the class paired off to dance, after all the squeals and grumbling of eleven-year-olds with the thoughts of dancing with those of the opposite sex, only one boy, Arman Mazie (he was White—there were no Black boys in our class), with whom I had been friends, offered to be my partner. I *thought* I was the same, yet my inclusion in the constituent "we kids" was questionable. There were few reflections of me in the Gregory elementary school curriculum. I cannot remember class materials or stories that validated my existence. In both the school and public library, I searched long and hard only to find a very few literary works that included little colored girls as their protagonists.

In these and many more early moments, I took my sameness with the dominant society for granted, but learned of the narrow and pejorative visibility assigned to Black people within the dominant culture. I lived between the "how to" versus the "never being able to" reconcile or acquire positionality within this imposed subordinate existence. While this impositional lens took its toll on me, the duality within me resisted and rejected viewing myself in the pejorative paradigms of the dominant society. This resistance got me through the high school and undergraduate years of my academic career. College was baptism by fire at Yale during the mid-1960s. I needed New Haven to experience living in an urban Black community, not to idolize it from a distance, but to live it with all of its possibilities and dangers. From these years I learned much about my self, my own voice, and my relationships with the Black community. These and countless more experiences shaped my commitment to the Black community; however, I still needed the academic tools and skills to make my contribution. Graduate school provided me with what I needed.

Invisibility in the Academy: Discourse, Positionality, and the Struggle of African-American Women Scholars on Campus

Graduate work at the University of Wisconsin–Madison began in the wonderful and tumultuous times of the late sixties. This was a wonderful time to find discourse, dialogue and theorizing to help sort out the world. My advisor Herbert Kliebard, along with other faculty friends such as Carl Grant, Mike Apple, Tom Popkewitz, John Antes and many more, provided the heuristic tools that helped me examine critically the taken-for-granted everyday life in schools. My teachers also helped me understand the political nature of schooling in society: how educational institutions operated; how mechanisms of normative standardization endured; why the power relationship within society was presented as immutable, objective, commonsensical and impervious to change; and, most importantly, that social institutions were not monolithic, that resistance and change could begin in the smallest cracks and fissures of the dominating structures.

During this time, personal revelations and experiences coupled with graduate studies influenced my ability to contextualize my life experiences and those of other family members and friends within the history of the African diaspora in the Americas. Most assuredly, the concept of deviancy influenced my research emphasis in graduate school. Deviancy and other deficit paradigms as defined in educational literature were accepted as part of the social structure of the minority community. Furthermore, this deficit framework was accepted as the normative, legitimate lens through which conceptualizations and interpretations were made, and diagnoses and prescriptive and remedial interventions were fashioned to assist African-American learners. Reading educational history (Church 1976) that describes how blame for the failure of American schools to produce a well-educated polity shifted from focusing on the issues of a weak, insufficient and ineffective curriculum, to focusing on student deviancy as the source of the problems of schooling. This is one way of knowing, albeit impersonal and cursory. To know through one's own lived experience how such distortions, misinterpretations and fabrications influence societal consciousness, values and responses, and how perceptions manifest themselves in the daily lives and practices of school personnel as they relate to students of color—this is a very different way of knowing. For example, I remember reading how school counselors steered minority students away from college preparatory courses. But I also remember what it meant to fail Latin and have my own high school counselor respond by suggesting to my family that I would make a lovely secretary and that even if I got into college (which was doubtful), how could they afford it? Knowing by reading and knowing by the lived experience is the quintessential disparity between realities. The dominant normative structuring has always implied that difference equaled deviancy. The concept of the "other" named by White middle class cultural standards, values, codes, and the impossible challenge of transforming "other" to "us" seemed to be the minority educational mandate embraced by the academy and endorsed through schooling institutions.

As a response to the pejorative way in which African-Americans were conceptualized, it is not surprising that my discourse, teaching, and research in the academy is dedicated to unmasking the paradigms and moral ethical systems that shape the thinking that determines and justifies minority deviancy as a normal and legitimate concept. Such critical discourse is provocative, particularly when so many within the dominant educational network have prospered by evoking the deficit model, either as an advocate of or having the appropriate remedial model to combat it. Even more thorny an issue is what constitutes an "expert" and who in fact are "the" experts on African-Americans and other people of color.

Within academia, there is a pervasive albeit an unspoken determination that White scholars, particularly men, are the ultimate experts of record when determining and explaining minority schooling and most other related issues. This has been my personal experience and that of many other Black colleagues, especially surrounding peer review as it relates to tenure and promotion. Likewise, in the ongoing struggle of people of color outside the academy to participate in the education of their children, particularly regarding the knowledge being disseminated to children in schools, suggests to me that the gatekeepers for legitimating African-American scholarship are predominantly White scholars, and particularly so if the scholar or scholarship challenges prevailing paradigms. Such validation by the dominant gatekeepers is indicative of the marginalization of African-American scholarly thought within the academy. These kinds of issues, plus my knack of not "knowing my place" as a colleague remarked, made my early life within the academy difficult to say the least.

As a new faculty member trying to find my way in unfamiliar landscapes, while challenging racism and sexism from both students and faculty, the critical question for me was with whom would I speak about such matters. As I left Madison, my advisor said to me, "Find a rabbi," and I understood what he meant. What never occurred to me was that those who had the influence did not care to be my rabbi. I had read *Games Mother Never Taught Me,* but it proved to be minimally helpful in preparing me for the struggle for academic survival. As the proverbial honeymoon period ended, it became evident that my struggle to survive would be an isolating experience. Isolation as opposed to solitude can be costly. I made foolish mistakes because I did not know the rules of conduct, nor the codes of jousting, nor the formal and informal rules of engagement within this institution. As time went on, the untenured faculty, myself included, became increasingly elusive, passive-aggressive, competitive and hostile. To say the very least, we were all running scared as we struggled for survival in the academy; at this point I hadn't come to terms with the falsely inclusive "we" that was emerging again.

At the time, there was only one other Black female faculty member in a department that consisted of approximately 40 percent White women, several of whom were also untenured. My relationship with most but not all of the White women could be summarized by a Groucho Marx line, "Who do you believe—me or your eyes?" Beyond the sisterhood and solidarity espoused in feminist literature, my eyes told me that the actions of White women remarkably resembled those of their White male counterparts when vying for power and control as senior faculty members or competing for promotion and tenure as junior faculty members. This is not a blanket diatribe or indictment of all the White women on my faculty; several with whom I worked were then and are today genuinely wonderful and supportive friends. Still, my *experiences* indicated that some of the White women with whom I worked treated African-American female faculty members in a way that reflected the White male power structure.

During this same period, I witnessed a transformation in the literature from addressing minority issues, to minority and women's issues, to women and minority issues. I experienced ambivalent feelings as I observed the advancing visibility of gender issues and their impact on American society. While I can only speak for myself, it may well be that other women of color, too, have grave reservations about the current configuration of gender issues in which White feminist agendas marginalize African-American issues. While neither time nor space will allow for an in-depth discussion of the interrelationship of gender, class, and racism, I submit that the tensions between women of color and Eurocentric women will fester until and unless such problems are openly and honestly resolved. The end of this essay will describe some of my own initial efforts to understand the complexity surrounding minority and majority gender issues through the works of African-American women scholars and artists.

During these early years, I did not have nearly enough formal or informal conversations about the requirements for promotion and tenure. Still clinging to the quickly crumbling illusion that work in the academy was an individual endeavor done in isolation, I was not forthright about asking questions, never mind that I felt I had few allies on whom to rely. In a word, I was "under siege." *Solitude* was not the issue. Rather I experienced the deadly weight of silence from *isolation*. Even though the college office sponsored general sessions in preparation for faculty going for promotion, I received the critical information, "the real deal" by accident, through eavesdropping, from whispers, and occasionally from a few friendly colleagues. There were moments when the lines between isolation and alienation intersected, especially when I realized there were other ways junior faculty were getting survival information about the tenure and promotion process inaccessable to me. Beyond the everyday work setting and seemingly beyond my grasp were weekend and evening activities that I was not invited to that acquainted my junior faculty peers with the culture of the department, the institution, and other accompanying issues such as the negotiation of and settling academic business, mentoring, publishing, collaborative research efforts, and accessibility to national and international networks.

Marginalization with regard to student–Black faculty relations was another area of anguish. Having been told repeatedly by the department elders that I was the cause of the tensions, distrust, and hostility between myself and my students, I was instructed that it was incumbent upon me to accommodate the students. Coming to terms with my White students, particularly White undergraduate females who had never had an African-American faculty member, meant learning how to speak in yet another tongue.[3] During a college reorganization, with the support of a senior Black faculty member and another faculty group, I transferred to another department. Overall, the faculty in the new department took a wait-and-see attitude toward me. While I was clearly more optimistic about my new home, feelings of self-doubt and fear were still present. Was I an affirmative action misfit? Had I been placed in a revolving minority slot and then broken the rules by having the audacity to believe that I was good enough to be successful? I clearly recall job descriptions anonymously placed in my office mailbox. Colleagues advised, "If you fight and leave here kicking and screaming, you will never get another job worth anything," etc. Well-meaning friends would tell me I needed alternative job plans, just in case. Several Black students were apprehensive about my serving on their doctoral committees. One Black student commented that there were few Black professionals who had successfully come up through the ranks to acquire promotion and tenure. While my responses to these and various other situations required multiple tongues, my indignation was still evident.

There were many dark days during the struggle for tenure. Clearly, I learned how to fight, while being simultaneously engaged in a war for survival within the academy while not sacrificing my own voice or commitment to my community. My resilience was generated from the spirituality of my solitude. I turned inward and listened to my ancestors speaking to me in their tongues. In addition to their voices, strength and words of encouragement came from other African-American women in academia from around the country. One friend put into words what I knew in my heart to be true. Her response to my query about leaving one institution for another was, "Where are you going to go? We (referring to African-American scholars in general) are under siege all over the country." There were many African-American faculty that I knew or heard of who had become academic nomads, wandering from position to position with no tenure nor the accompanying stability to their lives. They became a kind of institutional affirmative-action prostitutes being passed around from one job to another. My decision was to stand and fight.

There were three critical people in my life during these times. Together we sustained each other while learning how to negotiate the straits of the academy: two were African-American women who were my age and in doctoral programs at my institution, and the third was an African-American male faculty member in another department. In the collective solitude of our lives outside of the institution, we were able to speak in tongues on topics that had to be left unspoken within the institution; these friendships and alliances sustained all of us through our ordeals. My friends and I chose to endure the protracted and painful struggle, and although bloodied and scarred, we endured.

My female friends successfully completed their doctoral programs, and my male friend and I acquired the precious commodities of promotion and tenure. Now we smile knowing that victory (with good health) is the best revenge.

As I reflect on my present situation, I feel very good about my life, my colleagues and my work. There is still much work to do. In a department of thirty-two full-time tenured and tenure-track faculty, consisting of eighteen White males, eleven White females, two African-American men and only one African-American female (me), there are issues of faculty recruitment that we need to address. On the other hand, as new faculty arrive, new program area configurations emerge that are giving rise to legitimating the scholarly lenses and paradigms other than those dominated by the gatekeepers. I find myself in the company of White women colleagues in my department and African-American women colleagues around the country with whom I have been able to engage in rich and illuminating conversations about issues raised earlier in this paper. These conversations and collaborative efforts are yielding important theoretical and methodological topics for work in our respective fields.

Perhaps the most important point of this truncated life history is that my struggles and those of my peers and friends are ostensibly the same struggles African-Americans students experience in society's schools. From preschool and kindergarten through higher education and professional schools, the institutional orientation produces a situation wherein people of color are under siege. The "fringe dwellers," those who occupy and struggle against being relegated to the fringe of the dominant society, are confronted on multiple levels with the following issues: understanding cultural codes; performance criteria; sustaining linkages with the community; success measured by normative structures set by a dominant and often hostile culture; defining and/or reclaiming our own words, dispelling the cultural particulars that imply a negation of one's humanity; and finding a contented and nurturing space for one's self.

At this point in my work, I have a need to give full attention to the critical business of serving my community. The voices of African-American women in scholarly and popular work; representation and leadership in and for the community; and selection and dissemination of knowledge that will provide the basis of the education for the African-American community are at least three critical issues for the African-American community in the twenty-first century. There is an urgent need for the next generation of children to acquire new lenses for critical understanding of the nature of self-inflicted destruction to the intricacies of advancing postindustrial global society.

Voice and Representation: Critical Issues Facing the African-American Community

For the past several years, I have been engaged in a humble effort to identify, articulate and delineate what I have termed African-American epistemology. This the cultural knowledge[4] generated out of the experiences of the African diaspora in the Americas, and the implications of this knowledge for the African-American community. In an earlier work, I identified endogenous emancipatory currents of thought that are pervasive in African-American philosophical, sociological and educational scholarship over the past century and more: self-help, service, nationalism, economic automomy, and political power (Gordon 1985). However, my work lacked the perspectives of African-American women scholars and artists.

I was introduced to the works of Alice Walker while inquiring about African-American epistemology as a descriptor at the Schomburg Research Library in Harlem. One of the male patrons suggested that I read Walker's (1983), "The Unglamorous but Worthwhile Duties of the Black Revolutionary Artist, or of the Black Writer Who Simply Works and Writes" if I wanted to know about African-American epistemology. That was an understatement. This was one of my early entry points into the world of African-American women scholars, authors, filmmakers and literary writers such as Hazel Carby, Joyce Ladner, Gloria T. Hull, Patricia Bell Scott, Barbara Smith, Euzhan Palcy, Michelle Wallace, and Mary Helen Washington, among others. One interesting category that emerges from many of these authors is the problematic nature of the White feminist model that suggests oppression emerges from White male power domination. Making gender into a primary category from which to study oppression results in at least two points of tension for African-American women. First, when the issue of race is diminished, unpacking the idea that forms of gender hierarchy are both historically and culturally specific becomes extremely difficult. Secondly, the normative feminist formulations, those that have no particular need for the experience of race, empowers those women who are not disempowered by hierarchies of race, namely White, middle-class women.[5] Put another way, these formulations stake out a positionality that privileges some but not all of the "other" ways of knowing and being in the world. For women of the diaspora, the diaspora is the paramount experiential frame, and the African-American women's struggle has been for the humanity of an inclusive Black community.

Recently, this country witnessed the confirmation hearings of Supreme Court nominee Clarence Thomas, a Black conservative Republican. Although the end of the hearings were sensationalized by the charges of sexual harassment by Anita Hill, one of his former aides, the other consequential issue of Black conservative Republican ideology and what that would mean for the country in general and the African-American community in particular was overshadowed in the African-American community by the harassment charges. As reported by President George Bush and Robert L. Woodson, representative of the so-called "Black Neocon" (Black neoconservatives),[6] the rank-and-file majority of the African-American community was supportive of Thomas, while protests against his confirmation came from the progressive, liberal and well-educated constituency within the community. In addition, protests against Thomas's confirmation had also been raised by various others such as civil rights groups, pro-choice groups, women's groups, etc., during the confirmation hearings. The charge of sexual harassment and the ensuing fiasco seemed to galvanize the African-American people into the very old tradition of rallying around a community member under siege. The problem for the Black community was the question: In whose community and interest will Judge Thomas ultimately situate himself? The commonly assumed identification of group membership by race does not necessarily guarantee a mutual and reciprocal relationship, ideology or vision. A seemingly large majority of the community did not ask the hard questions about Thomas's political philosophy and agenda, his track record in the Equal Employment Opportunity Commission, and the implications of his decisions for the long-term well-being and advancement of the Black community. The societal conditions and challenges change, so the African-American community must be educated with the heuristic tools necessary to critique the sophisticatedly subtle and blatant racist challenges currently being presented to the American policy. This does not mean that all the common folk of the community cannot critique, but that "new occasions do teach new duties." The community will need different, more powerful lenses to decipher the constructed reality that they will be presented with and expected to accept. I suspect that while many people within the community have acquired such lenses from the lessons of life, the challenge facing African-American scholars, educators and popular artists alike will be how to disseminate the heuristic tools the community needs in various mediums, and to participate in societal decisions that are in the best interest of the community.

The community must also be encouraged to nurture its linkages to Africa. As people of the African diaspora, it is essential that the next generation have the previously mentioned critical heuristic tools to explore and evaluate their connectedness to the African continent as well as African people throughout the world. The controversy surrounding the concept of "Afrocentricity" is one of accepting a historical vision of how African-Americans are situated in the context of world history. Whose vision of how Africans and African-Americans are situated in world history is the essence of the controversy. Rejecting a Eurocentric view of the world and world history, many Black studies proponents and educators argue for an Afrocentric perspective that embraces interpretative and analytical paradigms that situate Africa and Africans of the diaspora as "subjects rather than as objects on the fringes of the European experience" (Asante 1991, 46). The current and subsequent generations of African-American children are in great need of ways to define themselves other than against a Eurocentric normative structure that views "other" in a pejorative context. Much of the senseless self-inflicted violence in African-American communities manifests a societal self-hatred that leads to destructive behavior.

Beyond critics such as Diane Ravitch and Arthur Schlesinger Jr., the controversy of Afrocentricity is not simplistic reductionist arguments such as if African-American students learn Yoruba math or believe the Egyptians were Black Africans, it will end teenage pregnancy or street violence. The stakes are much higher. As seen in the California social studies textbook adoption controversy, Afrocentricity demonstrates the broader issue of whose vision of history will be designated as the canon. Articulating an "other" vision of American and world history in school could change fundamentally the way in which Americans perceive themselves. Whose history is represented in schools and school textbooks is of no small import. The textbook adoption issue in California is a salient example of the various groups who argued that the textbooks embraced by the California textbook adoption committee were not multicultural because they represent a Eurocentric perspective of the world and the history of people of color. Regardless of the outcome of this struggle, clearly the ultimate responsibility of disseminating African-American cultural knowledge and the history of the African diaspora in the Americas and the world to the next generation of African-American children must be shouldered by the African-American community. The challenge will be to find a means of disseminating such information to the community in a way that provides both accessibility to and ownership of this knowledge.

Resolutions to these and other needs of the African-American community will not be monolithic, but will be issue and demographically specific. In response to these needs, service to the community even beyond personal need and interest may be necessary. The overarching concept that binds together the various strains of this discussion is "community." The idea of "we are therefore I am—I am therefore we are," is found in the ancient traditions of African civilizations. In the future, the concept of Afrocentricity may serve the community in ways that we cannot now even imagine; in this regard it is a force to be reckoned with.

In my solitude, I still hear Nina Simone singing words Lorraine Hansberry gave us, "To be young, gifted and black—what a lovely pleasure it is." In my heart, I know that the possibilities and potential in my community could only be rivaled by the scientific and technological genius it took to produce the ancient pyramids. The challenge will be how to awaken and galvanize this potential and possibility on a massive scale in the face of Euro-American cultural hegemony. Neither time nor space will allow for such a discussion. Suffice it to say that the passionate commitment of this tongue will continue to speak, propose, work, critique and acknowledge criticism that forces me to clarify my efforts at making some humble contribution to my community.

Finding My Own Voice:
The Process of Continually Being and Becoming
in African-American Discourse

The ongoing struggle for the development of my own voice, legitimacy of my discourse and feeling good about what I do even after promotion and tenure is still one of eternal vigilance, although my life is no longer hanging in the balance. My commitment to studying a variety of dimensions of the African diaspora in the Americas and their curricular implications provides personal meaning, satisfaction and self-worth and exemplifies for me what it means to be a scholar in the academy. Most importantly, I realize now why the old guard covets the academy and makes it so difficult for voices other than their own to endure and flourish. There are few jobs within any corporate structure in which you can raise your own questions and commit your life to answering them.

My life outside the academy, beyond the community, has continued through the duration of these experiences. At forty, I had my first child, now an almost four-year-old boy. I purchased a larger house, resumed some hobbies and in general have gotten on with my life.

Clearly having a child is one of my better decisions. Part of my decision to become a middle-aged mother was in response to something a colleague said to me years ago as we sat in a restaurant having dinner. In reply to my asking her if she wanted marriage and family, she commented that her books and articles were her children, and she would live through her works. The academy had become her entire life. I thought, quite the contrary for me: the academy as my *raison d'être* was not an option. Reflecting on the situation now, my colleague's statement scared the hell out of me. I distinctly remember promising myself that I would never allow articles and books to become my children.

After I received my tenure, I decided there was no time like the present, especially since my biological clock was ticking away. So, here I am with a three-year-old. Beyond wanting a child, I wanted a son; coming from a family with so many women, I thought it would be wonderful to have a boy. Yet the dangers of growing up Black and male in American society are real. When he was two years old, I ventured to an American Educational Research Association conference, leaving baby and father alone. As at every AERA meeting, I got together with friends who I had not seen in a year. One evening, a woman commented that she wanted daughters and not sons; the harsh reality of American society that confronts little Black boys increases their chances of being incarcerated or hurt or killed. Claude Brown was right: my son is a manchild in a promised land, albeit it very dangerous and deadly. Yet I know my ancestors endured under similar and even worse conditions. My son has love from both his father and me as well as the extended family and the community. Therefore, even in the face of all of the present and future difficulties and challenges ahead of him, he will understand the meaning of "Lift Every Voice" when he sings it; he will know his history as a descendent of great ancient African civilizations; he will be a spiritual being regardless of what religion he embraces; and he will develop his voice and accompanying tongues as he makes his contribution to the next generation. In turn, we will love and guide him as best we can and ask the ancestors to watch over and bless him on his way.

Perhaps I am not now what I should have become and maybe I am not working hard enough to be all that I can be, but I do know that I am in the process of being and becoming. As for speaking in tongues—the tongues that I have tried to describe in this essay—these are component parts of my collective voice. These tongues and this voice are all witness to and product of my own ongoing struggle for discourse and positionality in the today and tomorrow of my life.

References

Asante, M. K. (1991). Afrocentrism: Was Cleopatra Black? *Newsweek*, September 23, 46.

Church, R. (1976). *Education in the United States: An interpretive history*. New York: Free Press.

DuBois, W. E. B. (1990). The souls of black folk. New York: First Vintape Book/The Library of America Edition (first published 1903).

Gordon, B. (1985). Toward emanicipation in citizenship education: The case of African-American cultural knowledge. *Theory and Research in Social Education* 12: 1–23.

Henderson, M. G. (1989). Speaking in tongues: Dialogics, dialectics, and the Black woman writer's literary tradition. In *Changing our own words: Essays on criticism, theory, and writing by Black women*, edited by C. A. Hall, 16–37. New Brunswick, N.J.: Rutgers University Press.

Walker, A. (1983). *In search of our mothers' gardens*. New York: Harvest/HBJ Book.

Notes

1. For the purposes of this discussion, the term *intergender* will be used to describe relationships between Black and White women and the term *intragender* will describe relationships inside the community of Black women.

2. The phrase "Fringe Dweller" comes from the international film of the same title and examines the life of a young aborigine woman in modern Australia.

3. Just two years ago, the African-American faculty in my college formed a support group to engage in discourse on a number of research, teaching, and service issues that impact us as individuals and as a whole. Listening to the horror stories of other faculty members with regard to students, other colleagues, promotion and tenure struggles, etc., affirmed for me that I was not the only Black woman faculty member who had to struggle with continual challenges to my humanity from colleagues and students alike.

4. When referring to cultural knowledge, I am referring to the range of knowledge production in scholarly, classical, scientific, political, literary, economic, theological, artistic works, etc., focusing on but not limited to issues pertaining to the education and advancement of the African-American community.

5. Professor Sylvia Wynter, who holds joint appointments in the Departments of African and Afro-American Studies and Spanish and Portuguese at Stanford University, makes this argument.

6. There has been an ongoing and indepth discussion about the Black neocons and their agenda in popular magazines over the past year. See the following: A. Baraka and S. Steele, "A Race Divided," *Emerge* 2 (1991); P. Benjamin and T. Nivri, "Perspective: Neocon Artists, Negro Thought Police and Other Charlatans," *Emerge* 2 (1991); J. Davidson, "Perspective: A Backward Glance," *Emerge* 2 (1991); C. Lane et al., "Defying the Stereotype: The New Clout of 'Black Conservatives,'" *Newsweek*, 15 July 1991, pp. 18–19; also in the same issue see "Where Does He [Clarence Thomas] Stand?"; B. Turque and B. Cohn, "Black Conservatives Quarrel over Quotas," *Newsweek*, 24 December 1990, p. 20.

Chapter 14

Women, Single Life, and Solitude: A Plea to Rethink Curriculum

Susan Laird

> *I want to suggest to you that there is a more essential experience that you owe yourselves, one which courses in women's studies can greatly enrich, but which finally depends on you, in all your interactions with yourself and your world. This is the experience of* taking responsibility toward yourselves. *Our upbringing as women has so often told us that this should come second to our relationships and responsibilities to other people.*
>
> *Responsibility to yourself means refusing to let others do your thinking, talking, and naming for you; it means learning to respect and use your own brains and instincts; hence, grappling with hard work...*
>
> —Adrienne Rich, "Claiming an Education"

Alone in the Wilderness

In 1987, according to the U.S. Census, 8.7 percent of all women over the age of 18 were divorced, and 18.6 percent were never married;[1] altogether 39.5 percent were single.[2] I was myself *not* one of these women, accustomed nonetheless to doing my own "thinking, talking, and naming." Louise Bogan could have been writing about my own feeling life as the traveling and homemaking spouse in a weekend-commuter marriage when she wrote,

> Women have no wilderness in them.
> They are provident instead,
> Content in the tight hot cell of their hearts
> To eat dusty bread. (1968, 19)

The following year my husband elected not to follow me west to a new college teaching job. While recovering from the shake-up of a breast cancer scare (which at length, luckily, turned out to be just a scare), I memorized Bogan's poem in all its verses, read Emma Goldman's *Living My Life*, and took new responsibility toward myself.

My husband and I agreed to separate. I concluded my doctoral studies in philosophy of education and moved to my first full-time university teaching position, unfortunately far away from friends and family, in a little mill town on the edge of the northern New England wilderness. Here I began to live alone, by choice, for the first time in my life. Two years later my husband and I were amicably divorced. Like it or not, this basic story line is by no means particular to my own autobiography, but a commonplace of our time.[3]

So, too, is the rest of our story. Six months after our divorce, the nurse in whose home my husband had been living became his third wife, made him a stepfather of school-aged children, and followed him west to a new job, with plans of commuting daily to her own work, in a neighboring city. As I write this, I am still living alone, in the very same walk-up efficiency I rented when I first came to Maine, and finding it "hard work" indeed.

I believe that curriculum theorists need to take seriously the gendered asymmetries, reversals, and repetitions in this all too familiar story if girls and young women are ever to be educated to take responsibility toward themselves and if boys and young men are to be educated in ways that foster their understanding and appreciation of what that challenge can mean in a world that is often indifferent, condescending, unfair, hostile, and harmful, sometimes even murderous, to women. I am now thinking about this problem because my own experience of solitude following my marital separation has taught me to think of myself as a miseducated woman (despite the fine education I will be paying dearly for every month of my life until September 2009). No curriculum ever taught me anything about the challenges or joys of living alone; I have had to reeducate myself in order to survive the former and embrace the latter. And I am still only learning, but probably no more alone in this respect than I am in being single.

The textbook statistics about single women quoted to secondary and postsecondary students of family studies and human development do not distinguish homeless, incarcerated, or hospitalized single women; heterosexual, lesbian, or celibate cohabitors; inhabitants of nursing homes, boarding houses, dormitories, communes, convents, or houses of prostitution; or those single women who live with their children, siblings, parents, or other relatives from those of us who actually live alone. Nor do they even include women in "commuter marriages,"[4] who may live alone most of the time. Yet the statistics do make clear that, however varied, the experience of single womanhood is not unusual in the United States.

This experience furthermore holds significance for all women's lives. Not all single women have chosen to be single; husbands do suddenly die, and others do leave their wives. The prevalence of wife-initiated divorce moreover does bear witness to the fact that many married women do seriously consider single life an option that may be preferable to remaining in their marriages.[5] Of course, most (I wish I could say all) of us begin adult life as singles, and most (like both my own grandmothers) end it as singles, too, even if married most of their lives. Material constraints almost always limit, and sometimes even forbid, single women's self-determination. But, contrary to the impression of the "singles lifestyle" that students may get from their textbooks in school,[6] the situation of singleness does usually allow (in fact it may require) a woman's choice among several possible ways of living other than marriage. These ways of single life include the difficult one that my grandmother, resisting all family advice, chose for herself at the age of seventy-six when my grandfather died; this is the same way I have recently chosen for myself, at least temporarily: the option of living alone.

Today preoccupied with "cooperative learning" and "critical pedagogy" and with profoundly political disputes over "basic" requirements and the nature of "cultural literacy," theorizing about curriculum has yet to take this life context and choice into account in its considerations of educational ends and means.[7] Yet over twenty years ago, Jane R. Martin urged curriculum thinkers to consider conceiving curriculum more broadly so that it might include the subjects of "marriage and divorce" among others; she did not then consider the subject of single women's life among her particular concerns, but she did think of curriculum

> as encompassing forms of living or activity and not just forms of knowledge. Such a curriculum would have to give ample space to the arts, to the professions, to various sorts of work, and to all sorts of other practical activities; it would also have to leave room for a variety of social activities and roles—not just the role of inquirer and the one-time favorite role of citizen—and it would not be able to ignore things in what for want of a better designation I will call the personal realm, things such as character development. (1979, 84)

Yet thought about curriculum today continues to be framed in terms of the academic disciplines, the "knowledge base," and the structure of knowledge without addressing even those forms of living or activity that could cause, prevent, or help accidental mothers and fathers, battered wives and battering husbands, and unwanted, abused, or neglected children whom professional educators have lately became wont to label "at risk."[8] Thus narrowly framed by curriculum theory, educational ends and means often support and become "forces in society which say that women should be nice, play safe, have low professional expectations, drown in love and forget about work, live through others, and stay in the places assigned to us" (Rich 1979, 234).

We all know what these places are. What could the possibility of solitude mean to women in a world governed and miseducated by such forces? If we take seriously Martin's alternative conception of curriculum as embracing "forms of living or activity," what curricular value might solitude hold for women's efforts at learning "the courage to be 'different'; not to be continuously available to others when we need time for ourselves and our work" (Rich 1979, 234)? These are questions I am asking here.

Adrienne Rich in particular has faulted the central place given to "ethical models of the self-denying wife and mother" in the curriculum of girls' upbringing and schooling. For alternative ethical models of women, she has looked back to her own life as a student in an all girls' school,

> where the majority of the faculty were independent, unmarried women. One or two held doctorates, but had been forced by the Depression (and by the fact that they were women) to take secondary school teaching jobs. These women cared a great deal about the life of the mind, and they gave a great deal of time and energy—beyond any limit of teaching hours—to those of us who showed special interest or ability...we held those women in a kind of respect which even then we dimly perceived was not generally accorded to women in the world at large. They were vital individuals, defined not by their relationships but by their personalities, and although under the pressure of the culture we were all certain we wanted to get married, their lives did not appear empty or dreary to us. In a kind of cognitive dissonance, we knew they were "old maids" and therefore supposed to be bitter and lonely; yet we saw them vigorously involved with life. (1979, 237-238)

Thinking of my own experiences in church-governed girls' high schools and a women's college, I could say the same about not just the "old maids" but also the nuns, divorced mothers of grown children, and widows who taught me with uncommon moral passion, intellectual commitment, and physical vitality during the late 1960s and early 1970s. Rich does recognize that, however helpful or necessary, such models are by themselves insufficient for a curriculum which would foster young women's responsibility toward themselves. A broader rethinking of curriculum will be necessary with this aim and such women's lives in mind, for "despite [these teachers'] existence as alternate models of women, the *content* of the education they gave us in no way prepared us to survive as women in a world organized by and for men" (1979, 238).

I will examine the concept "solitude," therefore, with the purpose of illuminating its utility as a critical and constructive tool for such a broad rethinking of curriculum. Drawing illustrative cases from my own experiences of solitude and from contemporary autobiographical accounts of other single women's experiences living alone, specifically those by May Sarton and by Alice Koller, my examination will begin with a close look at the concept's ambiguity. In the critical light of Martin's more recent curriculum inquiry, about what it has meant in the past to be an educated woman, I will untangle two distinct meanings of solitude, its "task" sense and its "achievement" sense,[9] and clarify their complex relationship to each other. This chapter will then conclude by drawing from my conceptual case studies of women's solitude some curriculum questions that merit further consideration by curriculum theorists and designers who care about the quality of women's lives. In sum, what could it mean to become educated about, in, and for women's solitude? Without such education, whatever its curriculum may be, how can we women learn to choose our own lives? And how can men learn to respect, understand, and support our choices?

Solitude as Task:
Being Alone, Living Alone

In its simplest sense, solitude means being alone. Like being married or being a good friend, being alone usually requires some work, no matter how, why, or where one is alone. For it is possible to be alone miserably, tolerably, or well. Avoiding and curtailing unwanted solitude while uncoupled can be work; making and sustaining wanted solitude within a caring life is work; indeed, coping with or enhancing the quality of any substantial solitude takes work. Definitively, being alone imposes a demand that one claim responsibility toward oneself, which usually entails some "grappling with hard work," as Rich has recognized.

Though at its best often playful or restful, solitude is in this sense a task, and the task can take many forms, depending upon its context and purpose. A woman can be alone in "a room of one's own" for pursuit of her own authentically chosen purposes, as Virginia Woolf has urged; a wife can take time out from a busy life of caring for husband and children to be alone, as Anne Morrow Lindbergh does in *Gift from the Sea*—if, like Woolf or Lindbergh, she has the privileged means to do so. One can be alone in meditation or in relationship to the natural world, as Annie Dillard is in *Pilgrim at Tinker Creek*; one can be alone as one's own psychoanalyst, a writer and reader of one's own journal, as Joanna Field is in *A Life of One's Own*. A woman may, like Barbara McClintock, depend upon her own "capacity to be alone" if engaged in scholarship that others resist taking seriously, as Evelyn Fox Keller recounts in *A Feeling for the Organism* (1983). A woman can be alone in her sexual or racial identity, or in the courage of her moral commitment, even among her sisters or comrades; such is the case of Anna Julia Cooper in *A Voice from the South*, an early advocate for the education of African-American women; such too is Goldman's case in *Living My Life*, for she was a lone woman and feminist among sexually exploitive men anarchists. A woman can be alone in bearing responsibility for others, as single mothers usually are, and even married ones can be. She can find herself alone, jostled by mean crowds on a city street after a violent marriage and abusive psychiatric treatment: a shopping-bag lady. One can be alone on a stage or in a library, alone within a stressful marriage or difficult family, alone in any number of ways. The possible kinds, qualities, and conditions of solitude, in this simple task sense of being alone, are perhaps nearly endless. The task's meaning for women inevitably depends upon its context and purpose.

Living alone is therefore obviously not the only way of being alone, but it is one clear case, one that can encompass many other ways of being alone. It is the one instance I focus upon here because of its particular significance for single women. May Sarton wrote about the task of living alone almost twenty years ago, during the Nixon-Watergate era, in *Journal of a Solitude* (1973). Alice Koller has written about it in *An Unknown Woman* (1981) and *The Stations of Solitude* (1990).[10] Of course, I am myself now living alone as I write this, albeit not with the same sure sense of wholeness and permanent commitment to this choice that both these women have expressed.

Whereas Sarton begins her *Journal* as a way of making "an open place, a place for meditation" (p. 12) within which she might find herself (or as Koller would say, "unbind" and "stand open") in solitude, Koller writes her book as a critical retrospection upon her lifetime's task of solitude: "a philosophical inquiry into what it is to be a person: how one becomes a person, and what it is that one has become. I am teaching, not by telling, but by displaying the process. By writing what it is for me to be solitary, I am sketching the outlines of the life of solitude everyone else lives. Can live, if you choose" (p. 67).

For me, at present, living alone is not an ideal end for either myself or women generally, but a transitional task, a deliberate rite of passage between "successive selves."[11] Like Maya, the divorced teacher whom Dana Crowley Jack quotes in her psychological study of women and depression, *Silencing the Self*, "I'm on a search trip for what a woman is really like" (1990, 183). A home of my own—that is, a tiny but solitary rented space for my own living—has seemed the first necessary place for conducting my search after ceasing to be a wife. Twenty or more years younger than Sarton and Koller, approaching my fortieth birthday, I do not know yet if such solitude is the only necessary place, or even if it will turn out to be the most important one for me to investigate on my "search trip." I need to know, first, what does it mean for a woman—perhaps I should say, for me—to live alone well, or at least tolerably, rather than miserably?

Jane Roland Martin has addressed women like Sarton, Koller, and myself, who are intent upon our own self-understanding, development, and education (if not also other women's self-understanding, development, and education) in *Reclaiming a Conversation* (1985). This work is her comparative philosophical critique of the ideal of the educated woman as variously conceived by Plato, Jean-Jacques Rousseau, Mary Wollstonecraft, Catharine Beecher, and Charlotte Perkins Gilman. Despite these classic and feminist Western thinkers' vast and illuminating differences of view, they all conceived the educated woman as distinctively *other*-centered: as guardians (with men) of the just state, wives, daughters, homemakers, and mother-citizens. In this idealized company, the woman living in solitude is clearly an anomaly.

Wollstonecraft, Beecher, and Gilman themselves all lived alone as single women for substantial portions of their lives, however. So women living in solitude would be foolish to assume without further inquiry that Martin's conversation about the ideal of the educated woman is necessarily irrelevant to our own culturally neglected life situation, even if this conversation has not made such relevance theoretically specific. What new theoretical turns could this conversation about education take if its participants specifically attended to the practical situation of women's singleness in solitude?

Martin's critical analysis demonstrates how, in all but the first of the ideals she examines, the "reproductive processes of society" acquire particular educational importance that is overlooked when women in the context of marriage, home, and family are philosophically neglected. These processes may at first seem irrelevant to single women's task of living alone. For within the marital familial context they are primarily *other-nurturing* in aim; they include "not simply conception and birth, but the rearing of children to more or less maturity, and associated activities such as tending the sick, taking care of family needs, and running a household" (p. 5). Martin points out that, for all the thinkers whose ideals she studies, the just state depends upon someone's performance of such duties, although the ends and means of liberal education today fail to take this fact into account. She has not yet considered what particular meaning or educational importance the reproductive processes might have if the experiences of single women undertaking the task of solitude were seriously examined. Does the task of solitude free women from participation in the reproductive processes of society? Or bind single women to reproductive efforts different from those required of women engaged in family life?

Martin's critique of the ideal of the educated woman cites a tension between the reproductive processes of society and what she calls the "productive processes of society," which include "political and cultural activities as well as economic ones" (p. 5). It is obviously possible (I would say even reasonable) to argue that the reproductive processes themselves have political, cultural, and economic purposes and consequences, or conversely that the productive processes can become settings for sexual activities and abuses, provision of means for children's livelihood, workers' own development, illness and injury, collegial care-taking and affiliation, even housekeeping. Yet, every ideal Martin considers in her account, except Gilman's, makes a strong distinction between these two kinds of processes the basis for division of labor within the just state: in Plato's case, division by class; in Rousseau's, Wollstonecraft's, and Beecher's, division by gender. Like Plato's female guardians, but unlike Rousseau's Sophie and Beecher's Sarah in Martin's account, a single woman who takes up the task of living alone inevitably confronts, even if she neither needs nor chooses to participate in, the political, cultural, and economic processes of life that Martin has named "productive." Does women's task of solitude impart any distinctive meaning or value to these productive processes?

As we shall see, the autobiographical cases of living alone that Sarton and Koller have narrated demonstrate the conduct of an interdependent relationship between the reproductive and productive processes as a difficult task that their solitude entails. These single women's cases also demonstrate critical differentiations among these processes' possible meanings and values within the context of their solitude. Hence this study may also suggest new notions of what it could mean for a woman to be educated, notions that are "new" insofar as they differ from those ideals which the participants in Martin's conversation have advanced.

Living Alone Miserably:
Sarton's Reproductive Processes

May Sarton, a poet and novelist blessed with independent income and rural property, justly views her own solitude as "the great, the greatest luxury," which means that "therefore my responsibility is huge. To use time well and be all that I can in whatever years are left to me" (p. 40). Yet as she approaches her sixtieth birthday, her whole life becomes miserable when the passionate difficulties of her sexual affair with X catapult her into a deep and relentless depression that brings her "close to suicide more than once" (p. 57). Her depression persists from one September to the next, at which point she finally ends the affair. Her entire *Journal of a Solitude* is her self-critical and socially critical record of the struggle she wages throughout this psychological depression, of her self-imposed domestic isolation while approaching the difficult decision to separate from X. Although Sarton has written other journals of happier times, her entries in this one form a series of almost Wordsworthian "conversations" (p. 11) struck up between a lone troubled woman and her well-kept country house, concluding with the haunting declaration, "Once more the house and I are alone" (p. 208). We might read this poet's prose text as a contemporary woman's artful revision of that familiar solitary male poetic figure who, once past "the hour/Of thoughtless youth," often hears "The still, sad music of humanity" (Wordsworth 1967, 154). Or we might read it with more practical purposes, as an educated woman's autobiographical case study of living alone miserably in "a corrupt country, of a corrupt vision," with "such a sense of death and of being buried under the weight of technocracy" (p. 62).

Read in this latter vein, Sarton's *Journal* demonstrates that when integral to single women's task of solitude rather than definitive of girls' and women's work as daughters, wives, and mothers, the reproductive processes of society may not be primarily other-nurturing as Martin's study depicts them; indeed, in the case of single women living alone, they must be *self-sustaining*. Although contraception, pregnancy, abortion, and even childbirth surely concern many single women, the reproductive processes need not entail, even within a woman's sexual life, these conventional feminine preoccupations with the conception, birth, nurture, and rearing of children that are central assumptions in those ideals of the educated woman which Martin has studied. For such preoccupations with children most typically (though not always) arise from the demands of marriage and motherhood. The task of living alone may or may not include resistance against such demands and against the ideology of "compulsory heterosexuality."[12] In Sarton's case, it appears to.

In her formulation, this task aims for a "wholeness" that conventional expectations of married women inevitably undermine: "We are whole or have intimations of what it means to be whole when the entire being—spirit, mind, nerves, flesh, the body itself—are concentrated toward a single end...wholeness does not, of course, mean being right in a deduction or an action. It does mean not being divided in spirit by conscience, by doubt, by fear" (pp. 55–56). Since men's wholeness so often depends upon their wives' and other women's performance of the reproductive processes that sustain men's spirits, their uncluttered space and time for mental pursuits, their nerves, their flesh, their bodies rather than their wives' own, Sarton observes this attribute to be typically "masculine." She further notes that it is typically accompanied by "a certain simple-mindedness," an inclination to "hew to the heart of the matter," perhaps even "a sensibility limited in some areas" (pp. 55–56).

Living alone to provide herself such space for her own wholeness, she still expends extraordinary effort to sustain herself against the force of her own psychological misery throughout her affair with X. In her *Journal*, moreover, she considers alternatives to heterosexual marriage for women who are intent upon developing their own work without loss of intimacy: "Professional women do need wives and many have joked about this fact. And we have seen instances of homosexual relationships where it seemed to work: Gertrude Stein and Alice B. Toklas come to mind. But the woman wife of a professional woman has to be extraordinarily selfless and still have a strong ego to keep her dignity—and Toklas really came into her own as a personality only after Gertrude Stein's death" (p. 56). In the absence of her own wife and of her own willingness to be anyone's wife,[13] Sarton's self-sustaining reproductive processes make up the most difficult aspects of her task of living alone. For her, solitude becomes an effort, against considerable odds, to claim her own sexuality without sacrificing her self.

The self-sustaining reproductive processes of Sarton's solitary life break down most dramatically for her in January, within the context of precisely this effort, to make for herself a long-distance, loving sexual life with X. Then, so too for a time does her productive capacity as a writer break down. She writes on January 12th of a "frightful attack of temper, of nerves, of resentment against X, followed by the usual boomerang of acute anxiety," and explains, "I was in such anxiety that my hair was soaked through. The only other time I have experienced this was during an attack of acute physical pain, when I had diverticulosis and was in a hospital for a week" (p. 82). Although this attack seems exceptionally strong and causes lingering "harsh thoughts toward [her own] anger" (p. 85), the depression for her is not exceptional. In the absence of any close friend with whom she might think aloud about what she is going through emotionally and thereby clarify her situation, she confesses, "I rarely sleep through a night here," finding herself once again "forced to try to come to terms with myself and to face the destroyer and breaker in me. I do not feel remorse so much as shame" (p. 85). Hurting from her explosive exchange with X, who "complains a lot about the job" and seems repeatedly unable to offer her own work the support she wants, she cannot read a critical review of it in the *Times* without feeling "bruised...like being tripped and thrown to the ground" (p. 85). She records three days later that "This has been a bad week. I have accomplished next to nothing, wasted time...and been depressed" (p. 86). Even receiving her latest book of poems fresh from the publisher does not lift her spirits, as she reports the next day, "I felt let down to be alone with this newborn babe, to have no one to whom I could show it" (p. 207).

Not surprisingly, she ends her *Journal* with a summary of her affair with X that describes it as fraught with "professional deformations" and as lacking a "foundation for understanding" as well as "time to make one" (p. 207). She therefore finally embraces her own isolation as "a return to some deep self that has been too absorbed and too battered to function for a long time" (p. 207). Her conclusion in September that "that self tells me I was meant to live alone, meant to write the poems for others" (p. 207), may reflect her much earlier assessment in January that

> I have been trying to say radical things gently so that they may
> penetrate without shock. The fear of homosexuality is so great
> that it took courage to write *Mrs. Stevens*, to write a novel
> about a woman homosexual who is not a sex maniac, a drunk-
> ard, a drug-taker, or in any way repulsive; to portray a homo-
> sexual who is neither pitiable nor disgusting, without senti-
> mentality; and to face the truth that such a life is rarely happy,
> a life where art must become the primary motivation, for love
> is never going to fulfill in the usual sense. (pp. 90–91)

Sarton never in any way signifies X's sex; perhaps significantly, her
portrait of X paints a perfectly credible lover as either man or woman
(even a perfectly credible husband in a commuter marriage). This
degenderization of the sexual lover X doubtless reflects Sarton's belief
that "roles should no longer be assigned on the basis of sex or of any
preconceived idea of marriage, but should grow organically from the
specific needs of two human beings and their capacities and gifts" (p.
122). Yet the "truth" she cites in this passage about *Mrs. Stevens* is
notably the same sad (and, I suspect, questionable) one she resolves
"to face" at the end of her affair with X and of her *Journal*: the necessity
of a solitude that abandons the possibility of love to the possibilities of
her work, that subordinates her reproductive to her productive life.

How can this be when Sarton paradoxically conceives the task of
solitude as "one of the ways toward communion" (p. 103)? She further
develops her concept of this task through her compelling metaphor of
the solitary artist as the New England lighthouse keeper:

> It is an age where more and more human beings are caught up
> in lives where fewer and fewer real choices exist. The fact that
> a middle-aged, single woman, without any vestige of family
> left, lives in this house in a silent village and is responsible
> only to her own soul means something. The fact that she is a
> writer and can tell where she is and what it is like on the pil-
> grimage inward can be of comfort. It is comforting to know
> there are lighthouse keepers on rocky islands along the coast.
> Sometimes, when I have been for a walk after dark and see my
> house lighted up, looking so alive, I feel that my presence here
> is worth all the Hell. (p. 40)

Personal isolation that confounds the public-private distinction thus
seems to constitute the parti of her literary work's design and, given
her view of the writer as "an instrument for experiencing" (p. 77), also
the parti of her life's design: "From my isolation to the isolation of

someone somewhere who will find my work there exists a true communion" (p. 67). With this theory of her own artistic ends and means, wedded as it were to domestic isolation, Sarton seems actually to think she requires the experience of living alone miserably, seems to think her art requires her depression: "With the return of cheerfulness I feel a sense of loss. The poems no longer flow out. I am more 'normal' again, no longer that fountain of tears and intense feeling" (p. 49). She furthermore holds to "the truth that whatever good effect my work may have comes from my own sense of isolation and vulnerability. The house is open in a way that no house where a family lives and interacts can be. My life, often frightfully lonely, interacts with a whole lot of people I do not know and never will know" (p. 115). She further analyzes her feeling that solitude becomes a source of "dismay" for her "when I lose the sense of my life as connected (as if by an aerial) to many, many other lives whom I do not even know and cannot ever know"; extending her lighthouse metaphor, she rhapsodizes: "The signals go out and some in all the time" (p. 40).

Thus Sarton's autobiographical reflections upon the task of solitude as a struggle for wholeness pose some complicated moral questions about women's sexual and artistic lives, about possible relationships between our reproductive and productive activities, about their privacy and public visibility. For a depressing isolation is the ultimate bedrock of her reproductive life, which she makes the foundational concept of her productive life, and upon which she defines the disparate human communions of sexual love, art, and solitude.

Sarton's *Journal of a Solitude* does, however, hint at other undeveloped possibilities for understanding the task of living alone, imaginable only in the absence of her anguish about X. Despite her romantic belief in isolation's necessity for artistic productivity, she does seem at times to take a more realistic view: that the self-sustaining reproductive processes of solitude definitively involve learning to recognize, take seriously, anticipate, evaluate, and attend to her own needs for health, truth, love, and moral purpose as well as for moments of beauty, serenity, play, and constructive achievement.

For Sarton, the aims and demands of her productive life define the shape of her reproductive life at its best, upon which their fulfillment depends. "Ordering seeds is my reward for finishing the income-tax figures," she explains, for "however terrible the storms may be, if one's life has a sufficiently stable and fruitful structure, one is helped to withstand their devastating aftereffects. For most people their job does this—provides a saving routine in time of stress. I have to create my own to survive. And now it is time to fetch the mail and get the car started" (p. 84). She feels "cluttered when there is no time to analyze experience. That is the silt—unexplored experience that literally chokes the mind. Too much comes into this house" (p. 160). She fashions some of her own self-sustaining reproductive processes in deliberate response to the persistent demands that come from her many productive affiliations, the excess of "books I am asked to read and comment on, manuscripts, letters, an old friend who wants my opinion about a journal" (p. 160).

The rare, brief moments when Sarton's depression does lift come with a break away from isolation, with meaningful human connections other than her affair; most of these are persons who, unlike X, somehow support her productive life or otherwise help to sustain the conditions it requires. Thus, the reproductive processes that abate her misery do not for her entail an absolute self-reliance, for they do include getting help when resources for her private self-nurture seem insufficient. In this spirit, Sarton takes a working vacation every summer at the home of Ann Thorp on Greenings Island in Maine, "the one unchangeable place in my life...the place of renewal and of safety, where for a little while there will be no harm or attack and, while every sense is nourished, the soul rests" (p. 171). In this spirit, too, though disdainful of *House and Garden* perfection that is "empty of poetry" (p. 51), she depends upon an "ambience [of]...order and beauty" (p. 12) around her as she works at home, a simple and unpretentious ambience visible in photographs throughout her *Journal*. This domestic ambience is, however, itself the purchased product of another woman's labors:

> Mildred is here cleaning. I think of all the years since she first began to come here and how her presence, so quiet, humorous, and distinguished, has blessed all that is here. The solitude is animated but not broken. I sit at my desk and work better because I know her sensitive hands are busy dusting and making order again. And when we sit down at ten for coffee and a talk, it is never small talk....She and I have lived through a lot of joy and grief together and now they are "woven fine" through all that we exchange. (p. 25)

Her friend Anne Woodson brings her flowers when her latest book comes out, another gesture that nurtures her productive life. Sarton further reflects, "I never see Anne without learning something" (p. 36). On other occasions, though not frequently, she welcomes this painter-friend, and other painter-friends, too, as house guests: "The criticism we give each other, the way we look at each other's work, is pure and full of joy, a spontaneous response" (p. 127).

At the same time, perhaps because of her inclination to learn by "being in relation to," the self-sustaining reproductive processes that constitute her task of solitude also include her occasional voluntary exertion to care for others who are not her own intimates or confidantes, but persons with whom she has had productive relations. For example, she tends her gardener, whom her *Journal* both narratively and photographically depicts as a sort of "solitary reaper,"[14] Perley Cole, during his "terribly lonely" dying days, separated from his wife, at a nursing home; she recollects that "while he scythed and trimmed, I struggled in somewhat the same way at my desk here, and we were each aware of the companionship" (p. 14). Similarly, she corresponds with her readers who express "the despair…of many middle-aged women" (p. 46), listens sympathetically to former students' and other young writers' struggles.

Such autobiographical vignettes suggest that Sarton may herself be mistaken about the artistic necessity of her unremitting isolation and misery. But she is surely right to question the value of a sexual life that is perpetually at odds with, rather than supportive of, her productive life. The task of solitude that Sarton represents through her own account of living alone miserably is to develop through practice those self-sustaining reproductive processes that can nurture a desirable quality in one's chosen productive life.

Living Alone Miserably and Well:
Koller's Productive Processes

In sharp contrast to Sarton, Alice Koller has upon reflection embraced "chastity" as "psychologically sound" (1981, 226) within her own context of heterosexuality and thus has avoided the erotic turmoil that frames and disrupts Sarton's solitary life. Whereas Sarton's house provides the central symbol of her solitude, Koller conceives the task of solitude as a journey: "A destination, some purpose sufficiently powerful, propels you into a journey. There are stopping places on routes designed by persons other than you for their economic profit. From the start of the journey to its end, you pay" (1990, x). The "stopping places" of this journey are *The Stations of Solitude*, which "mark out a repeatable line of travel" (p. xi). The task of solitude is a journey both philosophically and practically challenging for Koller, but one "that anyone can choose to undertake" (p. xi):

In circuiting the stations of solitude, your destination is the kind of person you wish to become. The line of travel is the process of shaping a human being, and the stations are stopping places in the process. Except perhaps for the early stations, the route is ad libitum: you move from one to another station at will, not because it is next in line. And there are circuits within the circuit: you will return to some stations many times because the person you yourself are designing is not yet completed the first time through. (p. xi)

Reflecting that "the station of solitude that seems to have my name on it" is "the moneying station" (p. 184), she emphasizes that "at every station…you pay" (p. xi). For she has suffered acutely from lack of the very same "luxury" that Sarton has had, the financial means to pursue her own work full-time at home alone.

Although Koller's books, especially *An Unknown Woman*, give accounts of what might be termed psychological depression, precipitated by her approach to middle age with Ph.D. but neither marriage nor career, her economic depression is most profound and enduring:

I've lived so long at the very edge of poverty, even for a time in its depths, that all erotic longing has vanished from me. I find myself not simply neutral but faintly repelled at the thought of physical contact. Other urgencies appropriate my attention: will I have money for food tomorrow, can I keep electricity and phone connected, pay the rent, repair the car, buy gas? My daily existence is far too insecure for me to have room in my thinking, my feeling, for a man, even to notice him more than fleetingly if he stood before me. (p. 197)

Such is the "privilege" of a single woman with a Ph.D. in philosophy earned from Harvard during the late 1950s, "when professors could arrange teaching jobs for their male students as deliberately as they chose their dinner guests" (p. 147). Koller observes that "long before they submitted their dissertations, sometimes five or seven years before, most of my male classmates were already teaching at Princeton, Berkeley, Michigan, Johns Hopkins" (p. 147). Not until after graduate school does she become aware of this active help that she has missed. What has been the upshot of this initial systemic injustice and its aftermath of futile academic job-hunting—even after she has published a widely taught and much talked-of scholarly work in philosophy of language?

The task of solitude has required Koller to learn to draw a conceptual distinction between two kinds of productive processes, her philosophical work and her jobs. Akin to the distinction that this task requires us to draw between the other-nurturing and the self-sustaining reproductive processes, this distinction between *self-defined* and *other-defined* productivity also has immense practical significance for women's solitude:

> It can take years, half a lifetime, to split apart the two ideas of work and a job. Once you know what your work is, you probably won't immediately be paid for doing it. To get the money that will buy time to let you do your work, you have to give up some of the rest of your time: you need a job. But you need it only to pay bills: rent, heat, electricity, water, phone, food, medical, car repairs, gas. People who work are constantly aware that time they spend at jobs is letting them buy time to work. (p. 139)

Koller therefore names and conceptualizes the productive processes of living alone as stations which force this split between work and job and engage her in conflict (brought about by this distinction): "working," "moneying," and "colliding."

After imaginatively hustling for jobs as a free-lance writer—"moneying"—for most of her twenty-five-year working life, Koller counts "only five years of having enough money to live on without constantly having to try to earn it so I could do my work. Since I consider people to be successful when their money comes only from their work, I can't at all count myself among them: I have had to give up 80 percent of my days merely to survive" (p. 184). The consequences of this ongoing, divisive crisis within the productive processes of Koller's life have reverberated through the reproductive processes of her life as well. Like me, she has never been able to afford the down payment or the accumulation of savings necessary to own her own home. The reproductive processes of living alone have thus for her included dealing with numerous landlords, moving in and out of numerous homes, learning how to repair them and prepare them for changes of weather, looking after her own physical protection against violence, becoming "at home" with herself under ever-changing circumstances.

"During the same twenty-five years, I have moved sixteen times" (p. 69), she explains, and "each moving on disconnects me further, loosens me link by link, from the continuities I still seek" (p. 94). More than the household management that most women are expected to learn and practice from girlhood onward, the reproductive processes of solitude have for Koller meant surviving mean bouts with poverty and homelessness: packing up her belongings, selling them or putting them into storage, inviting herself onto friends' couches and into their spare rooms, receiving their gifts and loans while hustling for a job. Koller appropriately names and conceptualizes her own self-sustaining reproductive processes as the stations of "homing," "loving," "singling," "connecting," and "recessing." Some may suggest that Koller's canine companions should disqualify her from the category of "living alone," but she herself has noted that her constant moving and hustling have left her little time for making and keeping a best friend or lover. Doubtless she considers herself a solitary because, whether living with her dogs as her only companions or mourning their deaths, she has spent most of her days "almost totally devoid of other human beings" (p. 263) and confesses that "some evenings I have very much wanted to be with someone close and cannot: he or she is too far away, forever gone, not yet found" (p. 264). Thus the quality of her reproductive life falls with the quality of her productive life. Through her account of living alone miserably, Koller represents the task of solitude as a journey marked out by certain economically fixed stations. Profoundly different from Sarton's solitude, her task is to find ways of resolving the contradiction between one's chosen work and one's paying jobs. It is to fashion, somehow, a kind of employment that can provide both productive fulfillment and adequate economic means to support those intimacies and continuities that are essential to any truly self-sustaining reproductive life.

Koller does meet the challenge of this enormous task for one uninterrupted interval of two years. She actually lives alone well when a government grant finances pursuit of her self-defined work at home:

> The project was one I had invented. It could proceed along lines that I alone could explore, modifying them as I worked, choosing what to read and when to read it, choosing whether to work in the libraries at Yale or Connecticut College or whether to carry the books and journals to my own study so that I might from time to time lay them aside to go outdoors and play with Logos, choosing which days to work and which not, choosing my own hours, responsible only to one single deadline: October 31, 1965, when I was to deliver to Washington a final report that would throw significant light on a problem of far-reaching importance that had not, until I outlined it, been adequately addressed. (p. 47)

Experiencing no contradiction within the productive processes of her life during this two-year interval, no opposition between her self-defined work and an other-defined job, Koller finds herself actually

> living in joy. A life of days in which my freedom was palpable; a life without other persons but also without constant longing for them; a life in which the motives of human beings were accessible for the asking or through patient observation; a life in which I weighed my small but obtainable goals and found them worth pursuing or else to be discarded; a life in which, secure at its very center, I looked out onto a world that was comprehensible, so that it was either malleable to my purposes, or else I was able to stop wanting the thing I could not have. (pp. 47–48)

Having purchased a second puppy to keep Logos company while she works, economically sustained in "the profession I invented, writing my thinking" (p. 69) and in "the life I was shaping to fit me" (p. 47), Koller makes her home her workplace. With her life thus arranged, she need not struggle against any frustrating division between the productive and reproductive processes of her life. Nor does she need to struggle against any division between the other-nurturing and the self-sustaining reproductive processes in which she is engaged. Her life alone in such circumstances forms a seamless, integrated whole, albeit only temporarily. This brief respite from her lifetime of solitary productive poverty is the only case of living alone well that I have met in this study.

Living Alone Tolerably: Learning Wilderness Wisdom

These two clear cases of living alone miserably teach us that a woman may drown in isolation as easily as she may (to repeat Rich's phrase) "drown in love." Such is not my own case now, but it was without question my case when I first moved to Maine, with help from neither family nor friends, emotionally exhausted after separating from my husband and handing in my dissertation, and still facing the divorce itself. By spring, my life had become entirely absorbed in the busy excitement of my new productive tasks. Being "from away" (as people say in Maine), I had still developed no sense of myself coming "home" to myself each night, and I could not help feeling depressed when greeted by the reproductive void that was my chosen solitude. I had no regrets about ending my marriage, but I did have nightmares about drowning off the coast of Mount Desert Island. Sarton captures the feeling well when she explains, "I feel myself sucked down into the quicksand that isolation sometimes creates, a sense of drowning, of being literally *engulfed*" (p. 107).

Hiking a mountain by myself on the same sunny summer day that I filed my divorce complaint and summons with the Maine district court, I had to hide from a truckload of drunk, loudly joking and cursing, barebacked men on the peak; I feared what they might do to me. On the way down after they had left, I was shaken. I tripped on a rock, my whole body fell, and I sprained an ankle. My ankle took months to heal because I did not care for it properly at first. I had a lot to learn about the task of solitude. But this wilderness hiking event supplanted the feeling of drowning to become a metaphor by which I began to conceptualize that difficult task for myself as I set about figuring out what I must yet learn.

Utterly alienated from all notions of homemaking and leisure-making after my marriage, even for myself, I found it helpful to think of these obviously necessary activities together with, rather than separate from, my working life. I started to think about my task of living alone as a complex, deliberately thought-out wilderness expedition, or series of such expeditions. I thought of the task's reproductive activities as akin to those of preparing my body and backpack for a long hike, talking with more experienced hikers who knew something of the region's beauties and hazards, studying my maps and compass, getting the best possible weather predictions, outfitting myself appropriately in view of them, trusting myself to judge my own fitness and skill for various paces and ways of going, looking after my own safety as well as the environment's, setting up my own camp with or without carefully chosen trail companions, taking care not to stray beyond earshot of the stream's rapids, and so on. I thought of my productive working life as my actual movement along a precipitous but beautiful wilderness trail toward some destination which I could locate and make some educated guesses about, but had not yet glimpsed. The height of the destination, I reflected, would matter to me very little, but what I could see and hear there must be worth seeing and hearing.

Studying Sarton's and Koller's cases of living alone miserably have proven instructive for me as I have used this metaphor to develop my own self-taught curriculum in solitary living. I am still engaged in this pursuit, at a level of metaphoric elaboration that, however helpful to me, would be tedious to explain here and should in any case be more or less discernible beneath the surface of my autobiographical case. For, disquieted by Sarton's and Koller's cases of living alone miserably, I am now also critically studying two instances of living alone which are for the present unburdened by so much isolation as theirs: my friend Kate's and my own. She and I take day hikes together frequently.

Our reproductive and productive lives partly overlap with each other—which is not to say they are well integrated or easy. She lives alone, and I still live alone, too—sometimes amazingly well and sometimes miserably, but in general we both live alone neither well nor miserably. We live alone tolerably. We do so with an acute, shared awareness of possibilities at both extremes, and we approach the task of solitude accordingly. On one hand, we repeatedly take prudent cautions against the everpresent threats of psychological and economic depression; on the other hand, we continually question and imagine what it might mean, for each of us with our different purposes, characters, and tastes, to live well. Such inquiring dialogue is mutually educative, animated by our different nationalities and class backgrounds. Though our religious backgrounds also differ, we do have in common unforgettable experiences of sex-segregated schooling by nuns, and we both teach in the same college of education.[15] Although our subject specialties within the education and women's studies professions differ, we both are engaged, as a matter of conscience and sometimes precipitously, in gender studies of education.

Unlike Sarton and X, we are not lovers contemplating the possibility of becoming a couple. I am more obviously like Sarton at her *Journal*'s conclusion, since I have lately uncoupled with the intention of trying to effect "a return to some deep self" (p. 207) by living alone. Rather than seeking for a way of accommodating each other, Kate and I are separately engaged, just as Koller advises, in a "course of thinking, feeling, understanding, deciding" that each of us is herself devising "to shape to [herself], to make fit [herself], as only [she] know[s] how best to do" (p. 5). But neither of us acts from a defensive premise of "Lone Ranger" omniscience about our own life situations, either. Instead, unlike both Sarton and Koller in this respect, we seek greater clarity about our own thoughts, feelings, understandings, decisions by sharing our experiences and different views, examining them together, and questioning each other daily.

In such conversation, Kate has aptly characterized our solitudes in exactly the same way that others commonly characterize the day-to-day existence of working wives and mothers: as a "juggling act." For in some sense, each of us is her own wife and mother. In terms of my own metaphor, some stretches on the trail are so rugged I can't keep my balance if I don't take off my backpack and somehow push it a distance beyond where I am actually standing, so that I can move forward unencumbered. For although we are each other's friends, constantly nurturing and learning from each other, we are responsible to and for ourselves alone. Each of us housekeeps for, decides and provides for, feeds, washes, clothes, shelters, drives, disciplines, looks after, and lives with, herself alone. Neither of us can afford to pay for the sort of household help that Sarton is able to hire for herself, nor do our productive lives afford much time for us to do such extensive household work ourselves, so rarely during a university term do we achieve the domestic "order and beauty" (Sarton 1973, 12) upon which she depends for comfort; I have come to think of such household work and its marvelous results as a vacation treat to look forward to. We have, however, shared with each other our common need for what Sarton most deliberately seeks in solitude, away from "the interruptions, nourishing and maddening," which inevitably occur in our jobs as university faculty: that is, "time alone in which to explore what is happening or has happened" (p. 11).

Thus, despite our friendship, we do spend much of our time at home completely alone—oftentimes not as much as we would like, but sometimes perhaps too much. Given an entire week alone, I punctuate my work with a lot of reading. But when I come home to my empty apartment after teaching nightshift classes, overflowing with thoughts and feelings too complicated and too many to name in one phone call to Kate or anyone else, I now soothe myself by learning and practicing simple folk songs and classical themes on a rosewood recorder before going to bed. After my cat wakes me up for her morning affections, I often write and draw in my journal, have a sort of breakfast conversation with myself while listening to music or the news. Three mornings a week, though, I join two friends and a half-dozen other women agemates at ballet class instead, a euphoric ritual in itself, upon whose joyful rigors they and I have come to depend for inner resistance.[16] Kate has spoken in a similar vein of devouring novels, watching BBC on PBS, listening to opera and rock, writing letters, cooking experimentally, entertaining guests, pumping iron. Like Koller's runs with her dogs through the woods or Sarton's gardening and visiting, such stopping times for leisurely activities that are aesthetic, physical, or expressive are part of the reproductive task of sustaining ourselves in solitude. But they are not all of it.

However alone we are, neither of us lives in isolation as profound as Sarton's and Koller's. We engage in many reproductive processes that are *simultaneously* self-sustaining and other-nurturing. I have become friendly with my neighbors, a couple in their eighties, across the street. Kate and I each have friends and family with whom we particularly work at staying closely in touch across the country (in Kate's case also around the world), whom we attempt to care for long-distance. She and I also share a small, growing circle of agemate friends here in eastern Maine, single and uncoupling university women, feminists of various sorts, whose comings together make us not yet quite a community. These are special friends with whom Kate and I separately share particular intellectual interests related to our work or politics, with whom she plays squash or I study dance, with whom we both take long walks and drives down to the coastal islands or to Portland or Boston; one or two friends with whom we occasionally go to meetings, lectures, plays, concerts, art shows, bookstores, suppers—as the severe limits on our time and money permit. We regularly keep tabs on each other's health and spirits, on each other's work, our difficulties and successes at caring for ourselves and "coping."

With these few friends, we make our birthday and holiday celebrations, have weekend dinners, and talk and talk into the early morning hours, thoughtfully sharing our lives with each other. We tell each other about our past marriages, our divorces, families, friends, jobs; we discuss our sexuality, scholarship, feminism, politics, the arts, the university. We ask each other questions, sometimes serious and difficult, sometimes whimsical and ridiculous: Should Kate return home to Australia and run for public office? Should I temporarily return to high school teaching so that I can pay off my student loans? How and when could she and I best go about developing a graduate program in gender and education at Maine? Should we try? Could and should our friend try to return to scientific research? Could we make *Women of Summer* happen again, in Maine? Should all of us together leave our academic careers and commit ourselves to collective work with the pro-choice movement? Could we do something more imaginative than we are now doing with our collective resources to counteract the present diminution and repression of intellectual vitality in and around academe? These are deliberate friendships, then, not just the "ragtag assembly of relationships…stumbled onto over the years…patched together from the leavings of others," that Koller warns about (1990, 5).

But this solitary existence within mutual, extended friendship is far from ideal; ours are not cases of living alone well. We live knowing our homes are neither permanent nor really ours, with the everpresent and disruptive prospect of have to move if the rent gets too high or the university faculty is forced by the state budget crisis to go on furlough. Even when we are fortunate enough to stay where we are, as I have been for the last few years, we find ourselves saying good-bye each year to close friends who move to jobs elsewhere. Thus we have to rebuild the circle of friends that sustains us again and again.

Furthermore, neither of us has tenure or savings, much less capital assets; our incomes are limited, in this recession no longer even rising with the cost of living; our debts and liabilities are substantial; and I struggle besides, as Koller and Sarton both once did and many women do, against the lingering ill effects of a miseducation concerning such matters.[17] So, although not so desperately poor as Koller is, Kate and I must struggle financially as well, not for luxury items like cable TV, VCRs, latest-model cars, homes of our own, or even meat in our diets, but for the barest means to do the most basic, healthy, human things for ourselves from one month to the next.

Unlike Koller, luckily, we have taken jobs that have some potential for permanence and pay us for doing our chosen work—albeit also for doing a lot of other assigned labors that do take substantial time and energy away from it. I do much of my work at home alone, and we each make our own decisions (insofar as we are free to decide) about how to juggle a tolerable balance between the self-defined work of our consciences and the other-defined labors of our jobs that together constitute our productive lives. But still, neither of us deliberates in isolation as Koller so fatefully does. Besides being "best friends," we are each other's colleagues, readers of each other's drafts in progress, partners in teaching a new "overload" graduate course in gender and education that we have developed together. Furthermore, each of us has our own mentors and supportive collegial cohorts on campus as well as in our own fields regionally and nationally. Our mentors advise us as friends, in inquiring rather than imposing ways, which show care and concern for the progress of our work, the quality of our lives, and the value of our conscientious self-determination.

Both the reproductive labors of making ourselves "at home" here and the productive labors we must do in our jobs challenge us to a constant struggle for scarce material resources, time, and energy to do our chosen work of conscience; to rest and play well enough to stay fit for coping with the stress of that struggle; and to stay closely connected with mentors, friends, and family. I still have my occasional wakeful nights, anxious about money troubles or just plain lonely;

Kate tells me she has some wakeful nights as well. It is a difficult balance we seek and insecurely keep as single women living alone, economically dependent upon a productive world still structured for men who live with self-denying wives.

How do we manage, most of the time, to avoid living alone miserably? What is the task of solitude in which we are engaged? Kate, our several friends, and I are sympathetically connected by both our reproductive and our productive tasks as single university women who live alone. This sympathetic connection helps in a day-to-day way to heal much of the fragmentation to which academic women's lives are prone; it helps to ward off threatening low spirits, keeps us prudent, and makes other life possibilities imaginable. Profoundly educative, it thus helps us to define boundaries around our own purposeful solitary times and spaces and thereby keeps us from debilitating isolation; it helps us to clarify what we can see the world around us becoming, who we ourselves are becoming, and who we want to become, toward what ends.

Solitude as Achievement:
Responsibility toward Self

According to Koller, solitude is not just a complex task, not just the effort of living alone: "Solitude is an achievement. It is your distinctive way of embodying the purposes you have chosen for your life, deciding on these rather than others after deliberately observing and reflecting on your own doings and inclinations, then committing yourself to them for precisely these reasons" (1990, 4). In this achievement sense, solitude can be another name for that responsibility to self of which Rich has written in my epigraph. Koller further clarifies the meaning of this responsibility: "I am not simply carried along by the hours of the day. My doings follow a distinctive pattern that is composed of and by my purposes. My purposes are the things I do that matter to me above all else. They are of my own making. I commit myself to them. I make choices in accordance with them, and my commitment to them commits me to other choices that are consonant with them, that are often the means for bringing them about" (p. xii). Such responsibility entails a woman's participation in both self-sustaining reproductive processes and self-defined productive processes, no matter what other-nurturing reproductive duties and other-defined productive jobs shape her life.

Sarton does not write explicitly of solitude in this achievement sense even though her productive life could be said to exemplify it; the wholeness that she idealizes depends upon it. The relationship between solitude as achievement and solitude as task is varied and complex. Chance, or social and economic conditions, can make the difference between a woman's living alone well and her living alone miserably, but as Sarton recognizes, "the only thing that is not chance is what one asks of oneself and how well or how badly one meets one's own standard" (p. 54). Thus a woman's achievement of solitude depends entirely upon her deliberation about and execution of her own choices within whatever constraints are indeed beyond her control.

Although I would hesitate to say that a woman can live alone well without simultaneous achievement of solitude, my study so far lacks adequate cases of women's living alone well by which to test this possibility. Yet a woman's living alone miserably need not prevent her achievement of solitude. Even when Sarton fails to establish intimacy with X, her continued artistic productivity signifies her substantial achievement of solitude. Even when miserably failing to resolve her economic difficulties as she undertakes the task of solitude, Koller can still claim the achievement of solitude no less than she can when privileged to live alone well. For her approach to hustling jobs itself embodies her own thoughtful purposes. She makes rules for herself: "once you know what your work is, a job has to meet only two requirements. It has to give you enough money to pay your bills, and although it takes your time it must not use the creative energy you need for your work. Thereafter, the operative rule is: do anything for money that doesn't require you to break too many important laws" (p. 140). Willing on many occasions "not merely to remain silent when I would have wished to speak plainly but to lie outright" (p. 140) in pursuit of needed jobs, Koller draws an important line on issues of social conscience and responsibility. Even when unemployed and homeless, for example, she refuses to lie to an interviewer about her opposition to the use of nuclear energy, knowing it will cost her a potential job and prolong her misery. Solitude in this achievement sense is thus often a painful reflection of conscience.

But is solitude, the achievement, an inevitable consequence of solitude, the task? Can every woman who lives alone, whether well or miserably, claim solitude in its achievement sense? Koller asks her reader to consider herself critically, as possibly the figure of a particular sort of single person, who may or may not live alone, caught up in a fast life: "you will rush throughout the world to evade being alone elementally, searching everywhere for the person or other being who will make you whole again" (p. 7). Such evasion as a way of living alone is understandable; Sarton observes that "boredom and panic are the two devils the solitary must combat" (p. 94). Facing those devils in their first confrontations with solitude, the task, many women and men turn to marriage or remarriage, or another sort of sexual partnership, as if it were the only alternative to living alone, without ever asking about their decision's possible effect upon their future power to infuse their actions with their own chosen purposes.

This common situation raises other related questions. Is solitude, the task, a necessary condition of solitude, the achievement? Need a woman live alone to claim her achievement of solitude? In her *Journal*, Sarton herself often sets aside the importance of asking what it might mean to live alone well, to ask instead what it might mean to live well with a spouse: "Mine is not, I feel sure, the best human solution. Nor have I ever thought it was. In my case, it has perhaps made possible the creation of some works of art, but certainly it has done so at a high price in emotional maturity and in happiness. What I have is space around me and time around me. How they can be achieved in a marriage is the real question. It is not an easy one to answer" (p. 123).

Is women's solitude as achievement possible within marriage? This solitude demands self-knowledge and a sense of responsibility for one's own development. Yet, as Jean Baker Miller has explained:

> To concentrate on and to take seriously one's own development is hard enough for all human beings. But, as has been recently demonstrated in many areas, it has even been harder for women. Women are not encouraged to develop as far as they possibly can and to experience the stimulation and the anguish, anxiety, and pain the process entails. Instead, they are encouraged to concentrate on forming and maintaining a relationship to one person. In fact, women are encouraged to believe that if they do go through the mental and emotional struggle of self-development, the end result will be disastrous—they will forfeit the possibility of having any close relationships. This penalty, this threat of isolation, is intolerable for anyone to contemplate. For women, reality has made the threat; it was by no means imaginary. (1986, 18–19)

Sarton and Koller demonstrate that reality and prove reasonable that threat, for they accept the penalty, that Miller points to as intolerable for most of us even to contemplate. Like my own account of solitude, theirs are tales of sexual uncoupling. At the end of her stormy long-distance affair with X, Sarton at the age of sixty sadly concludes that she was "meant to live alone, meant to write the poems for others—poems that seldom in my life have reached the one person for whom they were intended" (p. 207). After an affair with a man that "came to nothing" (p. 138), Koller chooses to live alone permanently as well, having openly committed herself to loving her dogs Logos, Ousia, and Kairos rather than loving any more human beings.

Both their autobiographical reflections and my own quite different case corroborate the truth of Jack's claim that "cultural myths or images of how to be a woman offer little guidance for how to be strong, for how to be authentic in relationships, or for how to combine self-development with intimacy" (p. 27). Admitting that "there is something wrong when solitude such as mine can be 'envied' by a happily married woman with children" (pp. 122–23), Sarton searches in vain for guidance from cultural images, and questions the institution of marriage itself: "'Can one *be* within the framework of a marriage?' It is not irresponsible women who ask that question, but often...women with children, caring women, who feel deeply frustrated and lost, who feel they are missing their 'real lives' all the time" (p. 122). Marital obstacles to women's solitude in the achievement sense cannot be overemphasized; all the depressed women whose descriptions of emotional experience Jack studied in *Silencing the Self* are facing those obstacles. Sarton sympathetically considers the situation of the college-educated wife:

> She is expected to cope not with ideas, but with cooking food, washing dishes, doing laundry, and if she insists on keeping at a job, she needs both a lot of energy and the ability to organize her time. If she has an infant to care for, the jump from the intellectual life to that of being a nurse must be immense. "The work" she may long to do has been replaced by various kinds of labor for which she has been totally unprepared. She has longed for children, let us say, she is deeply in love, she has what she thought she wanted, so she suffers guilt and dismay to feel so disoriented. Young husbands these days can and do help with the chores and, far more important, are aware of the problem and will talk anxiously about it—anxiously because a wife's conflict affects their peace of mind. But the fact remains that, in marrying, the wife has suffered an earthquake and the husband has not. His goals have not been radically changed; his mode of being has not been radically changed. (p. 71)

Yet there are other forms of human love and affiliation than marriage. (Sarton finds the difficulties of heterosexual and homosexual marriage comparable, as already noted.) Neither she nor Koller considers alternative possibilities for human connection in the construction of her life as a single woman, thereby lending force to the mistaken assumption that single adults have only two life choices: marriage or solitude in its task sense. Kate, our several friends, and I are, I believe, finding that friendship poses no appreciable obstacle to our solitude in an achievement sense; indeed, quite the reverse. Now, of course, we are all living alone, but what if we all rented a large house together and formed a household? Would we then automatically be renouncing our "distinctive way of embodying the purposes" each of us has chosen for her life? I doubt it. Especially if some form of productive collectivity were a purpose to which we shared a substantial commitment. Even if it were not, we might find our reproductive collectivity an efficient means to the end of supporting each woman's own individual productive purposes as scientists, educators, art historians, activists, and so on. Of course, even within such a living-together arrangement, we might still claim to be living alone, too, each with her own set of private rooms and personal budget, for example, as necessary conditions for her achievement of solitude within our shared home.

Even allowing for such an alternative possibility, even allowing that solitude, the achievement, may not entail simultaneous, active or absolute engagement in solitude, the task, the question remains if the task is a necessary prerequisite to the achievement. In *The Stations of Solitude*, Koller theorizes that it is:

> To become genuinely solitary, to be alone well, you must first have been alone elementally. For that, no "here" will do. An island is not necessary. Only be away from everything familiar: every person, every relationship, every circumstance. Friends, a mate, an analyst, a priest, a teacher, your family to take you in, even one person you can talk to, liquor, drugs, the occult, the divine: if you have any of these you are not ready to undertake the interior journey that will let you confront the person you are. (p. 4)

She further theorizes that "at the early stations you throw out old choices and choose anew" (p. xi). She names these two stations "unbinding" and "standing open," and suggests that these are the only stations a person must circuit in the same order she has presented them. At the station of unbinding, which involves "being alone elementally," the lesson is "that your life is entirely within your own hands: to shape to you, to make fit you, as only you know how best to do, how to do at all" (p. 5). At the station of standing open, the unbound solitary claims her "own spontaneity," by "viewing the world and everything in it as though for the first time, each moment presenting itself as an occasion to be freshly sensed, perceived, conceived; saying, doing, wanting, seeing, understanding things you have not said, done, wanted seen, understood before" (p. 12). A woman's solitude in its achievement sense obviously depends upon a woman's having learned the lessons of these two stations. Can she learn them without "being alone elementally," which for Koller is their necessary condition? The lesson of unbinding could perhaps come about through a dramatic experience of betrayal or oppression at the hands of a trusted other, and the lesson of standing open could perhaps come about through travel to far-away places, I suspect. But who wants oppression or betrayal? And not everyone can afford such travel. Could childrearing and schooling, if they actually respected and fostered children's own choices and sensual openness rather than constantly curtailing them, nurture this learning that adults now commonly do only through confrontation with personal crisis?

Solitude, the task, may not be a necessary prerequisite to solitude, the achievement, but Koller's case and my own at least provide evidence that it can be one. Yet we would be short-sighted if we paired the task and the achievement of solitude together so closely that we neglected to ask what other achievements solitude, the task, may yield. For my own case makes plain that friendship may be an achievement that itself can follow from the struggle to be alone elementally. Sarton hints at this possibility when she reflects that

> when it comes to the important things one is always alone, and it may be that the virtue or possible insight I get from being so obviously alone—being physically and in every way absolutely alone much of the time—is a way into the universal state of man. The way in which one handles this absolute aloneness is the way in which one grows up, is the great psychic journey of every man. At what price would total independence be bought? That's the rub! I am conscious of the fruitful tension set up between me and anyone for whom I care—Ann Woodson for instance, X of course. I learn by being *in relation to*. (p. 107)

This is certainly true of myself. One thing I have learned from my own "absolute aloneness" in Maine has been a skepticism about any "total independence," its arrogance. The meanings and values of friendship, especially women's friendship within the contexts of single life and solitude, are matter for inquiry at another time. Could friendship provide an additional means of unbinding and standing open? Koller would argue against this view, I have no doubt, although I am not sure Sarton would. But friendship could be the one human relation which, because it is not an institutional relation (like marriage or motherhood) and must be defined anew each time we enter upon it, can enable rather than threaten both the task and the achievement of solitude.

Education and Women's Solitude:
Curriculum Questions

If single and would-be-single women are to make intelligent choices about our lives, we need to pursue inquiry about our lives' possibilities, for ourselves and with each other. It is perhaps noteworthy, however, that Sarton and Koller both generalize from their own particular female experiences of solitude to the solitude of all humanity, for as Sarton has protested, "Women certainly learn a lot from books oriented toward a masculine world. Why is not the reverse also true?" (p. 64). What human good might come of relationships between women and men if more men took up the invitation issued through Sarton's and Koller's generous gestures of gender neutrality? If men actually studied and learned women's practice of solitude, in both its task and its achievement senses, rather than idealizing and depending upon women's other-nurturing reproductive and other-defined productive labors? Moreover, if men, the self-denying women many of them live with, and the societal institutions that cater to men are not to constrain women's choices in hurtful ways, as they obviously have Koller's, men need somehow to learn what we go through when we are fending for ourselves.

"This is my solitude," Koller explains:

I do not cloak it among other persons, and I know how it appears. No sign of submission, in the eyes of most men; too assured, in the view of most women; not properly respectful, to the gaze of all those in authority. I have become that third gender: a human person, the being one creates of oneself. I fell in love with my work, became fiercely protective of my freedom, started to make new rules. In this, Sartre is surely right: persons are not born but made. The choice lies escapably within ourselves: we may let it wither away, or we may take it and run. (1990, 23)

Thus she is suggesting that there are at least two "genders" of women: women who are submissive to and "properly respectful" of men, and women like herself who claim their freedom. Not a feminist, she never draws the obvious distinction her poignant autobiography could easily justify: between two classes of "human persons," the white heterosexual male human person whose freedom to choose is his assumed right and the female human person whose freedom to choose is her contested right, one about which she should never dare to feel "too assured." These two genders of women and these two classes of human persons signified in Koller's text suggest the potentially radical significance, for relationships among women as well as relationships between women and men, of thinking seriously about education and *women's* solitude, rather than just Wordsworth's, Thoreau's, Emerson's, and others' famous solitudes. But what would it mean to think seriously about *education* and women's solitude?

We can turn our thoughts to education *about* women's solitude, to women's education *in* solitude, and to women's education *for* solitude. Each of these ways of thinking about education and women's solitude poses its own distinctive questions. My inquiry is itself a case of education and of self-education about other single women's solitude no less than it is about my own. It has involved my critical examination of our self-education in solitude. I have undertaken this study, moreover, with a sense of myself as uneducated and miseducated for the solitude I confronted at the end of my marriage; it has thus become part of my belated self-education for solitude. This critical sense of myself has led me to ask serious questions about my own education as a girl and as a woman, hence about education generally.

Education about single women's solitude in both its task and achievement senses could become part of childhood, adolescent, and adult education. Should it? Toward what ends, by what means, in what contexts? What would it mean to educate girls and women and boys and men about women's solitude? I think curriculum theory needs to address questions such as these. Textbooks in family studies and human development that I have seen in common use with secondary and postsecondary students show scarce signs of such foundational inquiry, with their short chapters and blurbs on the "singles lifestyle." Curriculum theory could take up questions about other possible contexts and means for teaching the subject matter of single women's solitude. Consciousness-raising about the history,[18] sociology, political economy, sexual and racial politics, psychology, and contemporary experience of single women's solitude could be an especially worthwhile purpose to develop such curriculum theory and such subject matter. That subject matter could include not only autobiographies, but also fiction, drama, poetry, song, film, architectural designs,[19] religious scriptures, philosophical treatises, archival materials, ethnographies, laws, policy documents, even slices of life as it is unfolding in the here and now. Research in family studies and human development has much to offer the development of this subject matter, too, but why should study of this subject of single women's solitude be confined to departments of home economics or colleges of human ecology?

Women's education for solitude is almost inconceivable without a curriculum that reflects such a thoughtful approach to education about single women's solitude. At the same time, would it not remain incomplete, insufficiently practical, if it consisted only of that? What would it mean to educate women for solitude in both its task and its achievement senses? One way curriculum theorists might approach these questions would be to investigate, both broadly and deeply, what education single women in different social contexts have made for themselves (as Sarton, Koller, and I have done) in face of the task, how and why. What has it meant for such women to become educated in solitude, by taking up the task of solitude, by attempting the achievement of solitude?

I have attempted to initiate such inquiry by recounting three different cases of women's self-education in solitude, from a particular concern to understand what aspects of such education in solitude might be considered the "basics" of education for solitude. Thus I have held up for examination, under the lenses these cases provide, the concept of the "reproductive processes of society" which Martin's philosophical critique of the ideal of the educated woman first brought to light. My examination has revealed that, whereas women's work within the institutions of marriage and motherhood have entailed reproductive labors that are other-nurturing, women's task of solitude may seem to contradict our education for such work insofar as it requires our learning to conceive and practice reproductive activities that are self-sustaining. "I often feel exhausted," Sarton ends one journal entry, "but it is not my work that tires (work is a rest); it is the effort of pushing away the lives and needs of others before I can come to the work with any freshness and zest" (p. 13). Koller meanwhile describes another sort of self-sustaining reproductive labor altogether, work that women have often been taught to expect from men in their households:

> You learn to listen for the sound of the pump. If you hear it churning away for a minute or two once or twice a day, all is

well. If it turns on and runs without stopping, or if it turns off and on every few minutes, you're in trouble. The water table could be low, a line or even the tank could be leaking somewhere, or the pump could be on its last legs. You call an electrician or plumber at once, if for no other reason than that your electric bill will be staggering until the problem is corrected. (1990, 75)

Koller herself sees the educational value of this experience, declaring, "No one teaches you any of this in graduate school" (p. 75).

My study furthermore suggests that women who lack Sarton's economic advantages must learn to make such varied and extensive self-sustaining reproductive efforts within the context of a struggle for productive freedom and integrity. Koller, my friends, and I face profound structural conflicts between our economic needs for jobs whose productive labors are defined by others and our moral and spiritual needs for productive work we can define in accord with our own capacities and consciences. The conflicts between our other-defined productivity and our self-defined productivity cannot only cause inner divisions which demand our reproductive energy and ingenuity; they can also impoverish our resources for such self-sustaining efforts. Resolving these conflicts is of course a matter of politics as well as of learning. But which of these basics of living alone can actually be taught by one person to another, and how? Which can one learn only when faced with the task of solitude? These are further questions for curriculum theorists to consider.

The history of thought that Martin has reclaimed, about what it might mean to be an educated woman, offers single women needed insight into the complex philosophical foundations of our situation, but little guidance for grappling with it. Sarton, Koller, and I have all searched our memories and knowledge of our mothers' lives for such guidance. But ultimately, whatever our conclusions about them, all of us have had to endure and examine our own pains and ignorance, strike our own metaphors, construct our own conceptual understandings of ourselves as women learning to live alone. For example, Koller has conceptualized her own education in solitude thus:

The stations are recurring circumstances in which a certain kind of decision, and then acting on it, are required of you. The decision you're called on to make will have far-reaching consequences for the person you are, the person you wish to become. It is the price of the journey: that at this stopping-place you must make a choice. At the early stations you throw out old choices and choose anew. At the other stations you reflect, you observe, you reassert an earlier choice or you revise it in the light of new observation, new reflection. At every station, therefore, you pay. But you also profit: you will learn, you will approach more closely who you want to be. Sometimes the choosing and the learning are painful; sometimes they are imbued with joy. (1990, xii)

At the station of "singling," for example, she confronts a logical inconsistency between her thoughts about hunting and her practice of eating meat, which ultimately leads her to defy her doctor's warnings and become vegetarian. The motives behind this choice come of an earlier choice made, to love her dogs as her most significant companions in life, and it requires her to learn about nutrition. From this experience of developing her own self-sustaining reproductive practices comes a stronger sense of self: "Thereafter I became the final judge of what to do with my body; I took back the authority over my own health that I long ago gave to medicine by not having known that sound alternatives existed. Now I look first to nutrition. It was nutrition that let me cure the disease medicine had told me I'd have to tolerate to the end of my days" (p. 220). This instance of her self-education presents a clear case of her solitude in its achievement sense, but what she learns could enhance living with others no less than it enhances her own task of living alone. Could she have learned it without having faced the task of solitude? No doubt, though this learning would surely not have been likely if she had been living with someone who liked to hunt! Curriculum theorists thus might examine women's education in solitude to determine which phases of its curriculum do and do not enable solitude in its achievement sense, which phases of its curriculum girls and women do and do not have to engage in the actual task of solitude to learn.

Beyond such rethinking of education about single women's solitude and such examination of women's self-education in solitude, curriculum theorists need to examine education itself more broadly with a critical recognition that, whether for ill or good, the education now offered to girls and young women is in most cases actually their education for solitude at some later date in their lives, if not for solitude in their present lives. Should the task of solitude itself become an integral phase of that education's curriculum, voluntary or required? If so, toward what ends, by what means, in what contexts? Should students' and teachers' achievement of solitude become a criterion of curricular value generally, regardless of its subject matter? If so, curriculum theorists will need to consider once again the complex questions that Martin long ago raised about what "learning to choose" might mean. She pointed out that what educators often regard instances of choosing are not instances of choosing at all. Freed from coercive curricular requirements, a student can pick an option from among others without any thought, or in a desire to conform to others, or from incomplete understanding of the options available to her. In such cases, she is not choosing but picking her course. Martin recommended that "guidance" is crucial to "a program of education for choosing," which an education for the achievement of solitude would entail, and it "would have to go beyond the mere guidance of curriculum choices lest students think that only in curriculum contexts do choice points occur or that all choices are at bottom curricular" (1975). The problems of women, single life, and solitude could reinvigorate curriculum theory by presenting a new phenomenological frame within which to set those difficult questions about free choice which current issues like cooperative learning and political correctness are posing for the field. Does education now foster the picking of marriage, or the choosing of marriage? What sort of education can foster choosing that takes into account what it means to live alone miserably, tolerably, or well? These questions are large and difficult, but women's lives are the price of not asking them.

References

Bogan, L. (1968). Women. In *The blue estuaries*, 19. New York: The Ecco Press.

Cooper, A. J. (1988). *A voice from the south*. New York: Oxford University Press.

Dillard, A. (1974). *Pilgrim at Tinker Creek*. Toronto: Bantam.

Field, J. (1981). *A life of one's own*. Los Angeles: J. P. Tarcher.

Goldman, E. (1931). *Living my life*. New York: Alfred A. Knopf.

Jack, D. C. (1991). *Silencing the self: Women and depression*. Cambridge: Harvard University Press.

Keller, E. F. (1983). The capacity to be alone. In *A feeling for the organism: The life and work of Barbara McClintock*, 15–37. New York: W. H. Freeman.

Koller, A. (1981). *An unknown woman*. New York: Bantam.

———. (1990). *The stations of solitude*. New York: William Morrow.

Lindbergh, A. M. (1955). *Gift from the sea.* New York: Pantheon.

Martin, J. R. (1970). The disciplines and the curriculum. In *Readings in the philosophy of education,* edited by J. R. Martin, 65–86. Boston: Allyn and Bacon.

———. (1975). *Choice, chance, and curriculum.* Boyd H. Bode Memorial Lectures, The Ohio State University. Columbus, Ohio: The Ohio State University Press.

———. (1985). *Reclaiming a conversation.* New Haven: Yale University Press.

Miller, J. B. (1986). *Toward a new psychology of women.* Boston: Beacon.

Rich, A. (1979). Claiming an education. In *On lies, secrets, and silence,* 231–35. New York: W.W. Norton.

———. (1979). Taking women students seriously. In *On lies, secrets, and silence,* 237–45. New York: W. W. Norton.

Sarton, M. (1973). *Journal of a solitude.* New York: W. W. Norton.

Woolf, V. (1929). *A room of one's own.* San Diego: Harcourt Brace Jovanovich.

Wordsworth, W. (1967). Lines written a few miles above Tintern Abbey. In *Wordsworth: Poetry and prose,* edited by W. M. Merchant, 154. Cambridge: Harvard University Press.

———. (1967). The solitary reaper. In *Wordsworth: Poetry and prose,* edited by W. M. Merchant, 646–47. Cambridge: Harvard University Press.

Author's Notes

Thanks to the Women in Curriculum program at the University of Maine for a 1991 summer research grant which permitted completion of this study. I am especially grateful for the questions and suggestions of Ann Diller, Mary E. Dolan, Susan Douglas Franzosa, Barbara Houston, Jane Roland Martin, Beatrice Nelson, Jennifer Radden, Kate Scantlebury, and Janet Farrell Smith, who all carefully read and discussed this chapter in working draft. A substantially different early version was presented to Division B of the American Educational Research Association in 1991, at which Maxine Greene, Glorianne Leck, Janet L. Miller, and our most patient editor, Delese Wear, offered truly helpful comments.

1. U.S. Bureau of Census, 1989, quoted in Robert H. Lauer and Jeanette C. Lauer, *Marriage and Family: The Quest for Intimacy* (Dubuque: Wm. C. Brown, 1991), 143–44.

2. Quoted from U.S. Census, 1988, in Bryan Strong and Christine DeVault, *The Marriage and Family Experience* (St. Paul: West, 1989), 151. Note

that "single" does not necessarily mean *uncoupled*; cohabiting couples, both heterosexual and homosexual, are included in this statistic.

3. On the metaphor of life as story, see Mary Catherine Bateson, *Composing a Life* (New York: Plume, 1990) and Phyllis Rose, *Parallel Lives: Five Victorian Marriages* (New York: Vintage, 1983).

4. In this category, I would include not only the bourgeois dual-career marriage that has come to be known by this name, but also the marriages of workers in the transportation and travel industries, armed forces, sales, and so forth.

5. Lauer and Lauer, 20, cite questionnaire findings of Hite (1987): "91 percent of women who were divorced said they, rather than their husbands, were the ones who had made the decision to break up the marriage."

6. See, for example, Patricia J. Thompson and Theodora Faiola-Priest, *Lifeplans* (Cincinnati, Ohio: South-Western, 1990), p. 77: "...most of those in the singles group anticipate marriage, if not in the immediate, then in the not-too-far future." Note that this book does offer instruction in activities of living that are basic to single life no less than they are to married life; yet textbooks of this sort might offer a different curriculum indeed if marriage were not assumed to be the most desirable life option generally and if the choices of single life were represented in more of their true complexity and variety.

7. This is not to say that studies of single life have no place in the curriculum, for they are indeed included in the university curriculum of family studies, human sexuality and development. I am indebted to Sandra L. Caron, a specialist in that field, for pointing this out to me. See, for example, two undergraduate textbooks which present single life as a not altogether satisfactory alternative to marriage: Lauer and Lauer, chapter 6; Strong and DeVault, chapter 6. The studies such textbooks cite do not consider the theoretical question of how curriculum in general might be conceived if the demands of single life, much less single womanhood, were considered constitutive of its structure and substance. The secondary curriculum in family studies treats single life similarly, albeit much more briefly, and more as a preface to marriage; see Thompson and Faiola-Priest.

8. See, for example, William E. Davis and Edward J. McCaul, *The Emerging Crisis: Current and Projected Status of Children in the United States* (Orono, Maine: Institute for the Study of At-Risk Students, 1991).

9. Here I borrow a conceptual distinction from Gilbert Ryle, *The Concept of Mind* (New York: Barnes and Noble, 1949), 130, 150, 152, 176. Note that whereas Ryle applies this distinction to verbs, I am applying it to a noun.

10. Thanks to Patricia F. First for introducing me to both *Journal of a Solitude* and *The Stations of Solitude*.

11. I am indebted to discussions with Jennifer Radden for this term.

12. See Adrienne Rich, "Compulsory Heterosexuality and Lesbian Existence," in *Blood, Bread, and Poetry* (New York: W.W. Norton, 1986), 23–75. Note that feminist theory has developed a cogent critique of compulsory hererosexuality but has yet to acknowledge the opressive ideology of compulsory coupling—an ideology to which it actually contributes, to the detriment of single women.

13. For a fictional reflection upon the reconstructed life of a woman widowed after precisely such a lesbian marriage, see May Sarton, *The Education of Harriet Hatfield* (New York: W. W. Norton, 1989).

14. See Sarton, 20–24, and Wordsworth, "The Solitary Reaper," in *Wordsworth*, ed. Merchant, 646–47.

15. All of this chapter's references to my working life predate my move to the University of Oklahoma in 1992.

16. An apt description of this ritual's incomparable character can be found in Judith Lynne Hanna, *Dance and Stress: Resistance, Reduction, and Euphoria* (New York: AMS, 1988), 145–46.

17. This miseducation is not unique; see Annette Lieberman and Vicki Lindner, *Unbalanced Accounts* (New York: Penguin, 1981), chapter 1.

18. I think it important to remember that during the Renaissance, Reformation, and Counter-Reformation, single women in Great Britain and Europe were, like Jews, the objects of a widespread inquisition and witchcraze, called The Burning Times. Michel Foucault unaccountably overlooks this fact in his *Madness and Civilization*, trans. R. Howard (New York: Random House, 1973), about the same era. See Susan Griffin, *Woman and Nature* (New York: Harper Colophon, 1978); Mary Daly, *Gyn/Ecology* (Boston: Beacon, 1978), chapter 6.

19. See, for example, Dolores Hayden, *The Grand Domestic Revolution: A History of Feminist Designs for American Homes, Neighborhoods, and Cities* (Cambridge: MIT, 1982).

PART III

Solitude and Work

Chapter 15

Private Spaces:
The Political Economy of Women's Solitude

Magda Lewis

I'm thinking about the ones who aren't here and won't be coming in late.

—Christian and Williamson (1983).

Kim Chernin once wrote that "it is a highly radical and subversive act to tell a familiar story in a new way. Once you start to do it you realize that what you call history is another such story and could be told differently and has been. And then the authoritative tradition starts to crack and crumble. It too, it turns out, is nothing more than a particular selection of various stories, all of which have at one time or another been believed and told " (1987, 59).

Women in the academy have not had our stories told very much one way or the other. First, our absence from and, then, our invisibility in the realm of intellectual work has meant that we have lived our condition as intellectual women mostly as an oxymoron. For women, the contradiction in applying the adjective "intellectual" to the social category "woman" comes from the concrete enactments of what it means to be either. Coded through the ideology of reproduction, women's capacity to labor has historically required us to sustain the work of production not only through the labor of our bodies but specifically by the labor of our hands. Encoded in language, as in for example, the Euro-American marriage ritual, it is women's hand and the labor that they promise which are "given" by the father to the groom. It is precisely in this exchange of "taking" a woman's hands that a man becomes publicly proclaimed and celebrated as the "head of household." Hence, mental work—the work of the "head"—is masculinized and defines intellectual labor as man's work against which women's intrusion is seen, at best, to be benignly irrelevant. More commonly the masculinized social forms of intellectual exchange overtly, sometimes violently, exclude and marginalize women (Lewis and Simon 1986).

While in the public realm, race and class may equally delimit the participation in mental labor of particular men, the fault lines that mark power relations within the private realm are socially institutionalized in deeply gendered ways. The power of patriarchy to realize the principles of heterosexuality and the nuclear family, whether or not one participates in these social forms, means that the engagement of *any* woman in intellectual work is by social-historical contingency named questionable. Despite our presence in the academy our commitment to intellectual work continues to be marked by the contradictory ideologies that give social meaning to these public and private worlds.

Thinking and writing are the stock-in-trade of intellectual labor. On the one hand the implied singularity of this work, as for example, in the academic requirement for the prioritization of noncollaborative authorship, is belied by the many hours of discussion, shared discourse, critique and debate in the public realm that precedes the act of writing. Yet the moment of setting pen to paper is a deeply private event requiring of the author an extended physical withdrawal from the tumble of daily life. As Madeleine Grumet (1988) suggests, "there is a dialectic of withdrawal and extension, isolation and submission to *esthetic practice* that requires both the *studio* where the artist harvests silence and the *gallery* where she serves the fruit of her inquiry to others" (p. 94, emphasis added). To the extent that esthetic practice requires the nonlinear spiraling of this dialectic in a mutual exchange between the public and the private, women's access to intellectual production is problematic. As I believe is the case for many women, for me the dialectic between the "studio" and the "gallery" not only holds open the possibility for creative work but, as well, articulates those moments of closure that define me through the terms of my participation in the social construct "woman/mother." Despite Grumet's tenacious and politically burdened resolve to identify the "artist" by the use of the feminine pronoun, women cannot claim for ourselves a safe public space of intellectual exchange, nor is it immediately obvious to me that we might take as given the possibilities for solitude in the private sphere. For women, both the public and the private aspects of intellectual work present a particular dilemma. Laced with contradictions and what elsewhere I have called the "double-cross-reversal" of phallocentric language regimes (Lewis, 1992), the discursive legitimation of our subordination hides the lived realities both of our public and of our private lives.

Women in the academy have been "allowed" access to the work of the intellect only to the extent that we agree to the terms suggested by the material realities of men's lives. Conversely, the very raising of questions regarding the processes of intellectual production leaves us named inadequate or indiscrete or both (Lewis, 1993). Yet that women bear children is not insignificant either to how the work of the household and parent-child relations are organized or to how intellectual work is accomplished. As Roberta Hamilton suggests, "children are a primary cause both of domestic labor and the sexual division of labor. It is not an historical accident that women are the domestic laborers; indeed it would have been a miracle of they were not. And it will require a major and sustained struggle accompanied by a collective and planned effort to go about changing it" (Hamilton 1986, 149).

For me, as for many women, the creative processes of writing are articulated through the specifics of my personal but politically charged realities that have a history and that bind me still to the materiality of woman-/mother-work. For many years, our house, full and noisy with young children, was, for someone who demands absolute quiet and solitude when she writes, inconducive to the task. Were it just the incessant chatter of young children learning language, themselves, and the world, I might have found there some quiet moments late into the night during which to read and write. However, my desk, the only possible writing surface that might have been consistently and privately available to me was, three subsequent times, converted to a baby's changing table and my study into a nursery. As a result, I still read Tillie Olsen's question with particular poignancy: "How is it that women have not made a fraction of the intellectual, scientific, or artistic-cultural contribution that men have made?" (1978, 27). If we have not, and I don't believe that we have not, it being more true that our contribution has gone noticed, unrecorded and unvalued (Smith 1978), it is, at least in part, because our desks—metaphorically or in reality—have had to hold both books and diapers, each threatening to overpower and consume the other while our minds have worked to mediate the struggle.

I was a graduate student during those years and it became a "habit" for me to return often in the evenings to the institution where I studied to work late into the night in the small office space to which I was assigned. After our shared moment of family dinners, riotous baths, story telling and tucking in I would return daily to this private space arriving usually around eight-thirty or nine o'clock to work often till one or two in the morning. The memories of that time still bring back deep powerful feelings of the pain of the contradiction yet mutual support of my double life. Sustaining the exhaustion of mothering three small children during the day was the knowledge that with the evening I could return to my books and writing; and sustaining the exhaustion of being a graduate student were my children who would with pleasure draw me away from those very same books and writing into the world of playgrounds, "mucking" in the kitchen and our weekly visit to the museum dinosaur display.

Nor has my body yet forgotten the pain that my ritual leaving of the private imprinted on my cells. My memory of "leaving home" is that of the image of my then young son, his body silhouetted dark against the pane of his upstairs bedroom window imploring me, night after night as I backed my car out of the driveway, to please not leave. I still don't know what compelled him to demand my physical presence "at home" even when he slept. Nor do I know how the neighbors understood my evening ritual of pushing the car out of the driveway and part way up the street before I turned on the ignition in hopes that my child might not hear me leaving and therefore not suffer the apparent trauma of my absence—or was it I, his mother, who was suffering the trauma of the projections of his unfulfilled desire that left me experiencing my work as "mother" invisible in its presence and yet indispensable in its absence?

The issue of women and our struggle for education is one which always bears more analysis. The good and ever more insightful work in our understanding of the dynamics of the challenge brought to phallocentrism by women's education is essential (Rockhill 1991). Indeed women's inaccessibility to the word in concrete terms—i.e., pen, paper, time, space and a coding system—has contributed profoundly to our silencing both materially and historically. Were this all of the telling of this story it might have stopped here with some self-reconciliation that as difficult as I might have found it I, at least, could negotiate those necessary moments during which to think and write. The story might have ended here with an acknowledgment of the privilege of my economic/social status which at the time did not require me to labor outside the home in order to provide for the physical sustenance of my children. To be sure, economic marginality *matters*, as do inequalities that define social/cultural/sexual difference in a deeply racist, classist and homophobic society. However, at the same time I want to note that not problematizing the terms under which any woman might undertake such work leaves unquestioned the embeddedness of the idea that women's creative engagement is something to be squeezed in without effecting our responsibilities for woman-/mother-work. Hence, my memory of those times is augmented in no small way by that young woman with whom, over the course of a year or so I shared long and frequent conversations late at night: I sitting at my desk with papers strewn, pen in hand; she pushing a cleaning cart and wearing the uniform of the cleaning company that cleaned the offices where my desk was located.

I realize of course that had I not been required to seek the necessary private spaces away from home infused with the contradictory reality of the ideology of familial comfort and closeness, this young woman and I might never have met and the questions that haunt me in this writing might have occurred to me differently. As it is, our conversations became the pivotal point for my own growing understanding of the material realities hidden in the ideology of "home." Her private world became the mirror in which I caught the ever more articulate reflections of the contradictions that create the nuclear family as the site of socially acceptable expressions of gender/sexuality set against the possibilities for women's intellectual/cultural expression. This young woman and I talked often, mostly about her: her aspirations, her future, her boyfriend, her home, her family, her job, her school. She had recently enrolled in a community college part-time upgrading program to improve her secretarial skills and to take accounting. She wanted to be a secretary, because, as she said, pointing to the trash can, "I wasn't meant for this job." Her boyfriend and, as plans were at the time, her future husband, did not mind her wanting to be a secretary, at least as she told me, until they have children. But he did not want her to go back to school. So her return to school was a secret she, with the support and help of her parents, was able to keep from him. Her parents frequently lied to him about her whereabouts, she told me, so that she might attend classes without his imposed constraint. Parents' complicity in supporting the gendered violations of heterosexual social/marital relations has a long and worldwide history. Historically and geographically the cultural imperatives requiring that parents, particularly mothers, undertake to make young women marriageable differ only in content not in intent. "If he knew I was going to school," she said to me on several occasions, "he'd get very angry. But I don't care, I have to do this. I just hope he doesn't find out."

In one of our conversations this young woman and I talked about her grandmother. Her grandmother, she told me, "is a very wise woman." "I listen to my grandmother," she said, "because she knows how things are. She told me women have to learn not to talk, they have to know how to keep quiet. A woman must never tell a man what she knows or what she thinks. Women must listen a lot, hear everything and keep quiet. Then we can do more because the man will never know":

> Let no one tell me that silence gives consent, because whoever
> is silent dissents. (Barreno, Horta, and da Costa 1975, 86–87)

Our silencing has been constructed simultaneously for us and by us not only in the emotional/psychological crevices hidden in the folds of the materiality of the phallocentrism of work organization and economic distribution but most profoundly by our relationship to the seat of phallocentric power—the patriarchic family.

I had images of this "grandmother" in my mind—what she might have looked like, what the sound and intonation of her voice might have been when she was telling this young woman these things. She related her grandmother's words to me almost in a whisper, moving closer into my room as if she were telling me a secret, sharing the profound wisdom of Mary Daly's hags and crones (1978). I thought at the time and think even more so now, that she must have thought me in need of such wisdom, surrounded as I was by my books, telling her as I did that she should not allow herself to be bullied by this man who had no right to control her life in the presumptuous ways he did. The irony of my relationship with this young woman still strikes me profoundly: each of us, mutually sharing the secrets of our different worlds, were simultaneously engaged in the genuine caring for one another signalled in our wish to impart the knowledge we thought the *other* needed in order to survive.

And yet the disquiet with which I have carried this story over many years has continually forced me to reflect not on our difference but on what we had in common made graphically concrete in that shared space and time. The same social forces that give patriarchy its power to silence, on that occasion brought us together in conversation when others slept. I don't intend this as support of some romanticized notion of women's developing consciousness. We both knew what we wanted: I wished I could have done my work differently as much as she wished to do different work. On the one had I continue to wonder: how typical was this young woman; of what particular social group was she a representative; to what extent did her realities and insights transcend class boundaries, social boundaries, race boundaries, age boundaries? I still don't know the answers to these questions. It would be comforting to believe that I and those women who form the circle of my social and political life don't keep quiet, don't just listen but are listened to, don't have a social and political existence shrouded in silence. Yet...I also continued to wonder: how much of my daily life is rationalized; how much is political strategy; how much is material, ideological, psychological and emotional constraint; how much is a particular discourse and a way of relating to the world that grows out of my appropriation of socially acceptable forms of femininity and my culturally contained reality as "woman"? Simultaneously, how much of what we do goes unnoticed, unaccounted for, forgotten, not seen to be "doing anything," considered unimportant or inadequate? And at what point might our "telling" overstep the boundaries of discretion because to speak about these things is like peeling back layer by layer the gauze that covers our wounds, gagging those who have violated us even as it exposes us to the healing powers of the wind and the sun.

It is these questions that have pushed their way through to the fingertips that hold my pen. For many months I have sat with this request to write a paper on the topic of women and solitude. For those same many months I have struggled with where I might begin. Carrying deep within me my commitment to the politics of feminism confirmed for me that I had to begin with where I am. The importance of the feminist focus on experience is not the vacuous and gratuitous telling of our private stories as a cathartic moment but indeed to emphasize that subordinate groups live subordination and marginality through our subjectivity. We live it precisely in the context of the details of our individual experiences which to the extent that they can be made to seem to be private cannot then offer the ground for a collective political practice. "Experience," says Chris Weedon, "has no inherent essential meaning" (1987, 34). Rather, we are able to uncover the politics of our subordination as we interrogate our experiences for how they delimit what is possible for us. The agenda of a feminist politics directed toward transformation is not only to validate the telling of our stories as the source of our knowledge. Rather, the political efficacy of a transformative politics based on feminist principles arises from the extent to which it can broaden the understanding of our experience to which we have access (Weedon 1987, 79).

On this occasion this political position has a profoundly concrete and historically significant meaning for me. On the one hand, like many women either in reality or by social/cultural definition, I find myself at this moment the mother of three children, whose growing up I sometimes catch myself actively resisting because my social category as "mother" has been one I have engaged with unqualified rigor and joy for close to eighteen years. It is a social position that locates me in universal time as unmistakably woman that both gives and denies access to social processes in particular ways (Kristeva 1986, 186-213). Thinking beyond these strong social forms is difficult and often painful work. And yet, on the other hand, I wait impatiently to be needed less in fulfilling the exhausting physical and emotional demands of such as relationship. Mothering, then—what it means to have conceived, birthed, nursed, tended to in infancy and now in their increasing independence, three newly created individuals—is a major and significant position from which I draw my understanding of social relations with other women who are mothers and with those who are not, with men in their relation to me, to each other and to themselves, with processes of work, with political and economic processes I have access to and those that I don't, and with envisioned, hoped for and real possibilities.

I now have a study that doesn't have to double as a nursery. And I have three growing children who no longer need one. It is a small room at the back of the house overlooking the lake on which my home is located. It is four in the morning and very dark. Although I can hear the waves crashing on the rocks I cannot see the lake. Indeed I cannot see beyond the circle of light cast by the single desk lamp that lights up this small space I call my own. I sit inside this circumference of light surrounded by the deep darkness of a world that for the moments of my being here disappears as a concrete reality: if there are dishes in the sink I do not see them; if there is laundry piled in their baskets I will neither wash nor fold them; the matter of whether children's homework is or is not done is at the moment irrelevant; I am comforted by the security of knowing that in their bedrooms no one moves; no one has to be picked up or delivered to any other place; no one is being anxiously waited on for having missed their bus; forgotten lunches and lost mittens are realities saved for the moment when the rising sun streams once again across the bay signalling that this pool of uninterrupted space is no longer my own. This room, this pool of light, this place where I can sit alone, is a space with which I am deeply familiar.

As I reflect on the familiarity of the moment and on my "habit" of finding most comfort when I write at night, I realize that the legacy of these early times, both as constraint and as privilege, has stayed with me for these many years. I still struggle against the contingencies of the contradiction in my life between the mental and the manual lived through the realities of the social category implied by the term "intellectual woman." My commitment to working as an intellectual woman has been, and in big ways, continues to be marked by the contradictory reality of these public and private worlds even as their fusion offers the rich tapestry out of which I struggle to carve out legitimate spaces for the solitary work of thinking and writing. How I might do this in the midst of raising three children is as problematic for me as my struggles to transform through my work our collective social understanding of the situation of women. I still negotiate the oppositional desires that continue to mark my double life. And I still struggle with the possibilities of "telling," aware that academic discourse precludes the putting to public scrutiny the moments of our private life, an act which not only judges us indiscreet but as well is seen to confirm our inadequacy.

The phallocentric imperative mandates that women be marginal to a discourse which arises form the material realities of our daily lives to which we are profoundly central. Gender struggles begin in the inequalities expressed within patriarchy and the competing interests of women and men forged in our condition of unequal access to the terms of our social relations delineated both materially and symbolically because "the governing of our kind of society is done in concepts and symbols" (Smith 1987, 87). Just as "the measure of power" within a capitalist economy is the control and disposition of property of all kinds" (Morton 1988, 257), so the measure of power within a patriarchic discursive economy is the control and attribution of meaning. Finding the transformative practice that both confirms the existence of these realities and breaks the symbolic/discursive code through which women's subordination and men's entitlement is articulated is the ground of a feminist politic.

And yet, in the act of taking up this text, I am struck not only by the enormity of the contradiction which its production requires me to overcome but by the memory of that young woman in her blue uniform speaking in hushed tones about her grandmother. By tradition women have not had and continue to be restricted in our access to the public forum of intellectual exchange (Luke and Gore, 1992; Bannerji et al. 1991; Lewis 1990). Hence to write about the blocks to women's artistic/creative talent is itself a privileged practice even as it is contradictory, for am I not a woman writing and am I at least, therefore, not silenced in my creative work? The political economy of creative work means that for women it is an intrusion into dangerous territory as much as it is a concrete and unambiguous claiming of the word to effect social change knowing all the while that "the economy of this system requires that women be excluded from the single true legislating principle, namely the Word, as well as from the (always paternal) element that gave procreation a social value" (Moi 1986, 143). Caught in the vacuum between the myths and the realities of our passionately political project, what private spaces might be found by those women for whom the potential of a desk caught in a pool of light is not a possibility?

Author's Note

I wish to thank Barbara McDonald for her valuable suggestions on an earlier draft for this paper.

References

Bannerji, H., L. Carty, K. Dehli, S. Heald, and K. McKenna. (1991). *Unsettling relations: The university as a site of feminst struggles*. Toronto: The Women's Press.

Barreno, M. I., M. T. Horta, and M. V. da Costa. (1975). *The three Marias' new Portuguese letters*. New York: Doubleday.

Chernin, K. (1987). In the house of the flame bearers. *TIKKUN* 2 (3): 55–59.

Christian, M., and C. Williamson. (1983). The ones who aren't here. *Meg/Cris at Carnegie Hall: A double album*. Oakland: Second Wave Records, Inc.

Daly, M. (1978). *Gyn/Ecology: The metaethics of radical feminism*. Boston: Beacon Press.

Grumet, M. (1988). *Bitter milk*. Amherst: University of Massachusetts Press.

Hamilton, R. (1987). Working at home. In *The politics of diversity*, edited by R. Hamilton and M. Barrett, 139–53. Montreal: Book Centre, Inc.

Kristeva, J. (1986). Woman's time. In *The Kristeva reader*, edited by T. Moi, 186–213. Oxford: Basil Blackwell.

Lewis, M. (1993). *Teaching beyond women's silence*. New York: Routledge, Chapman, and Hall.

———. (1992). Power and education: Who decides the forms schools have taken and who should decide? In *Thirteen questions: Reframing education's conversation*, edited by J. Kincheloe and S. Steinberg. New York: Peter Land, Inc.

————. (1990). Interrupting patriarchy: Politics, resistance and transformation in the feminist classroom. *Harvard Educational Review* 60: 467–88.

————. (1989). The challenge of feminist pedagogy. *Queen's Quarterly* 96 (1): 117–30.

————, and R. Simon. (1986). A discourse not intended for her: Learning and teaching within patriarchy. *Harvard Educational Review* 56: 457–72.

Luke, C., and J. Gore. (1992). *Feminisms and critical pedagogy*. New York: Routedge, Chapman, and Hall.

Moi, T. (ed.) (1986). *The Kristeva reader*. Oxford: Basil Blackwell.

Morton, M. (1988). Dividing the wealth, sharing the poverty: The reformation of "family" in law in Ontario. *The Canadian Review of Sociology and Anthroplogy* 25: 254–75.

Olsen, T. (1978). *Silences*. New York: Delta/Seymour Lawrence.

Rockhill, K. (1991). Literacy as threat/desire: Longing to be somebody. In *Women and education: A Canadian perspective* (Second Edition), edited by J. Gaskell and A. McLaren, 333–49. Calgary: Detselig Enterprises Ltd.

Smith, D. (1978). A peculiar eclipsing: Women's exclusion from man's culture. *Women's Studies International Quarterly* 1: 281–95.

————. (1987). Women's perspective as a radical critique of sociology. In *Feminism and methodology*, edited by S. Harding, 84–96. Bloomington: Indiana University Press.

Weedon, C. (1987). *Feminist practice and poststructuralist theory*. Oxford: Basil Blackwell.

Chapter 16
Opening the Closed Door

Ellen Michaelson

In many ways a loner, I have always sought solitude. Taking time for myself, preserving a sense of separateness is a way of preserving a sense of myself as an individual, as not just one of the crowd. In this way I have resisted undue influences. But while even as a child I enjoyed time alone in intellectual or musical or creative pursuits, I always wanted to be part of the crowd, too. And in order to function effectively in a professional world, even as a medical student, I had to overcome these loner tendencies.

I did overcome my loner tendencies and throughout my medical training, my life became a race from one concrete task to the next, one activity to another. I did not have time even to think about the notion of solitude. Only recently have I had the desire and need to relearn how to be alone in order to do other kinds of work. Finding solitude to do creative work amidst the pressures of being a physician has been a reconnecting to myself as a person, as well as to myself as a woman.

I was first-born, I was bright, I had my own room. These things were accidents of birth. My parents divorced when I was ten, and I had to mature even more than I already was. My parents held this notion that I could take care of myself, that I did not need as much supervision and as many rules as my two younger sisters did. This was probably my parents' need more than mine, perhaps my mother's need more than my father's, though I sensed he felt the same way. So there I was, in many ways on my own while still a child.

Not unlike many adolescents, I was moody and self-conscious. My moodiness and my battle for individuality and selfhood were complicated, however, by my parents' divorce. It was the mid-sixties, a time when divorce was not a common thing as it is today. In my case, most of my struggles were waged, when not against myself, against my mother. I was determined to be a woman who was not dependent on a man who would then leave her to raise three small children on her own. That is, I would not be like my mother. I decided then I would be independent and strong, and I would have my way. In this context, one image from my adolescence stands out: a closed door. The door is the one to my bedroom, the one I tried to keep closed.

In the house where we lived until I was fifteen, my bedroom was directly behind the living room. The bedroom had two doors through which one could pass from the front hall to the rest of the small house. To shorten the path to the rest of the house, both wood doors to my bedroom were removed and replaced with soft folding ones that were kept open, and did not close very well even in the few moments when I was getting dressed and undressed each morning and night.

In one corner of my bedroom, I sat on my single bed—a home-made one, a mattress resting on one of the wood doors that had been removed—and watched the members of my whole family traipse back and forth to their own bedrooms and the one bathroom in the house. The family pet, a caged white mouse named Ringer, sat on top of the dresser near the far door that was closest to the rest of the house; there was no place else to put him. My sisters visited him at will. At night I listened to conversations between my parents and visiting friends, and between my parents themselves before the divorce.

When I was fifteen, we moved to a larger house with two floors. My bedroom was now at the end of the hall on the second floor by the master bathroom, and it had only one door. In my new bedroom, I had a real bed, a trundle bed, in an alcove between two windows in the middle of the outside wall. A wicker canopy painted pink to match the wall paper that I was allowed to pick for the walls in the alcove hung above my head. Whenever I went into my new bedroom, I closed the door.

I sat in the alcove with the door closed and I listened. Through one of the windows, I listened to the cough of the chain-smoking-piano-teacher-mother-of-five who lived next door with her physicist husband and cowed Irish setter. Through the other window, the dog barked to be let in the back door. From inside, I heard the banging of pots and pans and garbled speech from the small black and white television, which was always on as my mother cooked in the kitchen just below. At night, through the far wall where my desk was built in, a longer version of the removed wooden door, I heard my mother's solitary snores.

Whenever I went out of my new bedroom, I closed the door.

Whenever my mother came down the hall to use the master bathroom, she opened my bedroom door whether I was there or not. And when my chair and the top of my desk were covered with a week's worth of clothes, she swept the surfaces clean, dumping all my clothes in the middle of the floor. She did not close the door when she went out.

My mother meant well (and still does) but she never understood my need to be alone. To her the act of closing my bedroom door was antisocial. The label "antisocial" became indelibly stained on a socially (though never intellectually) shy teenager with the usual case of acne, a not-so-usual scoliosis (curvature of the spine), and an absent father. Being alone, wanting solitude was a blight against my personality that would take me years to overcome.

I live in a small one-bedroom apartment now, New York–style. My bedroom holds a loft bed under which is a dresser and a closet. Clothes hang from rungs of the ladder to the loft because the closet, the only one in the apartment, cannot hold the ten years' accumulation that I have carried with me since medical school. My bicycle rests along the short piece of wall that barely classifies as a hall between the bedroom and the rest of the apartment. The door to the bedroom is old and does not close. But since I live alone, that is of little concern.

I could live better, in a bigger space with more closets, with a bedroom door that closed, perhaps with two bedrooms so my guests would not have to sleep in the living room (which has no door), and I could hide all the piles of paper, the articles and journals unread, the copies of rewritten stories that collect dust in my living room, and the paperbacks that sit on the floor for the day when I put up additional shelving. I do try to organize. The compulsive doctor in me envisions a library-like system with every paper and book cross-referenced. The three-drawer black file cabinet that sits beneath the loft bed has only one drawer filled.

Periodically I take a day off from work and I remove piles of papers from behind the chair near the window seat in the living room. I tie the months-old fading Sunday *Times* into bundles to be placed on the street on Thursday night for recycling pick-up Friday mornings. I look through the piles of articles and stories intending to file or discard what I find. I read and reminisce. Then I make new, neater piles and put them elsewhere, usually on the floor in front of the bookcase alongside the paperback books for the day when I will put in place the brackets in the bottom two drawers of the file cabinet.

I choose not to afford a biweekly maid like many of my New York professional single friends. I choose not to live in a apartment and share expenses with a stranger. It is not that I love living in small, cluttered space. There are times when I grow impatient with the clutter and the lack of closets and the smallness of my three rooms. But at least for now, I have made a choice. I have chosen to write, and in order to have the time and the space, the inner space to do it, I do not chase dust and the almighty dollar that my doctor self has the capacity to do. Not everyone in my life understands.

"Does anyone want to explain the chapter to the class?" the teacher asked.

I had read the chapter he had assigned several times, not something I usually did when we started a new topic. But the concept the chapter introduced set my mind going, not unlike when I was ten or eleven and thought about the unendingness of the universe. I raised my hand, and the young teacher with thick, straight hair in a bowl-shape cut that made his hair swing when he walked, pointed across the lab table at me and I started to speak.

I went into a lengthy discussion of the principles of equilibrium. Once I was under way with my speech, I was not aware of the other students. Equilibrium was an amazing concept and I was totally enthralled. As I spoke, I visualized the molecules in front of my face. They hung in a cartoon bubble jumping to the words that flowed from my mouth and filled the air above the heads of the other students and the desks and the chairs. It seemed as though I were speaking in another tongue, communicating with another universe, the subatomic universe.

When I was done speaking, I looked down from the airy molecules. Every student in the class had turned in his or her seat and was staring at me. I thought that what I had said must have been unintelligible. Then I saw the teacher smiling. At least he had understood, or was sympathetic to my effort.

"Very good," he said. He was walking in the aisles between the desks. He stopped at my desk, put one hand on my shoulder. "You really did your homework. Excellent," he said. All the students were still facing me. One or two rolled their eyes and turned back to the front of the room as the teacher proceeded to explain further parts of what I had said. When the bell rang ending the class, the students all left quickly. No one said anything to me. The teacher smiled again and gave me a thumbs-up sign.

I had taken a lower-level chemistry class because the only higher-level one conflicted with advanced placement English. I was one of the editors of the school paper and was planning a career in journalism, or art history, depending on how I felt that day of the week. The following September, I registered as a freshman chemistry major. Later that year I declared myself premed.

As an adolescent, solitude was imposed upon me by circumstances of birth and personality. Being a loner stood me in good stead when it came to being a student. It was an asset: more comfortable in a classroom or with a book, I was not easily distracted by a need to socialize. In college I could sit for eight hours in the library studying organic chemistry or writing a paper. I always had a few close friends, but I was never part of the cliques.

When I went away to college, my days were filled with classes, usually an extra one, plus science labs and piano lessons and daily practice. I often sat alone in the cafeteria at lunch, not because I did not want to make friends, but because I was afraid I would get too caught up and not be able to pull myself away to do all the work I had to do.

On some level I knew myself back then, that I really had a desire to socialize, and this desire was seductive. But as my mother often told me, I had "things to accomplish in this world." I did not want to waste time. One of my friends told me that she admired me for being able to sit alone at lunch. She said she could never do anything like that. I had never thought of myself as brave, as someone to admire for choosing solitude over companionship.

It took me four years of college and several more of medical school to realize that I had to learn how not to be alone. After a full day, or several days of classes and activities that I enjoyed very much, I would look up for someone to talk to. But there were too few there. I was lonely. I had not spent much time creating a life outside my studies.

Still socially shy and timid in the face of authority figures, I had to learn how to talk, to connect with more than one or two close friends. I had to learn small talk, even to be superficial. And I learned much of that late, when I was a medical student. In fact, for a year or two my shyness and timidity became stumbling blocks to my finishing medical school at all. I had to make a lot of changes in order to learn to function effectively out of the classroom, away from the books and in the wards.

It was easier to talk to patients than it was to some of the other medical students and house staff, and the attending physicians who often had little time for the students. Especially the elderly patients: I could not talk freely with my own grandparents, but I liked these older patients. They were understanding and kind, and at first as a medical student, I identified with them. In my eyes they were poor and lonely. Many of them were women. No one visited them. Where were their children? Maybe they did not have any. They looked to me, they looked forward to the few minutes I would spend with them each day. I was their surrogate family. I looked down the road at my own life and saw myself as one of these lonely, abandoned women.

My first day of internship I told one elderly man whom I had just examined that I had to take care of a few things and promised to come right back to see him again. My beeper went off and I got caught up in the care of a number of other patients. That afternoon I did not get back to see him. When I entered his room the next morning, he kicked me out for not having kept my word. But by the end of a month of taking care of this elderly man, he would page me and I would come. He was my patient, I was his doctor. On the day he left the hospital he handed me an envelope. He was a man of limited means, he told me, but he wanted to give me something. Inside the envelope was a thank-you card and a five-dollar bill.

I soon realized the sense of empowerment and fulfillment that came from close relationships with patients. I found that it was often easier to be kind and loving to these strangers than it was to members of my own family. I also realized that patients and their families do not go home with their doctor at night, and they do not comfort their doctor when the doctor is sick or lonely. A doctor, a person, has to build a life of her own and learn how to comfort herself.

When I think about solitude, I think about eyes looking down intent on what hands are doing. I see my mother getting used to her bifocals, putting together a quilt in the upstairs master-bedroom-turned-sewing-room that used to belong to my sisters. My mother can work as long as her eyes do not dry out from an eye condition and her hands do not cramp from arthritis. Then she goes to her bedroom across the hall and curls up for a nap on the big bed that she has shared with a series of long-haired dachshunds for the past twenty-five years.

In a nook under another loft bed in an apartment not much different from my own, I think about another set of eyes scanning paragraphs, pages, chapters to see what next to rewrite. Eight hours a day for over seven months now, he labors to rewrite his second novel. Four years hard labor in all. Each night he creeps out of the nook and up the short set of stairs to the dark of his loft bed that he has shared for these months with an antibody that he cannot see or touch or feel but which he knows could, will probably one day take his life. "Yeah, I'm a gentle giant," he says and laughs. He knows this about himself, what other people see and touch and feel. He called me writer first.

I think about a young woman's eyes scanning the tiny face whose mouth holds onto her breast. "I told you never to call me at work," a man says to her. "I thought you'd like to know that I just gave birth to your baby," a woman doctor friend of mine says to her ex-boyfriend, also a doctor. They lived together for four years. They were separated briefly. Since her pregnancy, he is gone once again. She spends the first week after delivery home with the baby. Women friends visit during the day, but each night she is alone with her baby, changing her, pacing the floor with her, feeding her, trying to get a few hours sleep. "He wouldn't put his name on her birth certificate," she tells me. "I think it will actually be easier with a nursemaid than with a husband. That's it. No arguments. Easy."

Andreas was a twenty-eight-year-old male from Columbia. He was dying of Hodgkin's Disease, a cancer of the lymph glands that is curable in 70 percent of cases. He was not one of those lucky cases, however, and he was one of my patients when I was a hematology fellow. He was young and of Spanish origin and angry and tough and in pain. I was his fourth or fifth doctor. He did not know what to do with himself, and I did not know what to do for him. So together we struggled. His was the fiercer, more difficult struggle; I was merely his witness, and an active participant in his drama.

I held onto Andreas' story. It was Andreas' age, not much different than my own, the fact that his disease was usually curable and his particular case of it was not, his fight with himself, the disease, his girlfriend, with me. It was also the fact that as I became more involved, I saw my chiefs watching me, not interfering with what they saw but noting what went on between Andreas and me, that after a number of months Andreas would not see any physician other than me. I felt as though they were saying to themselves, "Her first patient to die so young. Let her go through it. It will be a good learning experience."

I first wrote a story about Andreas a few months after he died. It was very tedious. I put it aside and showed it to an editor-teacher six months later. He was interested in the material, though not in most of the writing. I tried to rewrite it. This second effort was worse than the first. I put it aside once again.

A year and a half later, without looking at the original, I wrote "Andreas." The first new draft came out in a flurry on the computer at home. Then I revised and rewrote. This work I did after hours on the computer in my office at the hospital. On Wednesdays after clinic, I stayed late, sometimes until nine o'clock. No one was in the suite, and I could work undisturbed.

For several weeks, pages and paragraphs of "Andreas" ran around in my head while I examined other patients, read their charts, decided on treatments. I worked hard in clinic on Wednesdays to finish on time, then waited for everyone to leave the office so I could get back to my patient. One night staring at the computer, rereading and revising, reliving and recreating what had been between Andreas and me, my beeper went off. I answered the page in a daze. I was busy with a patient that very moment. How could I attend to someone else? For those weeks I carried Andreas with me, I looked forward to the end of the day when I could re-enter our world. Even as I did, I felt odd. Somehow I betrayed myself, my patients, even Andreas. Getting back to the pages of his story was more real, more important to me than the patients down the hall.

Six months after I finished working on "Andreas," I visited another patient of mine in the Intensive Care Unit on a respirator. I had seen this sixty-year-old woman in my office every two weeks for a year and a half. We had been temporizing, trying to make the best of it, a balance between not too severe an anemia and not too much fluid in her lungs and her legs. We both knew we would not cure her hematologic disease, but it was her heart that was the more urgent problem. And we would not make that problem go away either.

Each day I visited Mary in the ICU where I could only make a few suggestions about her care. Other doctors were now in charge. Out of my allegiance to her and to our relationship, I chased after the intern who was caring for her, and badgered him for every detail. Lengthy discussions took place between myself and Mary's son, and myself and the head of ICU.

Then one day I remembered "Andreas" as I went to the ICU to see Mary. I stood by her bed. My eyes scanned her swollen belly, her exposed limbs bruised by so many needle sticks and lines. I took Mary's hand in mine, ran my other hand over the smooth surface of her taut skin. I placed her hand at her side, straightened the sheet that did not quite cover all her body parts, and I said goodbye.

When I finished my residency in internal medicine, I ran out and signed up for a writing workshop. A year later I was a part-time graduate student in fiction while also a fellow in hematology. A year and half into these two pursuits, I was confused and conflicted. I was a doctor and I also wanted to write. How could I do both? I could not ignore my patients, so I was able to let myself off the hook when my writing flagged. But my friends were getting published. What was I doing?

I left the M.F.A. program in fiction to complete my fellowship. Then at the urging of a doctor friend, I decided to work part-time as a doctor for awhile to give the writing a chance. It was a scary step, leaving the more-than-full-time rat race, the training that could still be continued and continued, and the safety of a prestigious institution. The early stages of my medical career.

And then, the solitude. What would I do with myself? After three years of residency and two more of fellowship, I couldn't sit still for half an hour without falling asleep. I hated to do nothing. I had to be busy. How could I sit all day alone and write? Or for half a day? What did I have to say? What if I had nothing to say? Wouldn't I be lonely? What if I couldn't write?

It has been three years since that decision. I still struggle with some of these questions. As I have worked on this piece that has temporarily taken me away from my fiction, I have struggled to put my struggle with this solitude down on the page. My writing is coming along, they call me "writer" now, published writers, my teachers and friends among them. Encouraging letters come in the mail from editors. I believe I can write.

Of course there are days when I waste time, when I have no good or interesting thoughts, when I do not want to write, when I find lots of things to distract me. There are days when I do not want to be sitting alone with myself. Why do I want to do this, I ask myself? What is it that I want to accomplish? Maybe I should be working harder, yes. And making more money. But, no. There are other weeks when I tire myself out, shifting back and forth between my computer and my patients and my medical students and my computer. I write a new story.

I am not afraid as I once was of being alone. I look forward to the full days when my only obligation is to sit at my computer and write. When one of these days is interrupted or taken away, I become irritable, cranky, resentful of whatever has intruded into my time and space. And then it becomes difficult to shift gears, to return to that inner space where I can think, read, feel. I am thrown off course. The pace of life outside my solitude is in such contrast to the rhythm that I define for myself. Often it is a struggle to maintain a balance, to be out in the world and then to get back to a place where I am more able to listen, and oddly enough, to let myself be more of a woman. It is acceptable in the world of fiction to be soft. It is acceptable to put my writing, my own muses above the pursuit of material objects and career advancement. Some days this is difficult, other days it is easy.

It is perhaps odd that this solitude has helped me to be myself. I retreat from the world of relations, away from my colleagues and patients and friends, away from my partner. And I return to them refreshed, more available. I have more to give, and at the same time I know better how to protect myself. I still struggle, however, with how much to give them and how much to save for myself. This will probably be an unending struggle now that I know how not to be alone, and I treasure my togetherness as much as my solitude.

But there is no doubt that through these struggles with my mother, my fellow students, my patients, myself with the need for solitude, that I have rediscovered the capacity for solitude and have come full circle. I have recovered parts of myself that I had to bury in medical school and through all those years of training. I do not think I am antisocial any more because I want to be alone to write, or even just to be by myself. Now I can freely choose to open the closed door.

Chapter 17

Solitude and Irony:
A Private Vision and Public Position

Elaine Atkins

As an English and curriculum teacher, I have, over the years, become increasingly comfortable talking about and providing opportunities for collaborative learning. I have read many texts on "community" and have based much of my own work on the hermeneutic concepts of dialogue and conversation. So when I was invited to contribute to this book, I immediately thought of Deborah Tannen's now famous paper on contrasting uses of silence. In 1984, Tannen compared the conversational style of New York Jews to other participants at a Thanksgiving dinner. Looking at the ways that different guests handled gaps in the conversational flow, Tannen noticed how uncomfortable she and the other Jewish New Yorkers were with silence, how they kept trying to keep the talk constantly going. She realized that her non-Jewish, non-New Yorker friends, on other hand, were much more comfortable with periods of silence and didn't feel it was their duty, for politeness' sake, to always make sure that there were no gaps in the conversation. Tannen titled her paper "Silence—Anything But" (1985). It occurred to me that an honest title for this chapter might be "Solitude—Anything But."

The idea of taking a serious look at solitude both challenged and discomfited me. I knew that in Spanish, the word "soledad" meant both loneliness and solitude. Although "solitude" and "loneliness" appeared separately in my lexicon, I don't think I had ever thought about them as distinct concepts. Solitude certainly did not carry a very strong positive connotation for me nor did it have a special or important resonance. I had grown up in an environment where it was as little prized as silence. Even the physical setup was wrong; living in an apartment house in New York City was not at all conducive to private, quiet encounters with myself; if I had known enough to want uninterrupted solitude, I would have had to have taken the bus to the library. The parks were busy.

As I approached middle age, a tacit, unacknowledged respect for solitude began to slowly creep into my consciousness, partly as a result of having read novelists such as Virginia Woolf, Kate Chopin, and May Sarton and partly from more recent conversations with friends, especially women who were steeped in feminist thought and had reflected on competing claims for privacy and community. On some level I understood that I had been escaping from even thinking about the role that solitude could, should play in my life as a woman and as a teacher. I remembered a conversation that I had had five years ago with a colleague at a curriculum conference. I was telling him about all the projects I was involved in, all the activities I was trying to complete and he simply replied, "When do you get the time to think?" I never forgot the question, even though I didn't do much about it. The discussion that follows is my attempt to figure out and clarify what solitude means (to me) and how this understanding can affect my life as a woman who is a teacher.

When a concept is grasped only vaguely, when it lacks sufficient experiential reference, a metaphor is needed. The poetry of Emily Dickinson provided me with such a starting metaphor. In a study of her life and art, Suzanne Juhasz (1983) points out that Dickinson spoke of the mind as an actual place in which to set up housekeeping. She refers to it as a house or room that she will keep in order (p. 14). In a poem that makes a strong statement about the power of the self alone, Dickinson writes:

> The Soul selects her own Society—
> Then—shuts the Door—
> To her divine Majority—
> Present no more—
> (from #303 in Johnson 1955)

Dickinson's most real life was her life in the mind, a place or kind of solitude that she made for herself. It was the occupied space she chose to inhabit (Juhasz, 171). As Juhasz suggests, when Dickinson describes mental experience in figurative language, she is incarnating the mind's ability to create, as well as codify experience (p. 177). Illuminating her conviction that the most important life is both interior and real, Dickinson writes:

> The Head is the Capitol of the Mind—
> The Mind is a single State—
> The Heart and Mind together make

> A single Continent—
> One—is the Population—
> Numerous enough
> This ecstatic nation
> Seek—it is Yourself.
> (from #1354 in Johnson 1955)

The metaphor of the mind as a place where an ecstatic nation of the self lives is the one I want to use to explore the power of solitude. I begin, then, with the idea of the mind as the scene of creativity, as the fertile house of the imaginative life.

This is a theme that weaves its way in and out of Anthony Storr's *Solitude: A Return to the Self* (1988). Storr echoes Dickinson when he suggests that by creating a new unity in a poem or other work of art, the artist attempts to restore or find a unity within the inner world of the psyche, as well as create something which has a real existence in the external world (p. 123). When I first read it, Storr's book jolted me and then helped me adjust my perspective. Before, I had thought of solitude as a retreat, as a way of sorting through or reflecting upon my life in the context of other relations. It had been a way of looking through the wrong end of a telescope, reversing the instrument so that I could see a whole picture from a greater distance. Being alone by choice allowed me to see myself on a smaller scale, in a more balanced perspective. Dickinson's depiction of solitude as a physical space was congenial to this: my mind was the refuge where I would figure things out before I went back "out there" to be with my family, friends, colleagues and students. Solitude was a tool for thinking about what I did or would do within the community.

Storr talks about solitude as a much more comprehensive, powerful force. He sees it as a direct route for achieving personal happiness, rather than as a tool for understanding relationships. He reminds us that the lives of creative individuals often run counter to the assumption that interpersonal relationships are the chief, if not only source of human happiness (p. ix). Just as Dickinson created her divine Majority of one, Storr speaks of individuals who have derived much happiness from solo activities (e.g., breeding carrier pigeons, playing the piano, setting up a cabin by a lake).

Storr questions assumptions that I have always taken for granted. He wonders whether the "burden of value with which we are at present loading interpersonal relationships is too heavy for those fragile craft to carry" (p. xiii), and speaks of the two opposing drives that operate throughout our lives: the drive for companionship and love, and the drive towards independence, separation and autonomy" (p. xiv). His book is an attempt to right this balance; not everyone does, can or should seek happiness solely or even partly within a community. Early on, he makes the case that human beings are directed by Nature, by adaptation, toward the impersonal as well as the personal (p. xiii). Later he suggests that good reasons exist for accepting the premise that humans are biologically constituted to possess an inner world of the imagination which differs from, though is connected to, the world of external reality (p. 69). Speaking about the later years of life, he reminds us that interest often moves naturally and increasingly toward pattern-making and the impersonal (p. 176). Storr is asking us to shift or at least enlarge our conception of happiness and fulfillment.

Citing Wordsworth's "Intimations of Immortality," Storr speaks of adults whose most vivid accounts of their childhood are captured in mystical unions with nature, in peculiar states of awareness (p. 17). Such moments of perfect harmony with the universe, he reminds us, are triggered by solitude and silence (p. 188). Storr is comfortable talking about religious and oceanic feelings; he describes the permanent, profound effects that such moments can have on the individual's perception of herself and the world she lives in (p. 38). Dickinson's ecstatic nation of one comes to mind here.

Storr is the most eloquent when he speaks of the power of creativity, not only in the more familiar terms of enriching or enhancing our lives, but rather as the essence of personal identity itself. He notes that the imagination has enabled human beings to use the impersonal, as well as the personal, as a principal means of self-development or growth (p. 75) and quotes De Quincey's assertion that "no man ever will unfold the capacities of his own intellect who does not at least checker his life with solitude" (p. 73). Speaking of "great introverted creators [who] are able to define identity and achieve self-realization by self-reference," he shows how they interact with their own past work rather than with other people (p. 147). Storr sees the artist or philosopher as maturing primarily on her own, defining herself through the changing and mattering nature of her work, rather than through her relations with others (p. 154). Emily Dickinson's solitary life is an example of this self-definition and maturation. For a creative artist like Dickinson, the search for coherence and sense takes place in the mind in solitude. In another passage suggestive of Emily Dickinson's life and work, Storr notes that for creative individuals who are introverted and have a difficult time making close relationships, developing their own point of view autonomously is of particular importance. Such thinkers are especially protective of their inner worlds, are often resistant to premature scrutiny and criticism, and in fact may be more than usually impervious to the ideas of others (p. 154).

Storr's study is so valuable to me not so much for the strength of its individual studies of creative figures but for its cumulative effect; I read it as an invitation to reconsider the role that solitude might play in my own life, and in the life of my students. It shows how the capacity, ability or art of being alone can be a rich resource for generation and creation, for maintaining contact with the inner world of the imagination.

I began this paper by revealing my distance from, my unfamiliarity with solitude as a positive, let alone necessary force. It is still a struggle for me to figure out how (not if) I will be able to make changes in my own life that will allow me to test what I can do in the place of my mind. Even more problematic for me, at this time, is to come to terms with how this shift in perspective will affect me as a teacher. I have readjusted my lens but I don't fully underhand yet what that will mean in practice. I am still working on fitting the concept of solitude into a broader philosophical framework, into an integrated world view; it is not a concept that I can productively think about in isolation (no pun intended).

As I mentioned earlier, for a number of years now, I have worked within European hermeneutic and American pragmatic traditions and have written about what a fusion of these two approaches might look like in education (Atkins 1988). Influenced by thinkers such as Hans-Georg Gadamer and Richard Rorty, I have focused my work on the importance of conversation, on the concept of dialogue in interpretive communities. As a result, I have been comfortable speaking of learning in terms of collaboration and shared meanings. Placing knowledge within the context of social or communal institutions, I had never thought seriously about how solitude allowed an individual to interact with her own thoughts rather than with other people, other texts. Nor had I ever thought self-consciously about how I could build on my own thoughts, my own imaginative creations.

When I first read Richard Rorty's recent book, *Contingency, Irony and Solidarity* (1989), I was struck by the attention he paid to the private person and the importance he attached to what he calls a private, final vocabulary. Rorty, after all, has long spoken in terms of community and solidarity, of socially constructed meanings and shared understandings. *Contingency, Irony and Solidarity* turns in interesting ways to the individual's internal, private life. It speaks of her "final vocabulary" as the set of words she carries about to justify her actions, her beliefs and her life: "These are the words in which we formulate praise of our friends and contempt for our enemies, our long-term projects, our deepest self-doubts and our highest hopes. They are the words in which we tell, sometimes prospectively and sometimes retrospectively, the story of our lives" (p. 73). Rorty stresses that these vocabularies are final in the sense that their user has no noncircular argumentative recourse if the worth of the words is challenged (p. 73). There are no ultimate truths to back them up. This, of course, is consistent with his previous work on contingency.

Rorty draws a very clear line between the private and public self. The citizens of his liberal utopia, which he refers to as a "poeticized culture", would give up the attempt to meld their private ways of dealing with their finitude to their sense of obligation to other human beings (p. 68). He says that John Stuart Mill's suggestion that governments devote themselves to "optimizing the balance between leaving people's private lives alone and preventing suffering" seems to him "pretty much the last word" (p. 63).

Rorty calls himself a liberal ironist. It is this concept that helps me locate my understanding of solitude within the hermeneutic and pragmatic traditions that I find so compelling. As his conception of liberalism, which is somewhat naive anyway, is not central to this discussion, it suffices here to note only that he defines a liberal (borrowing from Judith Shklar) as someone who considers "cruelty as the worst thing she does" (p. 74). His conception of the ironist is much richer and more germane to this discussion. For Rorty, an ironist is a person who has a sense of the contingency of her own commitment (p. 61) and who fulfills three conditions: (1) she continually doubts her own final vocabulary because other vocabularies have impressed her; (2) she realizes that she cannot dissolve these doubts through an argument phrased in her own vocabulary; and (3) she does not consider that her vocabulary is closer to reality than others' or that it is in touch with a power other than herself (p. 73). Because she is aware of the continency and fragility of her final vocabulary, and thus of herself, the ironist can never take herself seriously (pp. 73–74).

As a nominalist and a historicist, the ironist also cannot claim that anything has an intrinsic nature, a real essence (p. 74). Her skill at imaginative identification has to do the work that the metaphysician would do by drawing on antecedent moral motivation, be it rationality, the love of God, or the love of truth (p. 93). So instead of spending her time searching for the truth, she spends it worrying "about the possibility that she has been initiated into the wrong tribe, taught to play the wrong language game" (p. 75). In such a contingent world, she thinks of final vocabularies as poetic achievements, and describes her own search for a better final vocabulary in the language of metaphors of making rather than metaphors of discovering (p. 77).

Rorty suggests that the ironist reads Hegel, Nietzsche, Proust for their final vocabularies, to figure out whether she wants to adopt their images, to recreate herself, wholly or partly in their images. Experimenting with the vocabularies of these "poets," she redescribes herself, her situation and her past in their language and then compares the results with redescriptions that use the vocabularies of alternative figures. The ironist hopes, by this continual process of redescription, to construct the best self for herself (p. 80). It is not surprising, then, that Rorty draws from Dewey's *Art as Experience* when he suggests that the imagination is the chief instrument of the good, that art is more moral than established moralities. As Dewey (1958) suggests, the moral prophets of humanity are and have always been poets even though they speak in free verse or in parables (p. 69).

The social glue holding Rorty's liberal society together is little more than a consensus that the point of social organization is to allow everybody to have a chance at self-creation to the best of their abilities (p. 84). The reason why Rorty wants to preserve the institution of bourgeois liberal society is so that people will be free to work out "their private salvations, create their private self-images, reweave their webs of belief and desire in the light of whatever new people and books they happen to encounter" (p. 84). The task, then, is to equalize opportunities for self-creation, and then "leave people alone to use, or neglect, their opportunities" (pp. 84–85).

Ultimately, Rorty's argument rests on the individual, by herself, and in a permanent state of self-creation. As irony is inherently a private matter, the ironist is left on her own to create her own final vocabulary. This is the place, rooted in a contingent world, where I now locate myself as a woman and teacher. I see myself working on yet another final vocabulary, this time including solitude as part of my story.

As I mentioned above, I am not sure how recognizing and accepting this shift in consciousness will affect what I do as a teacher. I have taken a tacit concept, made it explicit, given it value, and placed it within a larger context or worldview but I have not formulated a program for action. I am just beginning to look at my students differently and ask questions about past practices. For example, if I regard each person as responsible for constructing her own story, her own final vocabulary, how can I guide every moment? If I value an inner spaciousness of the mind, what can I do to encourage or at least provide the room for the individual to construct her own meanings in solitude as well as in community? Are respecting and providing space sufficient or will I have to restructure the curriculum in ways that fundamentally change the way that my students and I relate to each other? What does an educational environment look like where students reconstruct their own knowledge in solitude, rather than always in collaboration?

Some of my favorite classroom practices now seem skewed if not misguided. Even an activity as seemingly benign as organizing collaborative writing groups will have to be scrutinized. It occurs to me that these peer revision teams, at least the way I have organized them, allowing almost no time for personal gestation, for private reflection, will have to change in structure and intent. I will have to design activities that encourage my students to come to their own terms with what they read, what we discuss in class. In short, I will have to look for ways to achieve a balance between the public and private. In the meantime, I also will have to continue to cultivate my own ability to think in solitude, to look for or create an ecstatic nation in my mind. I don't know if I agree with John Cowper Powys' claim that "all the nobler instincts of our race are born in solitude and suckled by silence" (p. 163), but I do know that without solitude and silence, we don't give ourselves much chance of creating a final vocabulary that can sustain us.

References

Atkins, E. (1988). Reframing curriculum theory in terms of interpretation and practice: A hermeneutical approach. *Journal of Curriculum Studies* 20: 437–48.

Dewey, J. (1958). *Art as experience*. New York: Capricorn Books.

Johnson, T. H. (ed.). (1955). *The poems of Emily Dickinson*. Cambridge: The Belknap Press of Harvard University Press.

Juhasz, S. (1983). *The undiscovered continent: Emily Dickinson and the space of the mind*. Bloomington, Ind.: Indiana University Press.

Powys, J. C. (1933). *A philosophy of solitude*. New York: Simon and Shuster.

Rorty, R. (1989). *Contingency, irony and solidarity*. Cambridge: Cambridge University Press.

Shklar, J. (1984). *Ordinary vices*. Cambridge, Mass.: Harvard University Press.

Storr, A. (1988). *Solitude: A return to the self*. New York: The Free Press.

Tannen, D. (1985). Silence: Anything but. In *Perspectives on Silence*, edited by D. Tannen and M. Saville. Norwood, N.J.: Ablex Publishing Co.

Chapter 18

Solitary Spaces:
Women, Teaching, and Curriculum

Janet L. Miller

I am alone in the house. But for me the world does not recede....Quite the contrary. The world is given point by my solitude. For even as I sit alone in my room, I feel a pull on my attention that necessarily attaches me to the world. Our intellectual work ought to give point to and signify those attachments. Our attachments ought to give point to that work.

—Jo Anne Pagano, "The Claim of Philia"

And when is there time to remember, to sift, to weigh, to estimate, to total? I will start and there will be an interruption and I will have to gather it all together again. Or I will become engulfed with all I did or did not do, with what should have been and what cannot be helped.

—Tillie Olsen, "I Stand Here Ironing"

One of my mother's favorite Perry Como renditions is "In My Solitude...," and I remember her humming that tune as she ironed, her swaying body keeping gentle time with the music drifting from the radio that was permanently anchored on a shelf above the kitchen sink. That particular form of solitude, a reverie laced with static from both the radio commercials and her two young daughters and embroidered with household and child-care routines, could only have been fragmentary and fleeting. Yet I think that my mother wove together those moments for her own thoughts from strands of music and from breezes that barely puffed the white curtains shading our kitchen window, knowing that she never would completely sever her musings from the bustle surrounding her.

As I remember this particular scene from my childhood, I think that my mother's humming could have signaled doubled spaces—spaces of both insulation and inclusion. The humming keyed us into her desire for time "to remember, to sift," as well as enabled us to locate her within her own solitude. And, although I was busy playing with my sister, I know that I listened for her humming as she bent over the ironing board, creating those doubled spaces amidst our squabbles and the banging of screen doors and the squeals of neighborhood children playing on the swing set in the backyard.

As a young child, then, I learned to hum like my mother, trundling behind her as she swept through the daily household chores with Perry Como or Rosemary Clooney or Nat King Cole as her constant cleaning companions. At that point, replicating only her accompaniment, not her intentions, my hums most often melded into my sister's and my high-pitched inquiries and conversations. And, even though we had learned early that my mother's humming expressed, in part, her desire to be alone with her own thoughts, we often disrupted its melodic flow as we called for her to watch us play our games or, more often, to settle disputes over ownership rights of game pieces or a favorite toy.

Later, when my mother went to work outside our home in order to help with family finances, I took over the ironing and dishwashing duties, my adolescent alto replicating my mother's versions of "In My Solitude…" or "Mona Lisa" as well as Elvis' renditions of "Hound Dog" and "Blue Suede Shoes." And even as much as I loved those teenage moments when I could be alone in the house, vocalizing to my latest junior high school crush, I missed her as I hummed and ironed. I was waiting, in the midst of my industriousness, for her to come home from work so that we could talk about the latest incidents at my school or her office.

In the ensuing years, I too have had to learn to extract my own versions of solitude from the patterned inundations of daily work and responsibilities. Lately, my desire for solitude seems to increase in direct proportion to the amount of work and related stress that I am experiencing at any particular moment. That desire quite often demands that I literally separate myself from others and from a normally routine schedule that has jumbled itself into momentary chaos. During those moments, I often feel that isolation and separation are the only states of mind and being that can enable me to regain a sense of myself and what I want and need to do.

So, sometimes, especially at the end of a semester, I long to spend days alone, puttering in my study or repotting plants—doing anything, so long as it is not in any way attached to the required events of university life. The very few times that I have been able to carve out such spaces, I have withdrawn momentarily from the world. I have unplugged the telephone—the answering machine was not a sufficient barrier, because I eventually had to return calls or, if I didn't, to confront the seemingly inevitable question, "Where have you been?" I have built a fortress around me of books and music and unopened mail and catalogues from every mail-order business in the United States, I swear. Then, quite often, I have read, listened, or attended to none of these. Instead, I have waited and watched for myself to return and to enter into the spaces that I had been filling with the needs and desires and requests of others. And I think that, in those moments, I was protecting myself, not from the intrusion of others but rather against further alienation from myself.

I think my desire for that particular scenario of solitude as isolation also reflected a certain desperation on my part. That desperate feeling kicked in, I think, especially when I saw myself in either/or positions. Either I was in the university, with all of its related committee meetings and journal article deadlines and student papers to read, or I could be in a world where none of those pressures existed. The second part of that either/or construction is the idealized academic dream that I've only lately begun to unravel.

For years, when I felt as though I needed to withdraw totally from my schedule and work commitments at the university, I truly believed that, if I could just finish my perpetual list of things to do, I would be able to successfully remove myself from every obligation that accompanied my daily life. And I could have a form of solitude that was unencumbered by the pressures and attachments and commitments that constituted a large part of my work at the university.

Of course, what I have begun to realize in recent years is that this version of solitude is not only impossible, but also is not what I really want. I cannot, nor do I wish to disconnect myself from the students, colleagues, and friends with whom I work or from the ideas and theories and debates that we exchange. Instead, I want to spin and shape and spew out series of doubled spaces, overlapping and intersecting spaces that connect the many passions and commitments in my life and from which I can both replenish and share myself.

Thus, what I want and am still learning how to do is to construct moments of both solitude and connectedness for myself—those doubled spaces—in which I am fully present, neither sifted into others' spaces nor drained from my own.

And so, I still am working to construct possibilities of solitude as moments spun from webs of connectedness. But connectedness, I am still learning, is different from immersion in others' versions or demands of me. For that immersion threatens a suppression or sub-version of my own desires and needs to those of others. And that's when I lose myself, and have to concoct that isolated version of soli-tude as a way of connecting with myself before I can effect similar con-nections with others, with ideas, with actions in the world.

Connectedness and attachment, in ways that I want to construct them, entail spaces of shared as well as individual questions, chal-lenges, interests, intentions and actions. Those permeable spaces allow me both to enter into relationships with others and to maintain room for myself within those relationships. I watched my mother, seemingly alone with her thoughts as she embellished both her ironing and Perry Como, and she watched me, constantly aware of what my sister and I were doing at any given moment. Her particular versions of solitude, swirled together with music and children's prattle and the hiss of the iron as it flattened damp clothing, are not mine. But her versions con-tinue to teach me that I need not construct only detached or isolated forms of solitude in order to replenish connections to myself or others.

Thus, I still might wish for those isolated forms on days when stu-dents and meetings and deadlines threaten to squeeze me out of myself and into others' versions of who and what I should be. And I am sure that my mother also longed for those forms of solitude that could guarantee protection against children's interruptions and the constant juggling of demands from both her home and outside work-place. But my mother's versions of solitude, shaped within the midst of those demands and interruptions, have taught me that I can replen-ish myself, even as I acknowledge and participate in my attachments to others and to the work that connects us.

By extension, then, in my work at the university, I see ways in which those versions inform my interests in curriculum, teaching, and research as reciprocal and interactive, rather than as separate and dis-crete constructions. My mother's versions of solitude, in which she watched and responded both to herself and to her family, have enabled me, in turn, to both claim and question constructions of myself and the communities in which I participate, to both honor and challenge boundaries that can enclose as well as exclude, to both thread together and unravel moments of solitude and relationship that inform my life as a woman academic.

Like my mother, I juggle demands and responsibilities. For me, those come in the forms of teaching, of preparing classes and advising students, of writing and researching. And like my mother, I now attempt to create solitary spaces as pauses, as shifting and momentary respites rather than as definitive and constricted separations between myself and others. And as I work to create those doubled spaces, I now can see ways in which the tensions that erupted in me as I tried to construct an either/or version of my life in the university are reflected in the themes that have dominated my academic work. I have struggled to identify the fragmentation that I have felt in my life as a woman academic by looking at effects of separations of public and private, of authority and nurturer, of theory and practice, that historically have characterized not only the field of education but also of women's work within that field.

Therefore, I continue to explore these separations as representative of ways in which social constructions of women's work and voices, as situated within a private, domestic sphere, devalue teachers who wish to be both nurturing and facilitative in their work. And I am interested in ways that we might reshape the historically immoveable boundaries between the public and the private into spaces that might include notions of communities and collaborations without consensus. Instead of promoting educational communities and identities that promise unity and sameness, where we all will become "reflective practitioners" or cheerful "teacher-researchers," for example, what might we do to shape communities and forms of collaboration in which we could struggle together to create versions of curriculum, teaching, and learning that do not posit particular voices and experiences as representative of us all?

I continue to struggle to create solitary spaces for myself that do not replicate or reify historically and culturally constructed boundaries between self and other, or between particular selves and others. But I also am aware of the difficulties of constructing a doubled-spaced version of solitude that does not easily slide into silence or confinement or isolation or sameness.

And so, like my mother, ever watchful in her momentary solitude, I drive home from my evening's teaching, already casting an eye toward the next class discussion, mindful of a student's request for further reading, of the questions to which I want to attend in our next session, and of the students' papers that I must read before tomorrow's class. Like my mother, even as I savor the drive home as a small sliver of solitude, shaved from the day's schedule of endless meetings and teaching, I am watching and responding, aware of my connections to others whose varied and multiple interests and concerns inform, though often do not replicate, my own.

But as I teach, research, and write as part of my university responsibilities, I continue to confront myriad versions of ways in which schooling structures perpetuate the separations and compartmentalizations that keep us from ourselves and others. So just as I must work to create solitary spaces that both enclose and invite, that acknowledge my attachments both to the world and to myself, I also want to incorporate such doubled spaces into the ways in which I work as a woman academic. For me, the continuing challenge in all of this is to claim the connections and the differences created within such spaces while constantly questioning those boundaries against which I must push in order to claim myself.

For example, as I work with graduate students who are themselves teachers and administrators in the schools, we still must grapple with versions of teaching and curriculum that conceptualize pedagogy as a series of discrete skills and curriculum as content, as separate and autonomous disciplines, each with its testable facts and measurable knowledges. To create spaces in which to consider other possibilities for curriculum and teaching, then, we study conceptions of curriculum that extend traditional definitions of curriculum as content into analyses of social, historical, cultural, and economic forces that shape and influence the constructions of such content. And we try to examine those forces as they are occurring in the experience of our particular situations, in the contexts of our daily lives.

But, as we do so, teachers bring to class stories of daily confrontations with their school districts' central office mandates about students' raised achievement scores as evidence of "rigorous curriculum" and "effective" teaching and learning. Or administrators tell of pressures to squeeze curriculum into testable areas, so that chunks of material are "integrated" into conveniently measurable segments of knowledge. Or I talk of my frustration in working with a school administrator who wants to see, in a multiple-choice test format, measurable differences in students' writing. This "evidence" will inform the school district's decision to continue or halt a writing process inservice program for teachers and students in which I have been participating for eight years.

These various vignettes that my graduate students and I share and analyze and deconstruct illustrate the separations and distillations of curriculum, teaching, and learning into neat packages of measured and predetermined knowledges. And such conceptions propose that teach-

Solitary Spaces

ing and curriculum are actually separable from my students' or my own musing drive home after class, and from the relationships that spill from our classrooms and meetings into those momentary and moving solitary spaces. And those conceptual separations then threaten to become reified spaces that demarcate the public arenas of education as places filled with official words and actions of certain others who have been designated as "experts" or as representatives of us all.

Within such authoritative and restricted boundaries, my graduate students and I are officially separated from the interactions and relationships and cultural forces that we know frame and influence our curriculum and teaching constructions. And in those separated, autonomous, and reified conceptions of teaching and curriculum, my versions of solitary spaces, of curriculum, and of teaching as connected clearings in which to both watch and respond are shoved to the margins of educational practice. They are squeezed into distorted spaces of fragmentation and separation, of isolation and exclusion, or of totalizing discourses that certify only particular knowledges. Such reified constructions threaten my own as well as my students' attempts to clear solitary spaces in which we might reflect, question, replenish, and constantly transform our connections to our varied and multiple worlds.

And so, in order to create the kinds of doubled versions of solitary spaces that I initially experienced as I listened to my mother's humming, I also have had to increase my tolerance for ambiguity. In order to work in the schools, I have to deal with school districts' versions of curriculum as content that teachers must "cover" before they can turn their attentions to me and to the writing processes which I think can enable students and teachers to create curriculum. And, in order to work in the university, I still must struggle with my internalizations of how I "should be" in the academy. I am attempting to create versions of myself as a woman professor who is able to claim my own sense of authority as teacher and researcher and writer as well as my sense of connectedness to myself and others. At the same time, I still struggle with the "shoulds" that have been constructed from social, historical, and cultural framings of women in such positions. I still struggle with "either/or" versions of professor as "authority and expert" or as "nurturer and facilitator," for example. And, as I try to move into fluid conceptions of myself as possibly both/and, I remember my mother and her doubled versions of solitude that I still am working to create.

Thus, I continue to confront the silences and omissions as well as the possibilities within my emerging versions of solitude. For I still want to create solitary and communal spaces within teaching and curriculum that are overlapping and connected, but that also acknowledge and claim differences. And I know that my versions of solitude and of curriculum and teaching, constructed from my position as a white, middle-class woman academic, do not necessarily reflect the same ambiguities, conflicts, and exclusions felt by other women in similar positions. And I also know that the luxury of even contemplating such versions may not be in the province of many women who have little, if any time, to "remember, to sift, to weigh, to estimate, to total...."

And so, perhaps my early recollections of solitude, formed in the connected yet ambivalent spaces of my mother's work and reverie, can enable me to enlarge my understandings of my own privilege and of my particular constructions of myself as a woman academic. Perhaps my understandings of solitude as spaces forged in the midst of daily educational work and connected both to the relationships and the contents that are the focus of those activities also will enlarge. I want such enlarged understandings in order to work with others to forge educational communities and collaborations without consensus, without the pressure to merge into one position or one right answer or one identity.

I talked with my mother again about this paper and about her versions of solitude. We hummed a few phrases of "In My Solitude..." to one another, and then we laughed. "How did you ever remember that?" she asked, just as I voiced the same question to her, knowing that her remembrances and versions would not be mine. We talked for a few more minutes, as she recalled returning to work outside our home full-time when my sister and I were in elementary school, and really enjoying new forms of solitude on her daily bus ride into downtown Pittsburgh and in the work that awaited her there.

My mother recently has moved into a new apartment, and she was unpacking a box of photographs, even as we were speaking on the telephone. I could hear her humming a bit between the lines of our conversation, especially as she debated the best placement of the pictures of my father and my sister and me. She was both with me and not, both watching and responding, and that slight solitary space in the midst of our conversation hung in the air for a few moments after I hung up the phone, connecting us still across our separations and differences.

Chapter 19

Writing Autobiographically in Solitude about Teaching: Why To; How To

Ann Berlak

> *[A]lready bored, Lily felt that something was lacking; Mr. Bankes felt that something was lacking. Pulling her shawl round her, Mrs. Ramsay felt that something was lacking. All of them bending themselves to listen thought, "Pray heaven that the inside of my mind may not be exposed," for each thought, "The others are feeling this. They are outraged and indignant with the government about the fishermen. Whereas I feel nothing at all."*
>
> *Now all the candles were lit up and the faces on both sides of the table were brought nearer by the candlelight, and composed, as they had not been in the twilight, into a party round a table....Some change at once went through them all...and they were all conscious of making a party together in a hollow, on an island; had a common cause against that fluidity out there....It partook, [Mrs. Ramsay] felt, carefully helping Mr. Bankes to a specially tender piece, of eternity...there is a coherence in things, a stability; something, she meant, is immune from change, and shines out...in the face of the flowing, the spectral, like a ruby....Of such moments, she thought, the thing is made that endures.*
>
> —Virginia Woolf, *To the Lighthouse*

Long before I imagined myself teaching (while I was still in college), I was enraptured by this transformation of relationships and consciousness at Mrs. Ramsay's dinner table. Today, as I have taken myself away from friends and family to sort out this question of women and solitude, I recognize in that moment of transformation a central metaphor for what I have wanted (and have experienced, infrequently, unpredictably) in my classrooms, and in the classrooms of

253

students whom I "prepare" for teaching: a coherence—a thing that endures.

Such moments seldom occur in our classrooms. Most students of United States schools at all levels would be better off spending their days in well-provisioned playgrounds and libraries than sitting in the classrooms we offer them. I see the degradation of schooling as one of the effects (and causes) of a corrupt and unjust society and its institutions, and believe that significant changes in our social and economic structures must accompany if not precede the enlivening, creative, transformative classrooms we so desperately require. Yet in a world well on its way towards ecological destruction, where contrasts between the wealthy and the poor boggle the mind, while Rome is burning, I clear my calendar, carefully select my companions from the bookshelf, and remove myself from the world: I go off by myself to think and write about my teaching.

I do so because I need to take the time both to see the coherence of my teaching in the face of the flowing, and to see it critically, to analyze the parts: "(T)o think of things in themselves. That building, for example, do I like it or not?...Is that in my opinion a good book or a bad?" (Woolf [1929] 1957, 39), and also "to see the world as [I have] not seen it before, to hear people's voices and not only what they are saying but what they are trying to say...sense [a]...whole truth about them...sense existence, not piecemeal—not this object and that—, but as a translucent whole" (Ueland 1987, 53).

I know too many of the conscious and unconscious taken-for-granted assumptions implicit in the ways I think, respond and teach perpetuate things as they are, often blinding and desensitizing me to what's happening before my eyes, in my classrooms and beyond. As teacher and teacher of teachers—a transmitter and potential contributor to the transformation of the culture—I need to take the time to question what I take for granted more deeply than I ordinarily, in the flux of daily life, can do. It is currently fashionable and also, I think, of great importance, to identify the social, political and cultural assumptions deeply embedded in the full spectrum of curricular and pedagogical writings from right to left that are associated with maintenance of inequality and environmental destruction. Bowers and Flinders (1990), for example, identify some of the ways certain cultural assumptions about the nature and grounds of knowledge, the nature of language, and the nature of the individual permeate every capillary of our teaching theory and practice (see also Ellsworth 1990; Cherryholmes 1988). Yet, as I have written about elsewhere (1991a, 1991b), though I know these traps are there, I nonetheless fall into them (and I doubt I do so more easily than most).

To give another example, I know that as a European-American academic woman I receive and convey privileges of which I am at least partially unaware, and that I have also come to take for granted certain androcentric assumptions, just as members of other nondominant groups often take for granted some of the privileges of those who are more powerful than they. Is it therefore unsurprising that in my practice I transmit ways of thinking about the world that contribute to the reproduction of the very problems I intend to counteract?

I wish not only to question whatever dogmas I take for granted and reconsider my practices that flow from them, and to see how my part is related to the whole—as a person and as a member of that particular subset teacher—but also to *act* in ways that are consistent with my re-vision (though my actions will inevitably carry some residue of the oppressive ways I've learned of thinking and being in the world). I want to be more able to model to my students clear thinking, creativity, centeredness, no easy task, especially in the present circumstances of increased class size and workloads, and the political-correctness backlash, which urges constriction, not expansion of thought.

I ask, with Anna, the infant school teacher of Maori and European children, whose semi-autobiographical story Sylvia Ashton-Warner tells in *Spinster*, as she recollects having smacked a child, "How in heaven can I free myself from the tyranny of traditional thinking?" (1971, 37).

Some of Anna's most ecstatic teaching moments originate in some force or intuition that has no resemblance to what one ordinarily thinks of as self-reflection, or the questioning of taken-for-granteds:

> Sensuously and accurately I vibrate and respond to the multi-fold touch of my Little Ones....I am made of their thoughts and their feelings....I don't know what I have been saying or what I will say next (p. 22)....Some other deeper mysterious plan takes over. I look for it sometimes...if only I could put my finger on it beforehand. But I never can. I only recognize it when my intentions break astray, when something unexpected yet fundamentally gratifying takes their place. And I find myself wishing I was more accessible to this thing so that it could substitute for the brain I haven't got....I am as clay in the hands of this force, this something that told my delphiniums when to bud. (p. 28)

Both crying and singing have the same essential quality. They draw us together....Sometimes they [the children] cluster round the piano to sing....They sing themselves inside out....Then so strong is the air...that's about all I ask for in a moment of joy. (p. 51)

At other moments Anna does reflect upon the teaching process in the moment she is teaching. While sitting before her children she muses: "What a dangerous activity reading is....All the plastering on of foreign stuff. Why plaster on at all when there's so much inside already?" (p. 40). Later, also while teaching, she "pictures the infant room as one widening crater, loud with the sound of erupting creativity" (p. 41), while simultaneously reflecting on the criticism she would receive if the Inspector were to see her classroom at that moment, and feeling guilty about her nontraditional ways. Later she thinks, "What a lot I see, both behind my eyes and before, as I sit on this chair" (p. 41).

But this reflection in action, even though practiced by an exceptionally skilled practitioner, takes Anna only so far. "The mind flashes, many faceted....This thought, that thought...this memory, that. How can you keep track of the changes during an entire afternoon? Of the smile, the tear, the tenderness, the rage?...By the time I...take one last look across the plains to my favorite hill blurred with the enclosing rain...the storm reminds me of something I was thinking on early....I still register a mysterious feeling of a necessity to...prepare for a birth. But what was about to be born?" (p. 60). She is waiting for the birth, translucent and whole, of the secret to teaching all her children, European and Maori, to read.

In those times when I have gone off by myself for the purpose of thinking and writing about my teaching I have looked at what I think about while I am on the "shopfloor." I think of particular moments, lessons and courses I have taught, and ask myself what I was thinking as I made a particular decision or choice (Berlak 1989, 1991a, 1991b). I have learned that when I am at my best I, like Anna, construct my teaching while in motion, responding to the materials I am given: the moment in time, the news of the day, yesterday's argument, tomorrow's promise, the students who may show up and the moods they're in and, of course, the public knowledge I hope to teach. I have learned that I do, of course, sometimes reflect while in action. But my reflections are primarily about the subject—during a classroom conversation on the topic, I reflect with the students about the changing meaning of "politically correct." However, I ponder only fleetingly and infrequently on the classroom process while I'm teaching. Unlike

Anna, rarely do I, while teaching, puzzle about my pedagogical and curricular taken-for-granteds.

Later, perhaps an hour, a day, even a year later, while musing haphazardly about an event or a student, I may see something I had not seen before, why a particular course went well or badly, how my satisfaction with a class session was only possible because no one questioned the Eurocentric bias. Sometimes I ponder in a more focused way, particularly when prompted by students' criticisms or concerns. I might even talk about a situation—most often a troubling one—with a student or a peer. And perhaps as a result I come to understand the situation better; a light may dawn. I don't think, however, that at these times I follow the thread to its roots in some basic assumption I take for granted about curriculum, pedagogy, the learning process, the nature of human relationships, nor are the insights that result likely to be remembered and integrated; the social amnesia of teaching is both cumulative and individual. In any case, as with Anna, larger patterns of meaning do not become clear for me at such times. Like Anna, the vision of how the parts are related to the whole eludes me while I am in the process of teaching.

Writing Autobiographically in Solitude About Teaching

For three years, I have written autobiographically about teaching, in periods of solitude of varying lengths and degrees. In spite of the pleasure and satisfaction doing this has brought me, it's not an easy thing to commit myself to do. The impediments are both internal and external. Like primary and secondary teachers, I have no institutional incentive to write, so I am faced with the problem of finding some other justification to offer myself as well as others, for being unavailable as mother, wife, friend or teacher, every weekday morning in July, every weekend in February, or five days in August. First I ask myself, "Who am *I* to write about my experience as teacher?" Annie Dillard says, "Assume you write for an audience of terminal patients....What could you say to a dying person that would not enrage by its triviality?" (1989, 68). I fear to be the well-meaning Mary Carmichael Virginia Woolf writes about: "A skimmer of surfaces merely...[unable to look] beneath into the depths...[to] show the meaning of all of this" (Woolf [1929] 1957, 97).

It would be easier to claim the right to write autobiographically about teaching if more teachers, and particularly female teachers, had engaged in this activity in the past. Where are the classroom adventure stories? Where are the respectful gazes, the sustained looks that lay bare the splendor as well as the squalor of the teaching endeavor? There are very few, and *Spinster* is out of print. I was never assigned teachers' autobiographical accounts of their teaching in any education course through the Ph.D. Good writers of any genre (and I do not aspire to the masterpieces of which Woolf is speaking here) are not "single and solitary births. They are the outcome of thinking in common...so that the experience of the mass is behind a single voice" ([1929] 1957, 68).

Annie Dillard: "A writer...inquires not after what [she] loves best, but after what [she] alone loves at all. There is something you find interesting, for a reason hard to explain. It is hard to explain because you have never read it on any page....There you begin. You were made and set here to give voice to this" (1989, 76). In the absence of a tradition of autobiographical accounts of teaching, at a time when so many voices are silenced, and women's voices are still struggling to be heard, it's not easy for me to accept Dillard's dictum. And so when someone asks me where I'll be next week—as we pass a homeless man upon the street—I have to muster up courage to respond honestly, "I'm going away by myself to write."

And yet I'm here and am writing in the hope that many other teachers will also, literally or figuratively, pack their bags. What is to be gained? I come away to slow down, to get some distance on the work I do for a living, to await the muse; to try to make sense of my life and my vocation, not to find truths that will apply to classrooms or teachers across the board, but to understand my own individual experience, to see the macro in my micro, to see what's before my eyes and its significance, to learn more about what Anna calls "this thing," "this force," to find a way of teaching that might endure, to see what of eternity might be at my dinner table.

In my last sortie into solitude I looked closely at a course I had just completed teaching that was designed to encourage students to examine their racism, sexism, antisemitism, heterosexism, and classism. Months after the course was over, in solitude, I looked closely at a single class session that was powerful and disturbing for all of us. I looked at it from many different angles, considering the talks about it I had had with students, colleagues and friends, and I read. As I look now at what I came to understand and then to write about, I recognize for the first time that one thing I discovered in that class session was a moment of wholeness, though I hadn't recognized it as such until long after the course was over, and some understanding of the conditions under which such moments emerge. Only now, months after writing about the event, here by myself, can I name what I was then and have been searching to understand more about: moments of teaching that, like the moment at Mrs. Ramsay's dinner table, though only temporary, will endure.

Thus, I write not primarily to be understood, but in order to understand (Rico 1983, 29). I want to catch the paradoxes that have flashed through my mind during the semester, and consider them at my leisure, to puzzle, for example, at the absence of outrage at injustice so characteristic of my students (Berlak 1989), as Anna puzzles about teaching the Maori children to write, because, she thinks "the moment a man starts to write he ceases to live" (p. 154). I want to clarify the immense awesome complexity of teaching, to see some pattern in the interactions between those present in our classroom, interactions that shift from moment to moment, and from week to week. I want to impose my own particular way of looking upon the flux.

In solitude—away from distractions, from the dailiness—I may discover some things that parts of me don't really want to know: perhaps how I've betrayed a student, with a look, or with a word, and why. At such times the rewards of insight and understanding outweigh the private humiliation that confronting myself might otherwise entail. In solitude, without distraction, my more patient, more open, less defensive selves converse with the short-sighted, quick-thinking, less contemplative ones, the ones more likely to be governed by the taken-for-granted.

I go into solitude in order to change the way I teach, so that next semester I will respond to a student's question differently than I would have if I had not attended this seminar with myself (Berlak 1991a). Ultimately, I go in the hopes that I may be a better builder in the classroom of moments of wholeness from the bit of this and that I am given.

Why not just go and think in solitude? Why write? Why write for others? Would writing a journal do as well? For me, writing a "piece" forces me to search out the larger pattern, find an underlying story (and there are many "true" stories one might tell about the same events), makes me think harder, not be satisfied with first impressions, easy answers, facile ways of making sense. It involves me in mental conversations with potential readers, demands of me that I look at what sense I'm making from different points of view. I also write in order to preserve and dignify the classroom teaching/learning process: to leave a written trace in the hope that doing so will remind those who together construct transitory moments of significance to grant them the recognition and respect that they deserve.

HOW TO: First I read. I arrive in solitude (at a friend's house, a retreat in the woods, or a room in my house with the phone turned off, the answering machine silenced, and strict orders to myself and husband that I'm not to be disturbed) with carefully chosen books. Some books I have chosen because they will talk back to me, that is, unsettle my taken-for-granted views. Gloria Anzaldua is with me. She writes: I "live in a state of psychic unrest" as a result of being a Chicana and a queer. Living in that borderland is "what makes poets write and artists create" (1988, 11). I read more slowly in solitude; I allow my mind to wander. What does it mean to live in a borderland? What are the implications of what Anzaldua has written for a white, middle-class heterosexual woman who also wants to write and create? I select other writers (and Anzaldua is also in this group) because they have explored territories for which I am bound. I choose some whose prose I hope will lend some music to mine. The writer, says Dillard, "is careful of what [she] reads, for that is what [she] will write" (1989, 68). Such is my "review of the literature."

In the good company of Anzaldua and Dillard, I struggle to slow down. Anzaldua: "In my head I sometimes will say a prayer—an affirmation and a voicing of intent. Then I run water, wash the dishes... take a bath. This 'induction' period sometimes takes a few minutes, sometimes hours. But I always go against resistance" (p. 31). For Anzaldua the resistance is embedded in the pain she will explore as a writer because she lives in the borderlands. For me it is connected to my efficient quick reactive habits, and the fear I won't be able to find what I'm looking for.

I restrain the urge that comes almost immediately to begin to outline the "piece." I must encourage my mind to be idle, "not *willing* all the time. This quiet looking and thinking is the imagination; it is letting in ideas. Willing is doing something you know already...there is no imaginative understanding in it. And presently your soul gets frightfully sterile and dry because you are so quick, happy and efficient...you have not time for your own ideas to come in and develop and gently shine (Ueland, 29)." For Anna, it took six weeks of summer vacation, "complete possession of the days, and peace" (p. 168) for her to reach a new plateau of understanding in her great discovery of the key vocabulary.

Then comes the sustained, relaxed but focused concentration, the time to begin to distill the essence of a teaching moment, a class session, or a course. My mind alights upon a puzzle, paradox, contradiction, a painful, boring or exhilarating moment. If, like Anna was so frequently, I was truly present, "sensuously and accurately responding" in the moment I am seeking to re-view, I can more easily relive it. Annie Dillard: "...why so many books recall the author's childhood. A writer's childhood may well have been the occasion of [her] only firsthand experience" (p. 44). I reexperience the event or series of events with all the time in the world, turn it every which way, ask myself why I have come to call this particular series of images and sounds an event, why I see them as a series, simply, what was going on? If I feel inclined to read or reread a passage of a book, I do so, assuming my unconscious has its reasons. Gloria Anzaldua and Annie Dillard both speak of the beneficent effects of sensory deprivation at such times "so imagination can meet memory in the dark" (Dillard, 26). I prefer a room with a view opening out into the natural world.

Eventually arises the genuine—in contrast to the anxiety provoked—desire to put pencil to paper (or, recently, fingers to keyboard) of which other writers have taken note (Rico 1983). Tillie Olsen writes of "the work of creation and the circumstances it demands for full functioning...when the response comes, availability to work must be immediate" (1978, 11, 14), and, in telling of her struggle for solitude, reminds me how great a privilege it is to be sitting here alone. Later comes the process of revising, the continuing conversation with the self.

This process of discovery is slow, even for a gifted artist. Anna: "Why am I so slow to see these things? This has been with me for a year and I have not seen it until now. What a truly remarkable capacity I have for not seeing the obvious beneath my nose. It amounts to an infirmity, this blindness" (p. 193). During the period of time Anna tells of, she never completes the process of freeing herself from the tyranny of traditional thinking. At the end of the book, when she is not given a good grading by the Senior, she accepts his judgment: "I'm satisfied that I am no more than a vague incompetent artist, inadvertently and regrettably let loose among children" (p. 238).

I too continue to fight the power of traditional thinking and know that I will not, of course, ever finally win. Still, the process of reflecting in solitude changes more than my teaching—it helps me when I return to society to keep my eye on the ball, ask the grand questions, slow down, look, see.

The solitude I have found renewing and enlivening depends, of course, upon many moments of sociality in the rhythms of my life. First of all, for me there's no writing without teaching; the teaching is the experience of which I write. Second, I write to communicate with others, to initiate or continue reflective conversation about teaching, to "exchange a living current with a listener" (Ueland, 165). I write to enlarge a conversation. Third, my reflections on and writing about teaching are nourished by talking with, as well as reading the works of, others. Anna felt interaction with another was essential for understanding her work. "If only," she says, "I could relate this academic life of the infant room with the one of sensuousness beyond....[But to do this] I need something else, like the rain, like the sun: you need two for inspiration, but I am only one" (p. 43). The "something else" for her was the Inspector, who later in the year, provided the touch, the word "caption," that helped Anna crystalize the idea of the key vocabulary and bring it and the insights that supported it to birth.

What about those of us who do not have an other to help us look beneath the depths as Anna's sympathetic Inspector did when he provided what she needed to grasp how the whole of reading instruction was connected with its parts? What might Anna have meant when she spoke of the other that she needed as "something like the rain, like the sun?" Perhaps she means that something right here before me—the sun, the fallen apples on the path, the whirring hummingbird, a portrait of a dinner party—may, in undisturbed sessions of solitude, reveal itself as a metaphor that will disperse the weight of traditional thinking and illuminate my experience to me anew. Such revelations do not arrive on cue. But at least for me solitude is a prerequisite for their appearances.

References

Anzaldua, G. (1988). The path of the red and black ink. In *Multicultural literacy*, edited by Rick Simonson and Scott Walker. St. Paul: Greywolf.

Ashton Warner, S. (1971). *Spinster*. New York: Touchstone. (First edition 1958)

Berlak, A. (1989). Teaching for outrage and empathy in the liberal arts. *Educational Foundations* 3 (2): 69–95.

———. (1991a). Experiencing teaching: Viewing and reviewing Education 429. *Educational Foundations* 5 (2): 27–47.

———. (1991b). Anti-racist pedagogy in a college classroom: Mutual recognition and a logic of paradox. Paper presented to the American Educational Research Association, Chicago.

Bowers, C. A. (1990). *Responsive teaching: An ecological approach to classroom patterns of language, culture and thought*. New York: Teachers College Press.

Cherryholmes, C. (1989). *Power and criticism: Poststructural investigations in education*. New York: Teachers College Press.

Dillard, A. (1989). *The writing life*. New York: Harper and Row.

Ellsworth, E. (1989). Why doesn't this feel empowering? Working through the repressive myths of critical pedagogy. *Harvard Educational Review* 59: 297–324.

Olsen, T. (1978). *Silences*. New York: Delacourt. (First Edition 1965)

Rico, G. (1983). *Writing the natural way*. Los Angeles: Tarcher.

Ueland, B. (1987). *If you want to write*. St. Paul: Greywolf. (First edition 1938)

Walizer, M. (N.d.). Teachers' stories as research and reflection. Unpublished, undated manuscript, Princeton University.

Woolf, V. (1957). (1927). *To the lighthouse*. New York: Harcourt Brace.

———. *A room of one's own*. San Diego: Harcourt Brace. (First edition 1929.)

Chapter 20

A Time and Place of One's Own: Women's Struggles for Solitude

Linda K. Christian-Smith

It is harder for women, perhaps, to be "one-pointed," much harder for them to clear space around whatever it is they want to do beyond household chores and family life. Their lives are fragmented...this is the cry I get in so many letters—the cry not so much for "a room of one's own" as time of one's own. Conflict becomes acute, whatever it may be about, when there is no margin left on any day in which to try at least to resolve it.

—May Sarton, *Journal of a Solitude*

During my rereading of May Sarton's remarkable account of her struggles to achieve solitude and come to terms with the self-knowledge contemplation brought her, I relived my lifelong struggles to have both time and a room of my own. Solitude has always been important to me and a central factor in integrating my many lives as daughter, sister, spouse, friend, teacher, scholar and political activist. Unlike William Sadler (1974), I do not equate solitude with loneliness or alienation, although it can have those dimensions as revealed in Sarton's daily account of her solitary life of writing poetry. Like John Cowper Powys, I regard the cultivation of solitude as necessary to life in society (1933, 55). I agree with Anthony Storr's (1988, xiii) observation that solitude is as important as the interpersonal in making sense of relationships, fostering creative imagination, and as a preparation for a life of action. I describe in this chapter my journeys into solitude and back and indicate how solitude influences my public and private life. I begin with memories of my struggles for a time and place of my own.

I was born at the end of World War II in a small town in northern Minnesota. In my white working-class family there was little time to be alone with one's thoughts, although I felt a need to create my own spaces. I was influenced by my mother whose afternoon "naps" were minutes away from family and housework. Years later, she explained that her naps were not for sleeping, but time for thinking or repairing herself from the wear and tear of family life. Afternoon naps have been a staple of childrearing in the United States, but my mother did not need *Good Housekeeping* magazine to convince her of their benefits. I never had to be forced to take a nap. My first conscious memories at five years old are of laying quite still with eyes closed. I was not sleeping but listening to my thoughts. At eight, I discovered that my closet was a quiet refuge from being my mother's helper with my baby brother. I would say I was going out to play, but would slip into the house by the side door and glide up the stairs. For years I snuggled into the back of the large bedroom closet I shared with my grandmother. A book, flashlight, and my thoughts were my sole companions for hours. In the tart atmosphere of mothballed winter clothes, I dreamed of being a teacher, a writer and an independent woman.

At eleven I lost my precious space when we moved to a late 1950s ranch with cubbyholes for closets. At the same time I started junior high, which proved to be a large change from my small parochial elementary school where the adjoining church's choir loft offered quiet time. By the end of the school day, I was thoroughly exhausted from the noise and demands of the outside world. I longed to retreat into solitude to escape or muddle over the days' happenings. I soon discovered the possibilities of the neighborhood public library and the city bus ride to school. Although the bus was almost full when I boarded at seven A.M., the journey was quiet as passengers resumed their interrupted sleep or contemplated the day ahead. During my long ride, time unfurled like a ribbon upon which were embroidered my wandering thoughts interrupted only by the buzzer pulled by departing riders. The library was next to my junior high, and in no time I became one of their best after-school customers. Miss Stanley, the head librarian, had noticed me frequently sitting with fingers in my ears as shields from the whispering around me. One day she asked if I would like a quieter place. She took me to the last row of the adult book section. A small oak table and chair were hidden in a corner. Miss Stanley explained that this was her secret place where she often went to think or work on something important. I could sit here if I wanted. If I wanted?! I occupied that niche every school day until I graduated from high school. There I pursued my love of writing and healed myself from the many injuries of growing up. In the summer I found another sanctuary in the small woods near my home. The time I spent there away from college, work, friends, and family helped me to carry on and keep a sense of balance.

These memories contain the important virtues of solitude and indicate the role solitude plays in my life. Philip Koch's (1990, 200) five values of solitude—freedom, centeredness, harmony, reflective perspective and creativity—describe the importance of solitude for women and summarize how solitude has shaped my many selves. Implicit in each aspect of solitude is the notion of place and a modified sense of time. While it is possible to be "alone in a crowd," a crowd may not be the best place for the interior journeys I now describe.

In *Subject Women* Anne Oakley (1981) draws a map of women's lives that is bounded by others. Our time is their time. Our lives are spent caring for others, listening to them, and doing their bidding. This caring provides connectedness to others and creates bonds of affection. It is what makes living in an increasingly cold and exploitative society bearable. At the same time, this caring can sap our energies and leave little space to explore the other aspects of our selves. This is particularly the case when so many women now must clock in at their jobs, at home with the housework and in their positions as heads of families (Stallard, Ehrenreich, and Sklar 1983). According to Sarton (1973, 13), it is not "work that tires…it is the effort of pushing away the lives and needs of others." Women who try to carve out space for their own endeavors must constantly struggle for time of their own and may find the struggle itself exhausting. Women's freedom to push away other lives is often measured in fragments, a moment here and there during the busy day. My minutes are snatched at night when all are asleep or during the long work commute. I use moments in my silent house to strip my mind of thought. The miles and hours of familiar freeway stretch before me. My mind slowly spirals in cadence with the tires buffing the pavement. In Sarton's words, "I have time to think. That is the great, the greatest luxury. I have time to be" (1973, 40).

Women must constantly struggle to escape the overwhelming of their selves by others' personalities. Charlotte P. Gilman's *The Yellow Wallpaper* and Henrik Ibsen's *The Dollhouse* provide provocative examples of women fighting for their subjectivities. These struggles are especially acute for women because, according to Chris Weedon (1987, 105) women are to be many things to many people at different times. This view of subjectivity as ongoing and plural is a hallmark of feminist poststructuralist thinking. However, this view of subjectivity may romanticize what can become an exhausting process. Juggling teaching and writing with my homelife and friendships requires time to put these aspects of my life in perspective. Solitude can provide space for this centering, not in the sense of searching for an essential self, but for conducting conversations with many selves. This centering can bring calmness or upheaval through exploring one's interior spaces. During solitude I become a crystal whose facets refract the beauty of being connected with others. In the next moment, I am the volcano venting the smoke and fire of thoughts and emotions best let out when alone. Solitude is necessary for getting in touch with both aspects of myself.

Every day the world becomes more unjust as the gap between rich and poor widens. Harmony becomes an elusive dream. As the century closes, working-class women of all races still struggle for a living wage and life with dignity. As a teacher educator, I am guided by a vision of schooling in which all children can realize their hopes and dreams. This involves helping my college students to understand the ways knowledge is differently made available to students and the connections of schooling to the maintenance of the power and control of elite groups. Solitude was a key ingredient in my rethinking of schooling long ago and guides my struggles to attain a more democratic practice. However, I am often consumed by the struggle. Time away from the struggle gives me the courage to continue. From the vantage point of solitude, I imagine a world free from the violence of gender, class, race, and sexual oppression. The time and space to reflect on the meaning of events and my involvement in the struggle for social justice renew my dreams of harmony when I have become weary of the struggle. The different worlds I imagine come closer to reality and my conviction is renewed.

According to Carol Gilligan (1982) and Nel Noddings (1984), women from childhood are prepared for a life of connections to others. The days and weeks brimming with work and home certainly lend fullness to life. Yet I am reminded of my mother whose afternoon naps were equally essential to her life perspectives. She would agree with Storr (1988, 21) that "the capacity to be alone thus becomes linked with self-discovery and self-realization, with becoming aware of one's deepest needs, feelings, and impulses." Withdrawing into solitude sets in motion thoughts of self and the world seldom attained in the company of others. Although the perspectives of others often clarify thinking, solitary contemplation gives a clearer perspective on things. Home alone or commuting to work, I seize moments and become immersed in my own time. I let my thoughts wander into unexplored regions. I strip a problem bare and contemplate its various aspects without rushing to a solution. What has been baffling me for weeks about a relationship, my teaching or writing, is now magically resolved. The solution has been there all the time, but my busy eyes have not seen it.

As I write this article I am alone with my thoughts except for the humming of the overhead fan on this summer day. Philip Koch (1990, 204) speaks of creativity as a "flaming-up." This is an apt metaphor since encounters with others and happenings often fuel the first flames of creativity. Whenever I am working on a new project ideas and feelings whir inside as I go about my daily life. A friend's creative fires burn brightly as she writes in the kitchen with her children playing at her feet. However, my fires finally flame up and roar in my solitude. Every virtue of solitude I have thus far described—freedom, centeredness, harmony, and reflection—merge when giving thoughts a written form. Although like Sarton, I go up to heaven and down to hell every other minute when writing, I am compelled to express my thoughts. Writing returns me to the one quality implicit in solitude that describes why I create. Albert Camus (1961) saw solitude as social in character and the path to discovering the ties that bind people together. While my writing is a solitary act, my goals are to contribute to building a community of readers moved to action in the world. Readers complete the circle of meaning I began in solitude.

In the years since my childhood, solitude has remained as essential to me as my work and my relationships with others. However, like many women, I must struggle to carve out time and space for myself. I no longer have time for afternoon naps or to snuggle deep in my closet alone with my thoughts. As a white middle-class woman academic, I know my story does not encompass the realities of women of other classes and races who struggle against hunger and homelessness. However, I am linked with other women through my endeavors to build and write about teaching practices that emphasize reflection and community as essential to the struggle against social inequalities. In solitude, I build for myself and others.

References

Benstock, S. (1988). *The private self: Theory and practice of women's autobiographical writings.* Chapel Hill, N.C.: The University of North Carolina Press.

Camus, A. (1961). *Resistance, rebellion, and death.* New York: Alfred A. Knopf.

Engelhardt, T. H., Jr. (1974). Solitude and sociality. *Humanitas* 10: 277–87.

Gilligan, C. (1982). *In a different voice*. Cambridge: Harvard University Press.

Ibsen, H. (1965). *Four plays*, vol. 1. New York: Signet Classics.

Koch, P. J. (1990). Solitude. *The Journal of Speculative Philosophy* 4: 181–209.

Noddings, N. (1984). *Caring: a feminine approach to ethics and moral education.* Berkeley: University of California Press.

Oakley, A. (1981). *Subject women*. New York: Pantheon.

Gilman, C. P. (1973). *The yellow wallpaper*. Old Westbury: The Feminist Press.

Powys, J. C. (1933). *A philosophy of solitude*. London: Jonathan Cape.

Sadler, W. J., Jr. (1974). On the verge of a lonely life. *Humanitas* 10 (3): 255–76.

Sarton, M. (1973). *Journal of a solitude*. New York: W. W. Norton.

Stallard, K., B. Ehrenreich, and H. Sklar. (1983). *Poverty in the American dream.* Boston: South End Press.

Storr, A. (1988). *Solitude: a return to self*. New York: The Free Press.

Weedon, C. (1987). *Feminist practice and poststructuralist theory.* Oxford: Basil Blackwell.

CONTRIBUTING AUTHORS

Kal Alston is an Assistant Professor in Philosophy of Education in the Educational Policy Studies Department at the University of Illinois, Champaign-Urbana. She teaches courses in ethics, gender studies, and philosophical foundations of ethics. Her work is primarily in the area of the moral and aesthetic dimensions of teaching, centering on the moral significance of teaching practice and relationships. She is currently involved in two projects: one looking at representations of teaching in popular culture, the other examining the role of gender relations and desire in schooling.

Elaine Atkins is Professor of English at Community College of Philadelphia. She also teaches a course in curriculum theory at the University of Pennsylvania. Her research interests are in curriculum deliberations and in drawing from American and European philosophic traditions to understand and shape educational practice.

Ann Berlak has been fascinated with what goes on in all sorts of classrooms for as long as she can remember. She has taught in elementary schools, and interdisciplinary social science and teacher educational programs at the college level. She is co-author of a study of English primary schools, *Dilemmas of Schooling: Teaching and Social Change* (Methuen 1981), and has, in the past few years, been experimenting with ways of writing about her own teaching. She is co-chair of the Humanities Program at New College of California, and also teaches in the Department of Elementary Education at San Francisco State University.

Linda K. Christian-Smith is an Associate Professor of Curriculum and Instruction in the College of Education and Human Services at the University of Wisconsin Oshkosh. She has published widely on issues of gender, class, race, and sexuality in schooling, popular culture, cultural politics, feminist literary theory and the political economy of children's literature publishing. She is the author of *Becoming a Woman Through Romance* (Routledge) and co-author of *The Politics of the Text-*

271

book (Routledge) and *Becoming Feminine: The Politics of Popular Culture* (Falmer Press).

Elyse Eidman-Aadahl was a high school English teacher for seven years at Westminster Senior High School in Maryland. She has worked at Arizona State University and the University of Maryland in language arts, cross-cultural education, and curriculum theory. Now at Towson State University, she has directed the Maryland Writing Project and teaches in the M.A.T. and secondary education programs. She has facilitated research collaboratives in schools and nonprofit organizations: the Basic Writing Teacher-Research Network, the Gender Studies Project, and several action research/program evaluation studies.

Elizabeth Ellsworth is Associate Professor in the College of Education at the University of Wisconsin, Madison. She teaches courses that invite students to interpret, use, and produce educational media in ways that are situated within particular educational contexts, sites, and moments. These courses also focus on the meanings and operations of social and cultural difference within specific contexts of teaching, curriculum, and educational research. She is excited about trying to articulate what it means (to researcher, to the "field" of education, to business as usual in schools and universities) to do "Situated Studies in Education." That is, studies that raise questions of pedagogy, policy, curriculum, and inquiry from specific social and cultural positions within particular educational situations.

Beverly M. Gordon is an Associate Professor and faculty coordinator of Curriculum, Instruction, and Professional Development [Faculty] in the Department of Educational Policy and Leadership in the College of Education at The Ohio State University. Her current line of research involves exploring the social theorizing and discourse in the cultural and scholarly work of African-Americans, and describing the ideological, political, theoretical, and methodological implications of this work for reshaping social thought and classroom pedagogy. She is presently working on an edited volume that delineates the new challenges to the current regimes of truth within the academy for educational, political and economic agendas in the interest of people of color and a democratic pluralist perspective for all Americans.

Susan Laird is Associate Professor of Educational Leadership and Policy Studies at the University of Oklahoma. Through interdisciplinary studies in philosophy of education, feminist theory and criticism, and literature, her present research aims to clarify and evaluate taken-for-granted notions of the "maternal" and their consequences for teachers, teaching, and curriculum. Her articles have appeared in *Curriculum Inquiry*, *Harvard Educational Review*, *Educational Theory*, and *Philosophy of Education 1988*. "Women, Singleness, and Solitude" is her first attempt at explicitly autobiographical theorizing.

Glorianne M. Leck alternates between two residences, one, an inner-city apartment near Youngstown State University, where she teaches and the other, a cabin outside of Greenville, Pennsylvania. Her preoccupations are political and cultural, her recreation is minimal, and a cat named Sensai makes her city residence a home. The wonderful women with whom she shares a rural collective makes the earth their center and their home.

Magda Lewis is a Queen's National Scholar and Assistant Professor of Education, women's studies and sociology at Queen's University, Kingston, Canada. She earned her Ph.D. at the University of Toronto where she studied in the areas of cultural studies and women's issues. Her current work is in the area of feminist pedagogy and gender bias in education. She has published numerous articles in her area of research and is presently completing a book for Routledge, Chapman and Hall.

Lynne McFall teaches moral philosophy and philosophy of literature at Syracuse University. *Happiness*, a philosophical study, was published in 1989 by Peter Lang. *The One True Story of the World*, a novel, was published in 1990 by Atlantic Monthly Press. Her essays have appeared in *Ethics*, *The Review of Metaphysics*, and *Feminist Ethics*. Her fiction has appeared in *Story*, *New England Review/Bread Loaf Quarterly*, *Prairie Schooner*, and *Other Voices*. Recipient of a Wallace Stegner Fellowship from Stanford University and a James Michener Fellowship from the Iowa Writers' Workshop, she has also been awarded the Pushcart Prize and a National Endowment for the Arts fellowship in literature.

Ellen Michaelson was born in Maine, and grew up and was educated in Massachusetts at Brandeis University and the University of Massachusetts Medical School. Her medical training was completed in New York City, internship and residency in Internal Medicine at Downstate Medical Center and fellowship in hematology at Mt. Sinai Medical

Center. She has kept journals since age 11, has studied fiction privately and in the MFA program at Sarah Lawrence College.

Janet L. Miller is Professor in the Department of Interdisciplinary Studies at National-Louis University. She serves as Managing Editor of *JCT: An Interdisciplinary Journal of Curriculum Studies.* Her book, *Creating Spaces and Finding Voices: Teachers Collaborating for Empowerment* (SUNY Press 1990), narrates a teacher-researcher collaborative over a three-year period. She is searching for new connections among her teaching, research, and writing that might draw together her interests in curriculum and feminist theories, teacher research and knowledges and writing processes.

Jo Anne Pagano is Associate Professor of Education at Colgate University, and since 1990, Chair of the Department. Her publications include *Exiles and Communities: Teaching in the Patriarchal Wilderness* and, with Landon Beyer, Walter Feinberg, and Anthony James Whitson, *Preparing Teachers as Professionals.* Articles on curriculum theory, ethics and education, and women and teaching are published in numerous journals and edited volumes. She is serving currently as editor-in-chief of *JCT: An Interdisciplinary Journal of Curriculum Studies.*

Darshan Perusek is Assistant Professor of English at the University of Wisconsin-Stout, where she teaches, among other things, courses in women's studies and multicultural literature. She is also editor of *Kaleidoscope: International Magazine of Literature, Fine Arts, and Disability.*

Tuija Pulkkinen studied philosophy, political science, history and sociology at the University of Helsinki. She is the author of the book *Valtio ja Vapaus* (State and Liberty) as well as several articles in books and periodicals in Finland. She is currently Research Associate at University of California, Santa Cruz and is working on a book on postmodern political theory.

Jacqueline Jones Royster is Director of the University Writing Center and Associate Professor of English at Ohio State University. She is also a member of the editorial collective of *SAGE: A Scholarly Journal on Black Women,* who in addition to their semiannual journal have published an anthology, *Double Stitch: Black Women Write About Mothers and Daughters* (Beacon Press 1991). Her work in progress is a book, *Traces of a Stream: Literacy and Social Change Among African-American Women.*

Beth Rushing received her Ph.D. in sociology at Duke University in 1988, and is currently an Assistant Professor in the Department of Sociology at Kent State University. Her research focuses on health and health care, particularly as they are influenced by gender, race, and social class. She is learning to seek solitude in many different settings, with varying degrees of success.

Mara Sapon-Shevin is Professor in the Division for the Study of Teaching at Syracuse University. She has taught at the University of Wisconsin–Madison, Cleveland State University, and the University of North Dakota. Her areas of interest include teacher education, diversity, cooperative learning, the politics of gifted education and school reform. She is a member of Women in Black, active in local peace activities and the mother of two feminist, social activist daughters.

Delese Wear is Associate Professor in Behavioral Sciences at the Northeastern Ohio Universities College of Medicine, where she is coordinator of the Human Values in Medicine program and associate director of Women in Medicine. Her interests include literary and feminist inquiry in medical education and curriculum issues in the medical humanities.

INDEX